MEMOIR

OF

THOMAS HANDASYD PERKINS

Your Obedt Servt

[illegible] Darling[illegible]
with the compliments of
the author

MEMOIR

OF

THOMAS HANDASYD PERKINS

CONTAINING

EXTRACTS FROM HIS DIARIES AND LETTERS

With an Appendix.

BY THOMAS G. CARY

BOSTON:
LITTLE, BROWN AND COMPANY,
112, WASHINGTON STREET.
1856.

BOSTON:

PRINTED BY JOHN WILSON AND SON,

22, School Street.

PREFATORY NOTE.

In this volume, the Memoir prepared by request for "Hunt's Merchants' Magazine" has been extended, chiefly by additions, made at the suggestion of several readers, to the extracts from diaries and letters which appeared there, some of them descriptive of the manners of Asiatics, and of striking occurrences in the French Revolution. They will be found to have the interest which usually accompanies the statements of an eye-witness, while they casually indicate the character and habits of thought of the writer.

CONTENTS.

MEMOIR.

THOMAS HANDASYD PERKINS was born in Boston, Dec. 15, 1764, and named for his maternal grandfather, Thomas Handasyd Peck, who dealt largely in furs and the importation of hats. His father was a merchant, who died in middle age, leaving eight children, — three sons and five daughters, — most of them very young, to the sole care of their mother. She was a woman of excellent principles and remarkable energy, and undertook the heavy charge thus devolved upon her with deep solicitude (as appeared from a subsequent reference of her own to this passage of her life), but with firmness and ability; courageously assuming the business of her husband, who had been connected with George Erving, one of the principal merchants in the town. Letters from Holland are remembered which were addressed to her as *Mr.* Elizabeth Perkins; and when her eldest son, having attained the age of manhood, went some years afterwards to the Island of St. Domingo, where he established himself, he sailed from Boston in a ship, the "Beaver," of which his mother was part owner, and which had been chartered to the French government to transport part of their cavalry to Cape François.

This estimable lady discharged her duties successfully, rearing her children with such advantages as fitted them for stations of responsibility, which they afterwards filled with credit to themselves and to her; and at the same time taking an active part herself with the charitable associations of the town, which is shown by acknowledgments found among her papers, and in records of her services, as treasurer and otherwise, from those with whom she acted.

On her decease, in 1807, it was voted "that the officers of the Boston Female Asylum wear a badge of mourning for the term of seventy-one days" (corresponding probably to the years of her life), "in token of their high consideration and respect for the virtues of the deceased, and of their grateful and affectionate sense of her liberal and essential patronage as a founder and friend of the institution." She is still remembered by a few gentlemen, sons of her former neighbors and associates, as an excellent friend, of active benevolence, and as a lady of dignified, but frank and cordial, manners.

Numerous descendants of hers, under various names, now move in different walks of life in the United States, in Europe, and Asia; and not a few of them are distinguished for prosperity and the wise use of wealth, and for intelligence and refinement, as well as for the sound principles which she inculcated on all.

The success of several of the branches of her family was essentially promoted by the energy and warm-hearted sympathy of the subject of this memoir, who was the second son, only six years of age at the death of his father in 1771. The life of one like him, who, with only such advantages as are within the reach of many young men, acquired great power to influence others, and, using it wisely, left the world, within his sphere of action, better for his existence, affords a useful example.

His father lived in King Street, now State Street, where the conflict took place between the citizens and the troops, called afterwards the "Boston Massacre;" and, though he was little more than five years old at that time, the sight of the dead bodies and of the blood, frozen the next day on the street, made an impression on his mind that was never obliterated. The troops being quartered near there, many of the officers were afterwards visitors in his mother's family.

At about seven years of age, he was put under the care of a clergyman of great respectability, at Middleborough, about thirty miles from Boston, and was afterwards at school in Boston, until, intercourse with the country being stopped, his mother retired with her family to Barnstable, where she resided till the town was evacuated by the enemy. His grandfather, Mr. Peck, remained in Boston through the siege, but was nigh being sent home to be tried as a rebel for freedom of speech.

While living with his mother at Barnstable, both his legs were broken, by an unlucky accident, as he was returning from an excursion in the woods; and though the limbs were well set, and he soon recovered the use of them, he occasionally felt the effect of the injury when the weather was bad, even in advanced age. There, too, he formed an early and close friendship, that remained unbroken for nearly eighty years, until terminated by death, with one of his companions, whom he had saved from drowning, — the late distinguished lawyer and statesman, Harrison Gray Otis, nephew of the revolutionary patriot.

Some time after the return of the family to town, his mother decided on giving him a collegiate education; and he was sent, with other boys from Boston, — one of whom was the Hon. John Welles, now the oldest living graduate of Harvard, — to an instructor at Hingham, the Rev. Mr. Shute, noted for his success in preparing lads for college. After residing there three years, and being prepared for Cambridge, he was so reluctant to enter college, that it was decided that he should go into a counting-house. He was strongly inclined by temperament to active life. Vigorous and bold, with a frame peculiarly fitted for endurance, which was afterwards developed in fine proportions for strength and beauty in manhood, he saw less to attract him in the life of a student than in one of enterprise, where he might indulge a love of adventure, and exercise the courage, equal to almost every emergency, which characterized him. He was placed with Messrs. Shattuck, then among the most active merchants in Boston, with whom he remained until he was twenty-one.*

On leaving the Messrs. Shattuck, in 1785, not being well, he was advised to pass the winter in a warm climate; and visited his elder brother, Mr. James Perkins, in St. Domingo. He then went to Charleston, S.C.; and, in some memoranda made for his children within a few years past, he refers to this visit to South Carolina in the following terms:—

"As I had taken letters of introduction to some of the most distinguished inhabitants of Charleston from Gen. Lincoln and Gen. Knox,—the former of whom was the defender of Charleston during the war of the Revolution, and was a great favorite,—it gave me pleasant introduction into the best society under most favorable circumstances. As the inhabitants who have large plantations spend as much of their time on them as the climate will allow, I was an inmate in several

* Long afterwards, he recurred to this decision with regret for having relinquished such a privilege, and in advanced age repeatedly said, that, other things being equal (which condition he repeated emphatically), he should prefer for commercial pursuits those who had received the most complete education. In this opinion he seeems to have coincided with another experienced merchant, who once gave it as the result of his observation in a long life, that, as a general rule, applied to the whole class of commercial men, of whom it is well known that a considerable proportion fail, those had succeeded best who were the best educated. It derives confirmation, too, from a fact generally noticed, both here and in Europe, by those who know what goes on in the public schools where lads are prepared by different courses of study respectively, either for college or for mercantile life, as their friends prefer: those who are engaged in classical studies for most of the week, and give but a small portion of it to other pursuits, are generally found to be well up, in arithmetic, geography, &c., with those who bestow their whole time on such branches.

Without underrating the importance of a habit of attention to detail, or the knowledge of minute affairs and the qualities of merchandise, which may be acquired by early apprenticeship, it is to be remembered that men of high culture, who mean to effect what they attempt, show great aptitude for the minutiæ, as well as for the general scope, of any new business which they undertake, and that intellect well disciplined has considerable advantages in comparison with routine.

of their families, but passed the principal part of the time at the plantation of Mr. Thomas Ferguson, who had several rice plantations, upon which he numbered upwards of eight hundred slaves. The plantations were at a place called *Pon Pon ;* and in the vicinity was Gen. William Washington, who was a nephew of President Washington, and during the war commanded a regiment of cavalry. He gained a high reputation as a soldier, and was an accomplished gentleman. There was fine sport with the gun; geese, duck, teal, &c., being in great abundance. Every Saturday the gentlemen of the neighborhood met at a hunting-stand in a favorite spot for deer, hunted in the morning, and made good cheer after the chase, — dining in the woods, and, in case of not having success in hunting, always securing a succedaneum, in the form of ham, chickens, and other 'creature comforts.' The Saturdays were real red-letter days; and I could name twenty who were in the habit of meeting on such occasions, all of whom have long since retired behind the scenes."

He soon afterwards accepted an invitation to join his brother in St. Domingo, and they formed a house there which was very successful; but, finding that the climate did not agree with his health, he returned to Boston, and for some time attended to the business of the house in the United States, where their correspondence was extensive, — his younger brother, the late Samuel G. Perkins, Esq., filling his place in the firm.

In 1788 he was married to Miss Elliot, only

daughter of Simon Elliot, Esq. It was a union entirely of affection, and lasted for more than sixty years. His married life was commenced with necessity for strict economy; but the connection probably gave an important bias to his commercial career, as it led to intimacy with Capt. James Magee, a relative of Mrs. Perkins, who had made one voyage to Canton. He soon turned his attention to trade with China; and sailed from Boston, in February, 1789, as supercargo of the ship "Astræa," belonging to E. H. Derby, Esq., of Salem, bound to Batavia and Canton, and commanded by Capt. Magee. Difficulties were encountered, and inconveniences were necessarily submitted to then which are avoided now. The ship was not coppered; and, her bottom becoming foul, they made a long passage to Batavia. Being in want of water before arriving there, they stopped at Mew Island, at the mouth of the Straits of Sunda, for a supply. Referring to the voyage and this incident in some memoranda made for his children many years afterwards, he says, —

"The casks in which a part of our water was contained had been used in bringing coffee from the Cape of Good Hope; and although burned out, and, as was supposed, purified, yet the water put in them was most disgusting. The waters from the cascade on the Java shore were, of course, duly appreciated. We remained in this beautiful bay several days. There were, at the time I speak of (now fifty-seven years since), no inhabitants on this part of Java. I went on shore every day, and in one of my excursions climbed the precipice over which the cascade flowed, to examine its source; and, from what we learned on reaching Batavia, we were led to believe that we had run great hazard, as more than one instance had occurred of persons visiting the same spot having been destroyed by tigers who were slaking their thirst in this beautiful stream. Bats of great size were seen crossing the narrow strait which divides Mew Island from Java, and returning towards the close of day to their roosts on the Java side.

"I remember as if it were yesterday the fright I had in crossing a creek, the bottom of which was hard, about knee-deep, and but a few yards wide. My crossing alarmed half a dozen or more young crocodiles or alligators, which were farther up the stream than where I was crossing; and they came down upon us with a celerity which was inconceivable. Neither of them touched either my servant or myself; and I have no doubt they were quite as much alarmed as we were.

"No boats or vessels of any kind came into the bay while we lay there. Prince's Island was in sight; but the inhabitants, who had a bad name, were otherwise engaged, and we met nothing to alarm us. The pirates from Sumatra and the Eastern Islands made frequent attacks upon vessels in those days, even so far to the west as the Straits of Sunda; though their depredations were more confined to Banca Straits and the more eastern archipelago."

That part of Java remains uninhabited now, as it was at the time which he thus referred to, and both tigers and anacondas abound there. Quite recently, a botanist, engaged in making collections for a British nobleman, having crossed from Mew Island to the Java shore, his dog sprang from the boat as it touched land, and, dashing into the woods, was immediately seized by a tiger, as his master doubtless would have been if he had entered the thicket first. The enormous bats here mentioned are well known to naturalists. It is said that coal has now been discovered in that vicinity, which may lead to some settlement there.

They were among the earliest visitors at Batavia from this country, and he was treated with great civility by the governor-general and others in authority, but found some difficulty in obtaining permission to dispose of the cargo intended for that place. He kept a journal while there; and the following extracts from it exhibit some obstructions in business and deference to authority from which foreigners are now relieved: —

"July 13, 1789. — At five o'clock anchored in three fathoms water in the harbor of Batavia, where we saw Capt. Webb's brig. At seven the captain came on board, and gave us the most melancholy account of the state of affairs at the place, — of the prohibition and restrictions on trade, and every thing else which could serve to give us the dumps.

"14th. — At eight in the morning, took Capt. Webb in our boat, and went on shore. The entrance of the canal through which we pass is about half a mile from the ship. The appearance in the harbor beautiful. Canals, which cross each other at right angles through the city, are about forty or fifty feet wide. The water, which is always very dirty, must be unhealthy; they are continually filled with boats, which carry up and down cargoes.

"The variety of nations, which are easily to be known by their different countenances, astonishing. Great numbers of Chinese. Stopped at the custom-house, where the names of the captain and myself were taken, and other minutes respecting our passage, &c. As the canal is difficult to pass after getting to this place, which is about a mile and a half from shore, and through the centre of the town, we took a coach, which was provided us by the scribe who questioned us, and with whom I rode to the Shabendar's. Received with civility by him, but discouraged from expecting permission to sell. Represented our situation, the encouragement we had ever met with, &c. He told us he would do every thing in his power to serve us, but feared we should not succeed.

"Was conducted to the hotel, where all strangers are obliged to put up. Found Blanchard, who speaks of his prospects as distressing. Had been here a week, and done nothing but petition.

"According to common custom, presented a petition through the Shabendar for permission to sell. Waited upon the director-general, for whom we had a letter from Mr. L——, his nephew. His house a palace. He received us, Dutchman-like, in his shirt-sleeves, and his stockings half down his legs; took our address, and told us we should hear from him again; think he will be of service to us. Made other acquaintances through my knowledge of French, and endeavored to make some friends. To-morrow the council sit, when our fate is to be known.

"This evening the British ship 'Vansittart' arrived; and the captain, whose name is Wilson, with his second-mate, purser, and doctor, came on shore. Was very happy to find the doctor to be the gentleman for whom I had a letter, and whom I supposed to have been in the 'Pitt,' Indiaman: he seems to merit all which has been said to me of him. Feel myself drawn towards him more from his being a countryman than perhaps from any other circumstance, on so short an acquaintance.

"Thursday, 15th. — Anxious for the reception the petition may meet. At ten o'clock, Capt. Wilson and I went with the Shabendar, with our petitions, to the council-chamber. After walking the hall a long time, and being witness to a great deal of pompous parade, was introduced to the council-chamber, where the members, who are eight in number, were seated round a large table covered with silk velvet, with the governor-general as president. I made my respects and presented my petition, and then left them, to take another stroll in the hall, till the Shabendar, upon the ringing of a bell, once more introduced us to the great chamber, when Capt. Wilson had liberty to land his articles; but we, poor, despised devils, were absolutely denied the liberty of selling a farthing's worth. Whatever

I thought of the partiality, I very respectfully took my leave, but determined to persevere; and, after much difficulty, got leave to renew our petitions.

"16th. — Received an invitation to sup with the director, where we were superbly entertained, and met much company. Many speak French; represented our situation; music at supper.

"Friday, 17th. — Nothing to be done until Monday, when the council meet again. It is supposed we shall not have our future petition acceded to. Making interest.

"Sunday, 19th. — Dined with the governor, and received civility. An elegant place; the area, where we dined, superb, and the prospect round it not to be exceeded. Passed the evening, by invitation, at the director's, where were all the Council of Eight, the governor, the old director-general, and other grandees. More parade than before. Played cards. Custom of washing before and after dinner; the improvement in luxury; washing in rose-water; supper elegant, — superbly so; huzzaing, and the return from the owner of the house after any complimentary toast.

"I wrote a petition in behalf of Blanchard and myself, and had it translated into Dutch.

"Monday, 20th. — Dined with the Fiscal, who treated us with good fare; the British officers there, and many persons of consequence.

"Tuesday, 21st. — Supped with one of the Edelheeren; every thing in superb style; same company as before; the governor there; he does not honor them more than once a year with his visits. Twenty ladies at table; their dress, manner, style of putting up the hair; sitting by themselves; toasts, huzzas, bouquets, rose-water; superfluity of every thing which Europe and the Indies can give.

"Gained permission to sell."

This restriction on sales by foreigners has been removed since that time, and it is not necessary to wait for any such permission now. But at that time the United States of America were little known or regarded in that distant part of the world; and it is easy to see that the final success which the young merchant thus attained with the despotic authorities of Batavia, who had pointedly and formally refused his application in the outset, is fairly attributable to personal qualities which distinguished him even at that early period, and were characteristic through life. Few men could exert a greater influence over others with whom he had an important point to carry.

His notes on various subjects, in the same diary, show careful and general observation: —

"It is death to take spices; and an acknowledgment of having received notice of this is required, so that one cannot plead ignorance. The Chinese racked on the wheel for running spices; yet any of them will do it, bringing them to one's chamber in small quantities of twenty or thirty pounds. The Chinese are the principal husbandmen. All the Eastern nations are represented here in greater or less numbers, — Armenians, Moormen, &c. Murders frequent; Malays revengeful and cowardly, taking every advantage of situation, fearing to attack a man openly, and even afraid to hold a pistol. Gates of the city; strict regulations respecting the going out and coming in at them; four gates; walled all round; kept in good repair. Regularity of the trees. Chinese live in the suburbs, and obliged to be out of the walls before night.

"Every night, at a quarter-past ten o'clock, these gates are shut, and opened again at about four in the morning, when the Chinamen enter in great numbers with their greens, &c., to procure a good place in the market. An Edelheer — of whom I shall speak hereafter — has the exclusive privilege of passing and repassing these gates at what hour of the twenty-four he pleases; and the governor-general, who entertains company every Sunday night, sends orders to the officers on guard to have the gates kept open until eleven, for the accommodation of his company.

"There are particular gates at which you pass out in a carriage, and others appointed for entering the city, to avoid the frequent encounters which must necessarily arise were there no regulation of this kind. An Edelheer has, however, the privilege to pass at whichever he pleases; and his approach is announced by the sentinels at the gates, in order to stop other carriages from attempting the passage at the time.

"The houses, in general, at Batavia are of brick,

with a degree of neatness about them, but nothing of elegance. They all have very large glass windows, copied from the mode in Holland; though it is said the use of large windows in that country was intended to produce an effect that seems not to be necessary in this place, — which is, to admit the rays of the sun. Whatever the effect is, 'tis certain that their houses in front, almost without exception, are nearly half glass. The rooms are very high, and are spacious and well furnished. They have, in general, good yard room, and many good gardens behind their houses.

"The streets are wide; and on each side of the canal, which runs through each of them, are two rows of sycamore-trees, which have a continual verdure, are regularly planted, and are very much of a size. These trees give a beautiful appearance to the city, and afford an agreeable shade to those who are obliged to walk in the middle of the day. These canals communicate with the river Jacatra, which has nothing different from them in appearance; but has deeper water, runs from a great distance in the country, and empties into the sea. They are of great convenience for transporting goods, which may be brought in prows to within forty feet of any house in the city. The streets, which are not paved, are throughout the city sprinkled, morning and evening, with water from the canals. This is done often by private slaves; but, when they neglect to do it, it is done by the company's slaves, who traverse the city morning and evening, chained two and two, for this purpose. Upon first observing the plan of wetting the streets, I thought it a great convenience, which in fact it is; but it took away the pleasure of it when I saw at what an expense of human feelings it is effected.

"Procured two birds of paradise; the bird a native of the Moluccas or Spice Islands; valuable at Bengal, and on the peninsula of India.

"Birds' nests at Batavia at two thousand five hundred paper dollars the pecul. The birds that make these nests are shaped like the swallow, and fly with the same velocity, but are smaller. We saw numbers of them while at Mew Island, but did not know them to be the same at the time. The coast of Sumatra gives the greatest supply of them, called the Salignare, and found in great numbers in the Philippines. They always lay in the same nest, unless it be destroyed, and will keep continually rebuilding when their nests are taken away. Late method of insuring good nests, by destroying all the old ones. The nests are formed of a glutinous substance found in the water. They are about the size of the inside of a swallow's nest, and some of them almost transparent. The soup made of them is very palatable; but, as it is dear, it is not often met with. The old nests are of a black cast, and not near so valuable as the white. There are three layers or thicknesses in the nests, which, when separated, appear like three distinct nests: the first or outside layer brings the least price, increasing to the inside, which bears the amazing price above quoted.

"The shark-fins are also esteemed a great delicacy for soups, and are to many very palatable; but to me they were not so.

"There are at Batavia nine persons who bear the title of Edelheer, — that being a title of nobility which they have assumed to themselves. Among these nine persons are included the governor-general, who is the president of the Grand Council of the Indies, the other seven councillors, and the director-general of the company, whose post is second in the settlement. The old director also, who, being far advanced in years, resigned, holds this dignity of Edelheer, and has the same attention paid to him that the inhabitants are obliged to pay to the rest of them. Obeisance is exacted from all persons, without distinction, in one form which has much disturbed the feelings of some strangers who were not used to acknowledge themselves the inferiors of any one, and felt much galled at not being able to help themselves. It is this: The carriage of an Edelheer is, when in the city or on meeting any carriage of distinction, preceded by two running footmen, who carry each a baton or cane, with a brass head resembling the weight used with a pair of steelyards, and of an extraordinary size. This announces the carriage which follows to be that of an Edelheer; when the other carriage must drive up on one side the way, and there wait until his greatness has passed. They are very civil in returning one as low a bow as is given them. When no carriage of distinction is on the road, and the Edelheer's carriage is without the suburbs, it is known by those canes before spoken of being projected from the back part of the carriage in such a manner that they cannot but be seen. There is a heavy fine exacted for passing the carriage of an Edelheer without stopping.

"Some time since, there was an East India Company's ship at Batavia, the captain of which, thinking this a very great indignity offered him, upon his coachman's attempting to stop his horses, ordered him by signs to go on; which order not being complied with on the part of the former, the captain gave him a very severe prick with his sword. This made some noise at the time, but was overlooked. I think it did no great honor to the good sense of the captain, who must have been aware that the poor devil who drove him knew that passing the Edelheer would be attended with disagreeable consequences to himself; which should have alone been sufficient to have prevented the captain from wishing it.

"The captain of a French frigate who was here fell upon a much more eligible plan, and one which succeeded to admiration. On being informed that his coachman would stop on meeting one of the Edelheeren, he determined on endeavoring to overcome by civility what he had no hopes of averting by any other means. He had directions for distinguishing the carriage of an Edelheer; and, as soon as he saw one, prepared himself for descending from his carriage. As soon as his coachman checked his horses, he alighted from his coach, and made his respects to the Edelheer, who could do no less than dismount from his upon seeing a person of the appearance of the captain thus paying him his respects; and, after many ceremonious bows and testimonies of civility, they again resumed their seats in their several carriages. This piece of outstretched politeness was found to be the cause of some trouble to the gentlemen Edelheeren during the captain's stay here; which induced them to send an order to the hotel, giving leave to the coachman of the French captain to drive on without stopping for any one of the council, or indeed of the Edelheeren.

"In private companies, the greatest attention and studied politeness is shown them; and they always, when at table, sit opposite the master of the house, who divides the table lengthwise, and does not, like the host with us, take his seat at the end. They have a privilege of passing in and out of the several gates of the city at any time in the day; which is what no other person can do, as there are particular hours for passing and repassing the different gates."

These dignitaries, and the troublesome ceremonies attendant on their rank, are no longer known.

"There is at Batavia a great medley of inhabitants. The principal persons in business, after the Hollanders, are the Moormen. Many of them are very rich. They are distinguished by a peculiarity of dress, and a turban on the head. They wear square-toed shoes, which turn up and terminate at each corner in a kind of ear, which has a curious appearance. They are rather slippers than shoes, having no quarter or straps to them. In some respects, these people exceed any set of men whom I saw while at Batavia: they have an ease of address and an air of good breeding which one would not expect to find in their countrymen. In their houses they are courteous, and strive to make one's time agreeable while under their roofs. They are the best shaped of any of the Eastern nations whom I observed while there; their complexion nearly the same as that of the aboriginals of America; their features regular and well-set, with the most piercing eye of any people I ever saw. Their religion is Mahometanism. They carry on a great trade to the different islands in the Indian seas, and by their traffic make great fortunes. Their mode of saluting is by passing the right hand, with a slow motion, to the forehead, and at the same time bowing the head with a most graceful ease. They are, with the Chinese, the great money-changers. They are as remarkably quick in casting and making calculations, without any assistance, as the Chinese are with their counters. Some of these people support as decent carriages as any in the place, and live with a great degree of taste.

"They all chew betel, areka-nut, and chunam. This has the effect of rendering the teeth black and shining like ebony. They esteem it healthful, as it causes expectoration in a greater degree than tobacco. This, they aver, is absolutely necessary in their country. It is, however, a filthy, vile practice in our eyes, excusable in some degree in the men, but in the women truly disgusting. I never saw any European gentlemen use the betel; but many of the European women have adopted the habit of chewing it, and have their mouths crowded with it. The private secretary of the council, one of the most genteel men at Batavia, told me of his great aversion to the use of it in women; and observed, that his wife had so great an attachment to it, that all his powers of persuasion were not sufficient to wean her from it. She was quite young, — not more than nineteen or twenty at the extent. There is a child, of seven or eight years of age, always in attendance on those who chew the betel, which is deposited in a box, in some instances of very curious workmanship. This child is the bearer of the box, and ever waiting the wishes of the person so attended.

"All the people in this place seem very fond of being surrounded by domestics. One seldom sees a coach pass, particularly if there are women in it, without five or six slaves, — some carrying the batons, others the umbrellas, &c., the slaves being generally Malays; though there are some from all the inhabited islands in the India and China seas.

"The love of gaming shows itself in no place where I have ever been so strongly as here. It is, however, confined to the natives and other colored people; for, among the Europeans, they, for the most part, have a fixed bet, which is not large, and beyond which they do not go. But with the lower people it is the origin of almost all their quarrels, and frequently terminates in death. You will see, in whatever part of the town you visit, circles of those gamblers seated on the ground, and great numbers of spectators, who all seem to be deeply interested in the business, if we may judge from the smile of success which brightens up their countenances, and the look which, perhaps the moment after, bespeaks ill-luck. There are great numbers of houses, for the most part kept by Chinese, which are open as gambling-houses, and when passing which you continually hear the jingling of money, and the confused sound of many voices. They have a large table, like a tailor's shopboard, on which they sit in a circle and play their game. Even in private families, you will always see parties of slaves seated in some part of the house at this diversion; and, in short, this vice is the prevailing one, from the oldest to the youngest.

"The Malays are great cock-fighters, and have as fine birds as perhaps any in the world. They bet more deeply, and involve themselves more, in this barbarous custom, than in any other species of gambling; and there have been instances of their carrying it to as unpardonable a length as the Chinese do in playing away the liberty of their wives and children, and even of enslaving themselves; which last, however, is more excusable than to take that liberty with their connections.

"There are, in some of the Dutch settlements, Malay governors and chiefs; and many of their women are married to Europeans. The language of the Malays is the most known of any language in the several islands, and indeed may be called among the islands of the East what the French language is acknowledged to be throughout Europe. It is agreeable to the ear, and said to be the most musical and soft of any of the Eastern languages. It is very easily learned and spoken by every European who has been any time in the country.

"In most countries, the servant has to learn the language of the person in whose service he is: but here that custom is reversed; for there is not one in a hundred of the slaves who understands Dutch, nor one-quarter of that proportion who speak it; whereas every Dutchman and every member of his family speaks the Malayan language. Indeed, it is the first language the children here learn; as they get the dialect from their nurses, who are Malayan women, before that of their parents. Every child, when ushered into the world, has one of these nurses appointed to it, which is given to the child as its property, and generally serves it till their general master separates them.

"This language is used by the Chinese, who all speak it, as well as by the other Indian inhabitants of this place, who, for the most part, do not speak Dutch; so that it is absolutely necessary that they should know it.

"There are these advantages arising from the Malays not knowing the language of the Dutch, — that the latter are obliged to learn theirs, and that the conversation which is passing while they are in waiting is not liable to be carried out of the company by them. The Malays, without an exception that I was ever acquainted with, chew betel, and in greater quantities than the other Asiatics.

"The slaves, for the most part, have only a piece

of linen cloth over those parts for which modesty demands covering. There are some, however, who have long pieces of this cloth thrown over the right shoulder, and hanging down under the left arm almost to the ground. I could never see the use of this additional garment, as it only hid a part of the breast and the middle part of the back, and was always laid aside when they were engaged in work. There are others, who are body-servants, who have a kind of frock, or long skirt, buttoning round the neck with brass buttons, and hanging loose to the ankles. The Malayan women, in lieu of the petticoat, have a piece of cloth long enough to go twice round them, and made of a width sufficient to reach from above the hips to the ground; and, to cover the upper part of the body, they have a short white gown, which comes straight down to the hips, and has long sleeves, which set close, and show the form very distinctly. They seldom wear shoes, and, I believe, never stockings. They dress their hair, which is long and coal-black, with a most refined degree of taste and neatness. It is combed all to the back of the head, and, after being twisted, is fastened in a circular form on the back of the head with long pins. The juice of the cocoanut-tree, which is used in lieu of pomatum, gives it a gloss like japanned ware, and makes it appear very agreeably.

"Both whites and colored men and women pay great attention to the cleanliness of their persons. The white ladies ride a few miles out of town to their country-seats, past each of which runs a canal, with convenient steps made for descending to the water, where they strip themselves, except of a piece of cloth worn as the Malays do their common dresses, and a long piece of muslin thrown over the shoulders, and bathe, exposed to the eyes of every passer-by. They seem to have got quite reconciled to being thus exposed, as a stranger passing does not seem to disturb them in the smallest degree. The men who labor, being in general the colored people, and particularly the Chinese, towards dark strip themselves of their clothes, except a small piece of cloth round the waist, and go into the canals, which, in the town, are the receptacles for every kind of filth. They nevertheless dive under water, and sport as if in a clear river. The women also keep their piece of cloth, which encloses the lower part of the body, over them, and leave the parts above the waist entirely uncovered. They so early accustom their children to bathing, that they become in a degree amphibious, and appear to be as much in their element when in the water as when on land. Although the Chinese are the principal cultivators of the earth, the Malays bear some part in the burden. The former are, however, esteemed the best gardeners, and as the most industrious by far.

"I saw a Malay make use of an instrument for shooting birds, which it appeared to me impossible could carry with it the execution that in fact it does. It is a hollow trunk, about the thickness of our largest walking-sticks near the head. The hollow appeared to be natural. It was about five feet ten inches long; which I know by comparing it with my height. The hollow was about large enough to admit the middle finger, and had a brass ring round the end, —I suppose to keep it from splitting. This is directed towards the object against which you mean to do execution; and through it is blown, from the mouth of the sportsman, a piece of clay, formed round by the finger. This is shot with such force, and with so much exactitude, by many of the Malays and natives, as seldom to fail of doing execution. When I first saw this mode of shooting, I concluded that this piece of clay would not do more than stun the bird which it should chance to strike, and accounted in this way for the taking the immense numbers of birds which are daily exposed alive for sale in the market; but was assured, upon inquiry, that instant death was the consequence of the balls striking the bird. They are killed in this way from the tops of the highest cocoanut-trees; and from this we see that the rude state of the people produced some implements which they have found reason to continue since they are more cultivated.

"Many of the natives have their finger nails tinged with a vermilion color. They keep them in very good order; and this color gives them a very pretty appearance. They, in some instances, have adopted the custom of the Chinese, in letting the nail of one of their fingers grow to a great length, and, indeed, never cutting it, to show they are not used to labor. There are great numbers of the Malays and other colored people here who are clerks to private gentlemen, and many others who are differently employed by the company. They have the most unlimited confidence reposed in them in many instances, and show in not a few that they are not unworthy of it.

"The Malays, in a peculiar degree, are fond of music, and have a great taste and good judgment in performing. All the first people have bands of their own, who perform, as I was capable of judging, very well. Their instruments — or, at least, those which they use in the concerts above mentioned — are European, and the same as are usually played upon in the more western regions. Those bands which are brought to some degree of perfection, when sold bring a large price; but without any particular recommendation, and as they are taken from the vessels which import them, they are sold for about one hundred paper-dollars a head. I was astonished at the low price they bore in comparison to the Guinea slaves in America and the colonies; but it is to be accounted for from their being in less demand, and in greater numbers to be disposed of.

"The temper of the Malays is in a great degree vindictive, — never forgetting an injury done them, let what time will transpire between receiving the injury and having an opportunity to revenge it. Of the truth of this, there were, while I was at Batavia, many melancholy proofs. This revengeful temper of the Malays is more to be feared from its being so carefully hid by the person who harbors it. They do not appear to have treasured up the remembrances of an affront; and, when least suspected, take some means to deprive of life the person who has, or who they imagine has, done them ill. They are great cowards; though, in my opinion, made so by their state of servitude and entire submission to the wills of their masters. They always time their murders so well, that they are very seldom detected. They take the night for carrying their designs into execution; and the street is generally the place where it is effected. They use their long knives to such purpose when they set about it, that the unhappy victim of their malice or revenge is in an instant put beyond the power of calling aid, and thrown into the canals, where he is found in the morning, but without the most distant expectation of detecting the murderer. There is scarcely ever an instance of two being concerned in a single murder, so distrustful are they of each other.

"A few weeks previous to my arrival, there was a murder committed upon a person who was beloved and respected by almost everybody. He was an ecclesiastic, but had retired to the country, having exerted his good talent to the satisfaction of every one; and there was little doubt but that he would receive the rewards of a good and faithful servant, and have another talent added to his store. This universally acknowledged good man was shot dead while sitting at the door of his own house, in the evening, by whom, or for what reason, could never be found out; but it was supposed to be one of his own servants; though why or wherefore I never heard conjectured. Jealousy is not a passion that has taken great root with these people. However, when they have reason to feel this most dangerous of the passions which disturb the human breast, it affects them in a very high degree; and death with aggravations is the consequence of infidelity.

"When well used, the Malays are grateful, and would go great lengths to save their benefactor. Though they are great thieves, and must be very sharply watched, yet their thefts are never extended, or but very seldom, to house-breaking. They will pilfer every thing which comes in their way when there is little fear of detection; and, by their address, will steal from you before your eyes. Instances of this kind frequently occur in unlading prows; and when there is any thing that will sink, such as iron, steel, &c., they, with great dexterity, let a part fall into the water.

"Batavia, which is the warehouse of the Dutch East India Company, and the most important by far of all their possessions round the Cape of Good Hope, is raised on the ruins of the ancient city of Jacatra, where the English had a settlement, and from which they were ousted by the Dutch in 1617. It is about fifty leagues from the entrance of the Straits of Sunda, and about twelve leagues from Bantam. It has a fine harbor, which is well defended from the winds by the many small islands which surround it. It has good anchorage, and could accommodate seven or eight hundred sail of shipping. The latitude of Batavia is 6° south, and about 106° east longitude. The Dutch, after wresting this place from its proper owners, made many improvements in it. It is at this time well guarded by a stone wall, which is well built, and about twelve feet high. Without it is a canal, which quite encompasses it, and has several drawbridges over it, which are occasionally drawn up. On it are several watch-towers, where are continually soldiers kept on sentry. It has four gates, one to each bridge, which are all well secured and guarded, each gate having a guard-house adjoining it, which has a considerable number of soldiers in it. These walls are well stored with guns and the necessary appendages, which are always kept in order in case of necessity. They are very ornamental, — being well painted of a stone color on the outside, and being well built in a manner that does honor to the artificers who executed them. The bastions are so laid out, that they would be serviceable as well against an insurrection as an invasion. The one or the other they would have great reason to fear, had either the Chinese, who were inhumanly cut off here, or the original inhabitants, who have always been under the lash of the present possessors, courage enough to retaliate; but, fortunately for the Dutch, they have a people to deal with, in the Chinese, who do not appear to have the passions which govern men in general. They appear here to have no resentment in their composition. They have a placid countenance, which is very seldom seen to be acted upon by any of the passions. If they are vexed at what you say, they never will give you the advantage of them by flying into a passion of anger. If they are pleased in the striking a bargain, you will never know it from their looks, perhaps for fear the other party should suppose he has the advantage; so that, whatever thwarts them, they are on their guard: whether pleased or disgusted, merry or sad, you are not the wiser, such is the command they have of themselves. If any thing can raise their muscles into a smile, it is the seeing an Englishman throw himself into a passion on a trifling occasion. They will compose themselves, and remain seated until his anger has evaporated, and then inquire the reason of it, however apparent it may have been. You seldom see them laugh. 'Tis true, they smile; but it appears to be more out of complaisance to you than from a natural impulse. It is certain the softer passions are not so visible in them as with us. They have no fellow-feeling at the sufferings of those around them in distress; they pass by without a look, or even a thought,—if I may judge from appearances,—on the situation of those who are exposed to the arrows of misfortune; and view without a change of countenance objects of distress which would call forth the tear of sympathy from every eye that had a tear to shed.

"The Chinese, in general, will tell you, with all the seeming indifference in nature, of the loss of a wife, parent, or child; and although they make a parade of grief at their funerals, yet no sooner is the ceremony at an end than the brow which but a moment before appeared to be overwhelmed with grief now wears a placid appearance, and has not upon it the most distant trace of sorrow.

"I saw, while at Batavia, two of these interments;

or rather I saw the procession pass of one, and the return of another. In the first, the corpse was borne by a number of coolies, or porters, the coffin covered with a white pall: then followed a number of women, with hoods covering their heads, and in white from the head to the very shoes, who by their walk one would suppose had been taking too freely of their favorite betel, and had felt the effects of it in their heads. But this was only the show of grief; and I afterwards found out they were hired mourners. They were on each side supported by other females, who appeared with difficulty to uphold them. Those were followed by the *near* and *dear* relatives of the deceased; but in their countenances was no mark of grief; and they looked on this and the other side of them with all the indifference possible. Such is the effect of education. Their wives they treat with very little attention: nor, indeed, does any thing seem to be their object or pursuit but wealth; to obtain which they stop at nothing, however low and despicable. There are said to be forty thousand Chinese in Batavia and its vicinity. They are governed by their own officers, but are all restricted to the general outlines of the Dutch policy. Many of them are immensely rich, and enter very largely into trade; have stores in town, and elegant country-seats without the gates. They parade about in their carriages with a great degree of state, and seem to feel their consequence. The numbers of Chinese are daily increasing at this place: every junk which comes brings more or less, most of whom they smuggle into the city, as they have a duty to pay on all regularly imported, — the number of them to be imported annually is prescribed, — and have a rix-dollar to pay per month for having the privilege of wearing the hair after the manner of their own countrymen; so that, what was first adopted against their own wills, they have now to pay for the privilege of enjoying. Why more of the Chinese leave their country one year than another is, that, while they can find wherewith to exist in their native country, they choose to tarry there; but, when famine stares them in the face, — which is the case in a greater or less degree almost every year, — they fly to this place, in hopes of finding better fare than their own country offers them. They wear the same dress as at Canton, and live in the same retired way. They are the principal mechanics, and the best husbandmen. Their merchants deal for the largest and the most trifling article; for the same man who will sell you to the amount of fifty thousand dollars will bring you a pot of sweetmeats which cost a couple of ducatoons; and there are no risks they will not run for this darling treasure. A Chinese, if detected in vending one pound of spices, is racked on the wheel; and yet there is scarce one of them who will not bring them to one's chamber after a short acquaintance. Great care, however, is to be used in purchasing from them; for they are in some instances employed as spies upon the conduct of strangers by the Dutch Company; and in others they will deceive you in whatever they sell, if they find you are a green hand; so that it is necessary to have one's eye well about one to deal with these people, the character of whom is to me unfathomable.

"The Chinese are industrious to a very great degree. They farm the customs and the fishery which supplies the town. The former they make serve very valuable purposes to them, as they can wink at such things as will befriend their countrymen and are prohibited; and the latter, though apparently of no great importance, is of very great consequence.

"Although there is the greatest abundance of fish at this place of any I was ever at, yet not one is lost; for they are all brought to market alive, — which is the only state the inhabitants buy them in; and what are not sold while alive are pickled and saved against the rainy season, when fish of all kinds are very scarce, and the dried are in very great request.

"As the Dutch are ever seeking to turn to their own advantage the whims of every one who is under their government, they have not omitted taking the advantage of the Chinese in their mode of burials. As every man who dies among the Chinese must have a separate burial-placc, and must have his ashes left undisturbed, he has to pay well for it. Their burial-places take up miles in extent. Some of the tombs are very richly decorated, and must have been expensive. Where a great man is buried, the ground is thrown up, in the form of a small hillock, to the height of ten or twelve feet; and at one side of it is the tombstone, with a large flat piece of marble-work placed at the entrance, below the stone which marks who lies within. For these spots are exacted very large sums; and, as the numbers dying from seventy thousand cannot be inconsiderable, the income this produces is great.

"It is with the Chinese to raise the exchange of the paper currency or lower it as they please; they being great money-holders, and the greatest speculators in the place. The principal place of their abode is one called the Chinese Camp, without the walls of the city. The Chinese who are here pretty generally use betel, and, without an exception, have always tea ready made on a stand in their houses and shops. In whichever you go, you have a cup of it presented to you; which was very seldom refused by me, and which I found to be afterwards the general custom of the place.

"The Chinese are very cleanly in their persons. They bathe in the rivers often, and are, in a great degree, nice in their dress, which is the best adapted to the heat of the climate of any worn in this place. The trading men, in general, are dressed in straw-colored Persian. Their outer garment is a kind of frock, which hangs loosely over the shoulders, and extends as far down as the knees: it has buttons at the neck, and loopholes, by which they can, and for the most part do, fasten it. The sleeves are so loose as to go twice round the arm, if forced to, and reach down below the fingers' ends. I could not help — after being a little acquainted with them — assigning a bad motive for the construction of these sleeves. Besides this, they have a pair of loose trousers made of the same silk, which reach the ankles, and must be very cool and agreeable. They wear the Chinese shoe, which is clumsy and ill contrived. They are made of black satin, or rather covered with that silk, except when they are in mourning, when they wear white shoes, as well as every thing else of that color, — black being rather a rejoicing than a mourning dress. They wear on the head a little kind of skull-cap, about the bigness of a quart bowl, though not one-third its depth. This they take off, in the same manner as we do our hats, when they meet a person to whom they pay their respects; and they also give the hand in the same manner as practised with us. The wearing the hair as they do is what gives the most singular appearance. They shave the heads of their children as soon as any hair is visible, leaving only a round patch on a part of the back side of the head. The hair growing on this spot they take every pains in forwarding, and delight in having this favorite lock as long as possible. They plait it; and, when it is not naturally long, they blend in with it a kind of black silk, which resembles very much the hair, to give it what nature has denied. This lock is left hanging down the back, and, in some of them, reaches near the ground. When they are occupied with any thing wherein the hair interferes, it is wound round the head, and the end tucked under the thicker part, which keeps it from falling. They shave, for the most part, every day; and there is no part of the face, nor indeed any part above the middle of the neck, over which the razor is not passed. For the inside of the nose and indented parts of the ears, they have a narrow razor made for the purpose. The operation of champooing I never saw performed; though I am informed it is practised here as at Canton.

"The junks which come from China to this place always leave it by the 15th of July, and arrive in January. They are, to appearance, miserable things, and must stand a poor chance in a typhoon, — which is a heavy gale of wind, like the hurricanes in the West Indies, though said to be more violent. More or less of the junks are missing every year; and there is no doubt they are foundered in those heavy storms.

"The Chinese have a free trade to Batavia, where they bring tea, china, japanned wares, nankins, silks, &c., and take, in return, Spanish dollars and ducatoons, though the former are preferred. Spices, birds'-nests, pepper, tin, sugars, coffee, candy, beeswax, oil, hides, burning-canes, ratans, sandal-wood, and, when there is a probability of scarcity in China, rice, which will always pay a good freight, are exported.

"There is an old law which forbids the Javans from being made slaves; but they are in service, more or less of them, in almost every house. There are many sepoys in the service of the company as soldiers. They are stout, well-set men, in general about five feet eight inches high, and well proportioned, and their skins are almost as black as those of the inhabitants of the coast of Guinea. Their hair is black, and tied behind, though, in general, inclined to be curly. They have a sharp eye and fierce countenances, and are said to be fine soldiers. Their dress is a short, blue coat, made of thin cloth, with red lappels, and a waistcoat of the same, with a coarse shirt. Their breeches are made tight, buttoned over the hips, and do not come more than one-third the way down the thigh, to which they set as close as the skin itself. They have a sort of half-gaiter and shoes, and are more particularly employed as marines on board the spice-ships."

He proceeded to Canton for a cargo of teas. While he was there, a vessel arrived whose name has since become one of historical interest, — the "Columbia;" the ship which, in her next voyage, under the command of Capt. Gray, crossed the bar of the Columbia River, as it was always called afterwards, — the incident being referred to in recent negotiations of intense interest, as the foundation of a territorial claim on the part of the United States. Remaining several months in China, and attending assiduously to the business of the ship, he became well acquainted with the habits of the Chinese, and collected a fund of information concerning trade there in all its branches, and the value of sea-otter skins and other furs from the north-west coast of our continent, which formed the basis of action for him afterwards in planning numerous voyages and directing mercantile operations of great importance between America, Asia, and Europe. He was long remembered there too, particularly by one occupying a subordinate position at the time, who had observed him, though not known to him personally, and who afterwards became eminently distinguished in the commerce of the East, — the well-known Hong merchant, Houqua. Commercial relations of an intimate character and entire confidence were afterwards established between them, and existed for many years with mutual advantage.

Returning homeward, he found that the period of his absence had been eventful in changes that were to have important influence in the political and commercial world. They received news of the revolutionary movements in France from a vessel which they spoke in crossing the trade-winds. On arriving at Boston, they found our government organized under the new constitution of 1789; and though this led to heavy duties, particularly on teas, it was giving confidence and stability to trade. With the information which he had brought home, he sent a brig — the "Hope," Capt. Ingraham — to the north-west coast, with the intention of terminating the voyage at Canton. The most important result of this voyage appears to have been the discovery of the northern portion of the Marquesas Islands, as now laid down on the map of the Pacific. Its main object was defeated by untoward circumstances.

He soon afterwards joined his friend Capt. Magee, however, in building a ship, — the "Margaret," — of which the captain went master for the north-west coast, and, after an absence of two years and a half, brought the voyage to a successful close. Capt. Magee carried out the frame of a vessel, with three or four carpenters, and set up the little craft of about thirty tons under Capt. Swift, then the chief carpenter; and the schooner collected some twelve or fifteen hundred sea-otters during the season, which added much to the profit of the voyage, as the skins were worth thirty or forty dollars when Capt. Magee reached China.

In 1792, the insurrection began in St. Domingo, where his brothers had continued their establishment, doing a prosperous business up to that period. Mr. James Perkins, the eldest brother, and his wife, were in a perilous situation at the beginning of it, being in the interior on a visit to a friend who had a plantation, next to the one first destroyed, on the plains of the cape. They made their escape, however, from the frightful treatment which awaited all who lingered, and reached the cape. But things grew worse. The place was taken by the insurgents, and burned; and the inhabitants were obliged to get away in the best manner they could. This, of course, broke up his brothers' establishment. Their store was burned by the blacks, with its contents, which were valuable. This, however, was not the worst; as the planters were largely in debt to the house, and their means of paying destroyed. The brothers (James and Samuel G.) returned to Boston, having lost most of their property, to begin the world anew. He then formed a copartnership, under the firm of J. and T. H. Perkins, with his brother James, which continued until the death of the latter in 1822, though the name of the firm was altered on the admission of their sons in 1819. They used the information which had been acquired at St. Domingo with advantage, by keeping two or three vessels trading to the West Indies, and shipping coffee and sugar to Europe.

But their most important business was the trade of

their ships on the north-west coast and in China. They were concerned in numerous voyages in that direction; and eventually established a house at Canton, under the firm of Perkins and Co., which became one of great importance, and eminently successful.

In December, 1794, he took passage for Bourdeaux in a ship belonging to his own house and that of Messrs. S. Higginson and Co., in which firm his brother, Mr. S. G. Perkins, had become a partner, with a cargo of provisions; the demand for them in the disturbed state of French affairs offering the prospect of a fair result to such a voyage. But the depreciation of the assignats, and other causes, threatening to defeat their hopes, he found it best to continue abroad for some time.

His voyage to France was long, with boisterous weather, and some narrow escapes, as appears by the following extracts from the journal which he kept at the time:—

"Dec. 14, 1794. Sunday.—This day, at nine o'clock, got under way in the ship 'Charlotte,' with the wind at north-west, blowing a fresh breeze; and at half-past ten o'clock passed the light-house, and put the pilot (Knox) on shore: schooner 'Rambler' in company.

"15th.—A delightful breeze still continues.

"16th.—Still pleasant weather. Fell in with a shoal of porpoises, and took a couple. Capt. Hill, in the 'Rambler,' left us this day,—we being too dull company for his fast-sailing schooner.

"21st.—We did not omit on Saturday P.M., precisely at ten minutes before five,—which corresponds with four o'clock in Boston,—to remember the Saturday's club.

"25th.—A brisk north-west wind; the sea more smooth since we took our leave of the Bank of Newfoundland. It is supposed that the fogs, so frequent on and near this bank, are caused by the waters of the Gulf Stream, driven as they are from the warm climates of the West Indies to the cold generally prevalent here, which condenses the vapor as it rises; just, it is said, 'as the vapor from a cup of tea is hardly discernible in a warm room, but becomes visible in the cold air.' In observing the fog rise from the water this morning, I found that it continually issued directly to the leeward of the track of the ship,—which seems to prove the justice of the remark. The water is probably cooled on the surface in coming thus far eastward and northward; yet the stirring up the column below exposes it to the cold air. And, to follow the simile of the tea, we may observe even when that is somewhat cooled, and no evaporation appears, yet, if it be stirred with the spoon, vapor rises on exposure to the cold air, from which it had been defended by the surface.

"28th.—This day fortnight we parted from Boston, and this day at noon complete half our distance from the place of our departure to that of our destination. This is not doing bad.

"29th.—The number of rainbows we have seen almost daily since we have passed the Banks of Newfoundland is surprising. It is not uncommon to see five or six in a day, the beauty of which surpasses any thing I have ever before seen.

"31st.—The wind continues to the northward; and yet the weather is as warm as it generally is in Boston Bay in autumn. How kindly ordered is this by Him who orders and governs all things! Were the ocean, off soundings, as subject to snow and equal degrees of cold as the land, it would be impossible for vessels to cross it in the winter months, on account of the ice which would make upon them, and cause them to founder inevitably. Besides this, the sailors, who are without fire altogether, and who are in blowing weather continually wet, would not be able to stand the decks, and must leave them, to find security against the cold.

"This is the last day in the year, — a melancholy anniversary to my family. Our first-born child, Sally, died Dec. 31.

"On the deck of this ship it is now too warm for pleasure at mid-day; and we have the windows, or rather sky-lights, — for the cabin windows have been closed by the dead-lights ever since we sailed, — open at this moment.

"Jan. 9th. — 'Tis rather mortifying, to one who feels so anxious to get on shore as I do, to be rather worse off in point of situation than we were a week since; having lost as much in steering southward as we gained in steering northward.

"The wind this morning blowing very fresh, and a prospect of a heavy gale.

"10th. — Cloudy and unpleasant, with rain. P.M. — Blowing very heavy, and a large sea running. At ten, A.M., the wind, after a rainy night, shifted to the southward, and promised us a quick passage to our port, which we are now panting after; but, to our inexpressible mortification, it came out again at south-east, and continues to blow fresh.

"15th. — Well may inconstancy be compared to the winds. Our flattering prospects of a continuance of a favorable wind vanished when we had scarcely begun to enjoy it; and it has continued directly contrary through this twenty-four hours.

"16th. — An obscure, rainy day, with a head wind, blowing fresh. At meridian, tacked ship to the northward. When one becomes a voluntary exile from society, and takes leave of those on whose smiles his happiness depends, he is very apt to ask himself questions, which can be answered with very little satisfaction, when it is too late. This is strikingly my case; and, were it not unmanly to repine, I should feel quite a disposition to do so.

"18th. — At eight this morning, hove the ship to, to sound, but found no bottom. The occasion for sounding was the number of land-birds about us. A very beautiful crow was taken by the sailors; and many more were about the ship.

"25th. Three o'clock, P.M. — Just as we were about to heave the ship to, — the gale continuing to increase, — a fleet of ships were seen directly ahead. Nineteen sail were counted; and they extended their line as if it were a large fleet. A heavy squall passing us just before dark, the ship was kept away before the wind, to avoid falling in with any of these ships. This we flattered ourselves we had succeeded in, until about eight o'clock in the evening, when a light was discovered, which appeared like the false fire made use of by vessels of war for signals. We wore ship immediately, and continued to see the fires repeated for some time; till, to our great joy, they subsided, and we thought ourselves in security. Anxious, however, lest we should still run afoul of some straggler of the fleet, I did not venture to bed till twelve o'clock; and my mind had hardly got quieted enough to sleep, when a number of voices from deck cried, 'She is close aboard of us!' and, from all which could be heard below, the most fatal event was to be expected. A signal was thrown out by a lantern; when the ship saw us, and kept away. Those who saw her when nearest, suppose she was but a few rods from us. The rigging was very plainly seen even when I reached the deck; which I did with the utmost haste, and but few clothes on, as there seemed every reason to expect the ship would run us down; and those who could escape by getting on board of her would alone save themselves.

"It pleased Him 'who caters for the sparrow' that we should escape this sad alternative. I never remember to have passed such a night before, and hope I never shall such another.

"The gale was very heavy, and the night dark as possible. Had the ship not shown her light,—which she did every half-hour,—we should not have seen her, and of course not shown a signal; and the event would no doubt have proved fatal to us. We were lying to when we saw her. We were happy at the return of morning, when there was no sail in sight. The gale did not abate till about meridian.

"25th. Sunday. — 'Tis now six weeks since we left Boston; and we are doubtless supposed by our friends to have arrived ere this.

"26th. — This day makes but seventeen days of fair wind since we sailed; and of course we have had twenty-eight days' head wind.

"28th. — A strong breeze, but fortunately the right way. At four, P.M., the wind increased to such a height as obliged us to heave to, although a fair wind, — which is rather mortifying; but the immense sea which is running makes it necessary, the decks being continually loaded with water.

"At about eleven o'clock at night, it blew as heavy a gale as we have had since we have been out, and after that time began to moderate.

"At six o'clock, sounded, and got bottom in about eighty fathoms, — white and brown coral, shells, and small stones. The captain's reckoning hindered him from running the latter part of the night, as he did not like to be too near shore, should it continue to blow. Sounded at eight o'clock: eighty fathoms. Small, gray sand, with small pieces of dark-colored shells. Kept on our course.

"29th. — I passed a very anxious night; and sleep was a stranger to my eyes but for a short time.

"At daylight, saw the land, and considered ourselves about ten miles distant. At about eight o'clock, it began to snow and blow; the ship continuing south-east, and we under as much sail as the ship will bear, running off shore.

"'How happy a sailor's life passes!' says the song; but, if this is happiness, let me seek mine in another way.

"30th. — Hove to in a gale.

"Feb. 1st. Sunday. — At eight o'clock, stood in for the land, with a good breeze after midnight, in company with a Dutchman, whom we spoke, and who told us he had been five weeks in the bay. This served to reconcile us to the passage we have had, tedious as it has now become. At noon, saw a quantity of staves, the quarter-deck of a vessel, and other timber, floating on the water. Very anxious, for fear we should not get in with the land in time to get a pilot.

"Monday morning, Feb. 2, 1794. — At one o'clock yesterday afternoon, losing all hopes of getting in before night, all the vessels in company stood upon a wind to the northward. I little expected what were the dangers to which I was to be exposed this night; which I am certain was the most perilous I ever passed, or perhaps ever shall. The distance we were from the shore, when we hove about, could not be more than five or six miles at the extent. The wind continued to blow from four o'clock, and, from a fresh breeze, came to a most violent gale. The sea ran so high that we expected every moment to have the decks swept; and the ocean appeared like one continued wave breaking over rocks. All probability of our saving ourselves now depended upon carrying sail upon the ship; which we did so as to bury her in the waves. Our greatest apprehension was, lest we should have some of our sail blown away; in which case, inevitable destruction must have been our lot. The number of vessels in company, too, was another cause of uneasiness. We saw only one in the hardest part of the gale. After nine o'clock, presuming, from the course we had been obliged to run, that we must soon be on shore on that tack, we wore ship, and stood on the other tack; the wind blowing still directly on shore. After midnight, the wind abated, to our great joy. We were all truly sensible of the danger to which we had been exposed; and every one declared he had never seen such a night before. A lee shore within a few miles, and a heavy gale blowing directly on, to one who has so many blessings to live for, and who is so well satisfied with his lot in life, was to me distressing. For several hours I was in this awful state of suspense; and my reflections were not the most agreeable. Had necessity urged me from home, it would have been different. I should have been satisfied with having been in the line of my duty, and should have put a better face on it than I was now able to do.

"Tuesday morning. — We stood in shore, anxious lest we should again be too late. At ten o'clock, we saw many vessels standing in; and, at eleven, made the light, but saw no pilots come off. Finding ourselves in shore, and the wind blowing directly on, our only alternative was to go in at all events. Accordingly, we put our confidence in a chart, and were so fortunate as to get up the river past the light-house; when, doubling the point, a pilot came off to us when all danger was past. In this we are fortunate to a degree beyond our expectations. We were visited by a vessel stationed a few leagues up the river; and the officer took a note of our cargo, and left us. The pilot tells us there is an American brig lost on the rocks in the mouth of the river; and we are anxious for our friend Gray. He says we are very fortunate not to have been in sooner, as those vessels which arrived ten days since have been in imminent danger of being driven on shore by the ice, and have been obliged to cut their cables and run on shore to save themselves; so that we know not when we go too fast or too slow."

His observations while he remained in France, and the occurrences in which he became concerned, were of an interesting character. He made full notes at the time; but the following account is taken from the memoranda already referred to, in a week of leisure long afterwards, and commencing thus:—

"TO MY CHILDREN.

"SARATOGA SPRINGS, July 18, 1846.

"It has often occurred to me, that it would have given me infinite pleasure to have known more than has come to my knowledge of the early life of my father. He died when I was about six years of age;

and all I know of him is from report. My recollections of him are very faint; though I have an impression that I remember him in an emaciated state shortly before his death."

After narrating, for the information of his family, some incidents of his early life, — part of which have been already mentioned, — he proceeds to relate the occurrences that followed this voyage to France, as follows: —

"I remained in Europe from December, 1794, to October, 1795, — a very interesting period of the French Revolution. What was called 'The Mountain' in the convention, had been prostrated in some degree by the fall of Robespierre, the principal mover in the most bloody scenes of the revolution. He endeavored to destroy himself; but failed, and left the final act to the guillotine. This instrument had done execution on thousands through his influence; and retributive justice was satisfied in the fate which expiated his crimes.

"France was by no means in a quiet state when I reached Bourdeaux; and, in travelling with the courier day and night, we passed so near the theatre of war in La Vendée as to hear the reports of the cannon of the belligerent parties. If we had been fallen in with by the Vendéens, we should doubtless have had our throats cut, as public agents and bearers of despatches from one province to another. We escaped, however, unharmed; though the fate we feared befell the courier a few nights after we passed. During my stay in Europe, my time was passed principally in Paris, where I had rooms in the same hotel with my friend Mr. Joseph Russell. We kept a carriage between us, — always visiting or travelling together. It was a new English chariot, which had been left behind by some traveller on the breaking out of the war, and was in perfect order. We found it of great convenience while in the city; as public carriages were not easily had, and no private ones were kept by any Frenchmen. Indeed, they were kept by very few except by foreign ambassadors.

"There were in Paris several Americans of my acquaintance besides Mr. Russell. We used to dine at a restorateur, and breakfast at home; the wife of the porter of the hotel furnishing our coffee. There was a great scarcity of breadstuffs during the winter and spring. It was produced partly by the farmers having their ploughshares turned into swords, partly by the waste attendant on war, and in part by an unwillingness to sell for assignats, which were constantly declining in value. The whole population of Paris was placed under restriction; and each family received a certain quantity per day from the public bakers at a fixed price. The hotels gave in their number of guests, for whom they drew the stipulated quantity; and those who dined out had their bread carried to the place where they dined. I dined almost every Saturday with the minister of the United States, where I was in the habit of meeting distinguished men.

"I had little business to do in Paris; and leisure, therefore, to observe what was passing. Having sold the cargo, or the principal part of it, to government, I had little else to do for months than to dance attendance upon the bureau which had the adjustment of the account; and was finally obliged to leave the matter to the care of a friend.

"After the fall of Robespierre, the revolutionary tribunal, of which Fouquier Tinville was the accusateur-public, — like our attorney-general, — being abolished, he, with five judges and ten jurymen, in all sixteen, were executed in the Place de Grève by that operation which they had inflicted on men, women, and even children, for pretended crimes. I went with Mr. Russell, Mr. Higginson, and several others, and secured a room, the nearest we could get to the place of execution, that we might witness it closely. The prisoners arrived in two carts; from which they were taken out, and placed in the room directly under the scaffold. From there they were taken, one by one, and, by a ladder of eight or ten feet, were brought to the instrument, and decapitated. The attorney-general was the last to suffer, and must have felt at the fall of the axe in every execution as much as he felt when his turn came. They all met their fate without a struggle, except a man — one of the judges — who had been of the noblesse of the country, and whose name was Le Roi, which he had, by decree of the convention, changed to Dix Aout, or Tenth of August, after the assault upon the Tuileries on that memorable day, when the Swiss and the king's immediate attendants were so shamefully murdered by the populace of Paris. This man died game, but kept vociferating his execrations upon his executioner until he was silenced by the fall of the axe.

"This mode of execution is certainly merciful, inasmuch as its work is soon done. From the time the prisoners descended from the carts, until their heads were all in long baskets, placed in the same carts with the lifeless trunks, was fourteen minutes. Two minutes were lost by changing the carts; so that, if all the remains could have been placed in one basket, but twelve minutes would have been required for beheading the sixteen persons! The square was filled with people. Great numbers of the lowest classes — and the low class of women were the most vociferous — were there, clapping and huzzaing with every head that fell. These were the same people who sang hallelujahs on the deaths of those who had been condemned to the guillotine by the very tribunal who had now paid the debt they owed to the city; for their convictions were principally of the city. Other wretches of the same stamp were acting their infernal parts in different departments of France. Notwithstanding the deserts of this most execrable court, the exhibition was horrid to my feelings, however deserved the fate of the culprits.

"Mr. Monroe, the minister of the United States, told me that he wished a service to be rendered by some one, and felt great interest that I should give my aid to it. The object was, that I should aid in sending Mr. George Washington La Fayette to the United States. His mother, the Marchioness La Fayette, was then in Paris with her daughters, and Mr. Frestal, their tutor. Mr. Monroe gave me a letter to her; and I found her lodged in the third story, in the Rue de l'Arbre Sec. She explained her object to me; which was, to get her son sent to the United States, to prevent him from being drawn by the conscription into the army. He was then fourteen years of age. The proposal she made to me was, that I should apply to the Convention for permission to procure a passport for her son to go to America, for the purpose of his being educated in a counting-house. As the marquis was in bad odor in France, it was deemed necessary to sink the real name of the party, and to apply to the Committee of Safety for a passport for G. W. Motier, this being a name of his family which he had a right to assume. Madame La Fayette was intimately acquainted with Boissy d'Anglas, the president of the committee, and one of the old aristocracy of France; and from him she had assurance, that, if the application were made by an American, it would be favorably received. The marquis was at the time prisoner in the Castle of Olmutz, in Austria; and the object of madame was to go to him with her daughters, and solace him in his deplorable confinement, where his health was suffering.

"The application to the committee was complied with; and my friend Mr. Russell, who took an active part in aiding in the plan, accompanied George La Fayette to Havre, where was an American ship in which I had an interest, commanded by Capt. Thomas Sturgis, brother to Mr. R. Sturgis, who married my eldest sister. To him I gave letters, requesting that Mr. La Fayette might have a passage in the ship, which was freely accorded. Mr. Russell and myself paid the expense of the journey and the passage; and Mr. La Fayette arrived in Boston, where he was cordially received by my family, and passed some time there. He afterwards went to Mount Vernon, and lived in the family of General Washington, until, in the following year, he returned to Europe, when he entered the revolutionary army.

"He served with reputation; but, as the name was not a favorite one with the existing leaders, he was kept in the background by the influence of General Bonaparte; and retired, after a year or two of service, to private life. He is yet living (1846), and has been a member of the House of Deputies since the fall of Bonaparte.

"Madame La Fayette went to Austria, and remained with her husband up to the time of his liberation. Immediately after his being set at liberty, he wrote me a letter, dated at Olmutz, thanking me for the share I had taken in enabling his wife to visit him in his distress, and declaring that I had been the means of saving his life by the means used in restoring his family to him. This letter is now in the possession of Mrs. Bates, of London, to whom I gave it as an interesting article for her portfolio."

The following passages from the diary which he

kept in Paris at this time have considerable interest when taken in connection with what it appears was then done to promote the wishes of Madame de La Fayette. It will be observed, that there is no reference in this journal — written as it was with the hazard of its falling by treachery into the hands of some spy — to the subject which so deeply concerned that unfortunate lady. When he calls on her, when she breakfasts with him, or he goes with Mr. Russell to see him off for Havre, there is no allusion to the youth who accompanied the latter, and on whose escape her happiness and the welfare of the marquis so far depended.

"Old style. Paris, March 12, 1795. 22d Ventose. — I left Bourdeaux with the courier, and in six days and a half arrived at this seat of luxury and dissipation, where every thing is on a large scale, and the scenes of business and amusement are so numerous that it is apt to bewilder the head of a young traveller.

"My business has so much taken up my time since I arrived in Paris, that I have neglected to keep a note of the time as it passed, that at a future day I may have it in my power to recall to my memory some things which would escape it were this mode neglected.

"I am not a great lover of bustle and the amusements of the city, but rather admire the country round it, which is always cultivated and embellished in proportion to the magnificence of the city in the vicinity of which it is situated. The thousand ideas that have revolved in my mind within a few years, respecting this great theatre of the revolution, are all ushered into my thoughts together, upon coming into the part of the city which shows the places where the great scenes have been acted; such as the Palace of the Tuileries, the Elysian Fields, &c. The bridges in front of the palace are beautiful, and add much to the beauty of the prospect from the neighboring houses. The first time I walked over the Pont Neuf, I felt the force of Sterne's story of the notary, who, clapping his cane to his head, tipped the sentinel's hat into the river. My hand went instinctively to my head, and my hat had nigh gone after the sentinel's. There seems to be always a current of wind there; and every one takes the precaution the notary did in walking over it.

"24th. — The day pleasant. This day I dined with the American minister, whom I find to be a very gentleman-like, and, to appearance, worthy man. The celebrated Van Staphorst, who was exiled for his republicanism from Amsterdam, was there, and several other gentlemen of distinction. Mrs. Monroe is one of the finest women I ever knew; and she is said to combine the greatest worth with her personal accomplishments and beauty.

"25th. — The morning is again clear, for a wonder, and promises well for a pleasant day. Yesterday gave me news of the "Betsy's" arrival at Bourdeaux; and the same post informed me that the brig "Delight" was taken and carried to England. 'Tis well not to have extremes of good and ill fortune.

"I went yesterday through the Palace of the Tuileries, which was the one occupied by the royal family when at Paris, which I am told was but seldom, as their time was chiefly spent at Versailles. The apartment of the *ci-devant* queen was pointed out to me: it wears the marks of the violence of the tenth of August. The appearance of the palace is very majestic, and, when kept in good order, must have been superior to any other in Europe. The gardens in the rear, and the Champs Elysées, make one think one's self on enchanted ground. All the rooms in the palace are taken up with committees and the assembly-house. I had formed an idea of the room in which the Convention sit as immensely large; and indeed it must be large to contain seven hundred members on the lower floor; but the galleries and the tribunes are small in proportion to what one would suppose from the great noise they have made, and the terror they have created. The part called the Mountain does not appear to me to be capable of holding above four or five hundred persons. A large majority of the people in the galleries at the Convention are women, of all ages and conditions; most of whom are said to be hired to go there to approve or disapprove certain measures, as they may be for or against the party by which they are sent. It is certainly a very unfair influence; and I wonder at its being countenanced by the Convention.

"The members of the Convention wear their hats, and stroll about as their whims may call them. They begin business at about one o'clock, and finish at four o'clock, unless something of importance prevents them from adjourning. In the time of Robespierre, the majority of the people in the galleries were, as at present, women; but I am told they were very ill-dressed, and their vociferations at times were such as to prevent business. The leaders in the galleries at this time are the *Jeunes Gens*, who talk loud, and approve or disapprove with great warmth. The American and French colors are suspended over the chair of the president. I had an idea that every member who spoke was obliged to go into the tribune, — which is an elevation in front of the seats of the members; but I find that this is optional. Any one who intends to speak long, or wishes to make himself well heard, mounts the tribune; but they speak also from their seats.

"Barrère, Collot d'Herbois, Vadier and his colleague, have not yet had their trials. Their fate is pronounced, by every one I have conversed with, inevitable. That Collot d'Herbois merits it, no one will doubt who hears the facts related respecting his conduct at Lyons.

"Louis were two hundred and four livres two days since: they are to-day one hundred and fifty.

"26th. — The morning charmingly pleasant. A decree was this day issued to serve the inhabitants of the city with but one pound of bread for each individual in a family. This, to a Frenchman, is starvation; although children are entitled to the same as a grown person, and of course, in a large family where there are children, the quantity will be greater to adults than a pound per day, — which, to an

American, would be more than he wanted. Bread is given out at Paris for three sous per pound; whereas in all the other departments they are paying ten times that sum. This, however, has always been the case in this metropolis, where the poor govern, or where they would govern, and with a rod of iron, were they in want of the *staff of life.* This was done under the old government, when it was supposed that the will of the government could not be overawed by the people; and therefore it is not surprising that the Convention is obliged to do the same under the dominion of Liberty and Equality. This fact is not pleasing to the other great cities of the republic, which are obliged to pay twenty shillings per pound for the same article, and by the same government; but Paris, it seems, must be indulged in those things. The plenty in the markets in the city, of meats generally, and particularly of poultry of the best kind I ever saw, is surprising; and, in the public houses, every thing which speaks plenty is displayed in profusion.

"27th. — The morning fair; but the day, after nine o'clock, rainy and unpleasant. There are eighteen theatres open every night in this great, this immense city; and what is still more astonishing is, that they are all crowded; and, when a favorite piece is to be given, it is necessary to apply for tickets early in the day. The Opera House is the most beautiful I have yet seen; and the dancing is so far beyond what I had before seen, that it appeared to me like magic. The opera of 'Telemachus' was performed a few evenings since, to the delight of every one. The character of Calypso was supported by a woman of an elegant appearance and fine action, and whose *tout ensemble* is thought better than that of any other person who appears on the stage. I am told she was carried through the streets, in the reign of the tyrant Robespierre, in the character and as the representation of the Almighty. Telemachus was supported by the famous dancer Vestris. The nymphs, upwards of forty in number, were dressed with all the wantonness imaginable: their dancing, too, is, to us Americans, indecent in the extreme.

"There appears to be no want of persons to fill up the play, and to give it all its effect. For instance, the other evening, in some piece which was given, there was a well-disciplined company of forty-eight, rank and file, accompanied by another company of archers introduced on the stage, who went through a number of evolutions to a charm. Upwards of one hundred persons were on the stage at one time.

"Every piece is replete with patriotic sentiments; and since the fall of the Jacobins, who are styled the drinkers of blood, scarcely a piece appears which does not contain some severity against them. The *bonnet rouge*, which was once so much in fashion in France, is no longer worn: indeed, it would be dangerous for a man to be seen with one in the streets. The revolution which has taken place in respect to the Jacobins is astonishing. They who ruled France, and with a rod of iron, are now afraid to appear in the streets; for they are scouted wherever they are met, and it is as much as their lives are worth to be seen abroad. Whenever one has been found in the play-house, he has been made to run the gantlet, and was glad to get off so.

"28th Ventose. — The weather more unpleasant than yesterday; and, this morning, snow and rain fell in a small quantity. It is said that the Committee of *Salut Public* is occupied with some negotiations of peace with the kings of Prussia and Spain; and it seems to be the general opinion, that the 'conceited John Bull' (as the Parisians say) and the emperor will be obliged to hold the field, or rather to fly it alone. We are told here that the 'infatuated Pitt' is making great exertions to carry on the ensuing campaign with vigor. 'Madness cannot be greater than this,' say the Parisians.

"About eight hundred persons went yesterday to the Convention to complain of their allowance of bread, and used some expressions which three months since would have sent them all to the guillotine. The speaker for the multitude said, among other things, that they almost repented their exertions to effect the revolution, which was attended with so many evils. The reply of the president was spirited, and the Convention showed a great degree of indignation on the occasion. In lieu of having the honors of a sitting, as has been usual, they were advised to retire to their labors peacefully. The patrols have been increased since the deficiency of bread, and also the guards of the city.

"29th. — This morning it rained for an hour, and

the weather through the day has been very unpleasant. This day confirmed my opinion of the perfidy of some of the agents of the government. Although the contract I made with them was signed, they now make difficulties, and wish to alter the tenor of the agreement.

"I was this morning at the Convention, and was astonished at the intemperance which discovered itself in a debate which took place there. I was in the uppermost tribune, and could hear very little that was said, so distinctly as to understand the subject of debate. Lecointre, who was in the tribune, and had the 'parole,' was interrupted every moment. The two parties showed themselves *pro* and *con.;* and their gestures and tones would have led one to suppose that they would be at fisticuffs every moment. The president rang his bell for a minute at a time, but all to no effect; and I expected to see his hat go on every minute. Order was at length restored, and the orator proceeded. This, I am told, happens every day; but I doubt if it does to such a degree. Every member was up and speaking at the same time, in a tone of thunder; and the threats which their motions led me to believe they made use of would with us not have ended there. This kind of management in a legislative assembly is most certainly wrong and disgraceful; at least, it appears so to an American spectator.

"I am told most of the business of the Republic is executed by the Committee of Public Safety, which consists of but twelve persons. This committee may be called the Executive of the Government. It is appointed by the Convention, and is removable at the pleasure of that body; while its proceedings must be approved by the representatives of the people.

"Other committees are appointed for finance, commerce, war, &c., by the head committee of Salut Public, one of the members of which is president of the principal committee; so that all the doings of the several distinct departments eventually concentrate in the Committee of *Salut Public*, where they are matured and carried into effect when approved. I am told that the Executive Committee is the most indefatigable of any in the world; and that they sit at business until four and five o'clock in the morning, and are at it again at ten or eleven. In this way a great deal of business must be accomplished; and it is certain that they have effected wonders.

"Peace is still talked of with Spain and Prussia; and it is said that there is an emissary now in Paris, who comes to know if a commissioner would be received.

"My landlady tells me that I must go to the section to-day, and get a pound of bread, or I shall not be able to get any in the house. As bread is not the staff of life with me, I think I shall dispense with the bread, rather than be plagued with getting a card to entitle me to it.

"I am told that the daily guard, which mounts in this city, is at least twenty thousand in number. This is astonishing; and, at the time of the arrest of Robespierre, it is said to have been doubled. It consists principally of the citizens, who are all obliged to serve in turn; and no one is excused, or can find a person to serve in his stead, unless for very good and cogent reasons. They are generally armed with spears, fixed in the end of long poles.

"I see with great pleasure the national troops, which are sometimes paraded in the place before the Palace of the Tuileries. They are fine-looking fellows; and a band of music generally accompanies them on parade. The cannoneers all appear to be very young men, some of them not more than fifteen or sixteen years of age; and I am told that to them the Republic is indebted for some of the best victories she has to boast. May every man be a cannoneer when opposed to tyrants, and every cannoneer an army in himself!

"Exchange in silver seven hundred for one hundred.

"30th Ventose or Decadi. March 20th. — The morning more pleasant than for some days past. The churches may now be opened freely; and every one has the privilege of worshipping God as he may see fit. The suspension of this right has been one of the most unfortunate measures ever taken, for it is supposed to have been the cause in La Vendée of the loss to the Republic of three hundred thousand lives; and, what is even worse than that, it produced an animosity between those who ought to think and act like brothers and friends, which it will be very difficult to eradicate. An eventual peace is at last established in that quarter, which for two years past has been a scene of blood and carnage. Freedom of thinking is a privilege which, when once enjoyed, will not be tamely given up, particularly in matters of religion; and it is, in my opinion, wise and prudent in the Convention to take off the shackles which fettered this darling right.

"As I was taking my usual walk in the morning, I was induced, by the sound of music, to enter a building which was once used as a church, but which had been shut up by Robespierre for upwards of ten months. My friend Sabonadaire was there, with whom I took a seat.

"This discourse was the first one delivered since the opening; and the subject was principally the sacred liberty of religious opinion. The society was Presbyterian. The women seemed particularly affected by the discourse, which was very pathetic. Mr. Sabonadaire pointed out to me Miss Helen Maria Williams; and, as I had an inclination to be acquainted with her, he introduced me to her after church. She seemed to be a sensible, sprightly woman, but too much of a politician.

"1st Germinal. 22d March. — The weather appears to change with the introduction of the month, and speaks the approach of spring and its attendant beauties.

"There is a general agitation in Paris this day. Large assemblies of persons were seen in the streets; and the cause of this is supposed to be the approaching trial of the four members of the Convention, — Barrère, &c. It is said that the Jacobins wish to raise a party to rescue them; and the fear of seeing them again in power sets every one alive and on the watch. In the evening there were blows given in the Palais d'Egalité; and I am assured that several hundred Jacobins appeared there, and put the Jeunesse de Paris to flight. They returned to the charge with increased numbers, and beat their opponents off the ground. Large numbers of the young men paraded the streets in the evening, chanting the new, patriotic, anti-Jacobin song of 'Réveil du Peuple.' The guards in Paris, who I am told amount every day to twenty thousand men, are double that number to-day.

"The trial commences to-morrow.

"2d. — Cloudy and unpleasant. This day will be an interesting one, and will show whether Jacobinism dare raise its hideous head.

"Midnight. — The commotions of the last evening, and the fear of seeing Jacobinism once more triumphant, brought out every man this day. The number of patrols that paraded the streets and the gardens of the Tuileries was astonishing. The guard of the day was forty thousand; besides which, the reserve guard, which may be called in half an hour, numbers sixty thousand. In addition to this, almost every man has girded on his sabre to-day, and paraded the gardens and palaces. The number of people in the Tuileries was very great; and every one was armed, and showed a spirit of determination to overthrow any thing Jacobinical that might show itself.

"Barrère, Collot d'Herbois, and Billaud de Varennes, were this day brought to the bar of the Convention. The crowd was so great that there was no getting in.

They are to make their defence to-morrow, or rather they will begin them; for it is supposed that they will procrastinate as much as possible, in order to give their party time to show itself. But it is too late: the general opinion dooms them to death; and there is but little doubt of their meeting it. If the condemnations finish with those now at the bar, the public will be very much disappointed. Incendiary pieces are stuck up, setting forth the necessity of taking off forty or fifty of the Convention, ere peace and security can be restored.

"3d. — This day has been more tranquil than was generally expected. Nothing shows itself which is opposed to the fate of those at the bar. In passing through the court of the Palace of the Tuileries this morning at ten o'clock, I saw the attention of the crowd attracted to a coach which entered; and, as it passed me, I perceived that one of the prisoners was in it, guarded by three *gens d'armes*, who rode in the coach with him. It was Billaud de Varennes. He jumped from the carriage as soon as the door was opened, and from where it stood to the door of the Convention, with great agility, as if not to be seen by the people, who were gathering in crowds round the carriage. Perhaps fear induced him to wish not to be seen by the public; and, had it been Collot d'Herbois, I should not have been surprised at his fear of assassination, if a thousandth part of the barbarities attributed to him are true. He (Collot) was the deputy at Lyons, where every kind of enormity which shocks humanity was committed. All ages, sexes, and conditions fell victims to his savage disposition, and without an opportunity to defend themselves. One instance of his unheard-of cruelty was printed in our American papers; but it was supposed to be a fable of the aristocracy, and had not the public faith. This was his ordering the military to fire on the populace, whom he had summoned into a square; and all sexes and conditions were inhumanly slaughtered. The charges against him are many and great; his chance but small of saving himself.

"This evening, Mr. Monroe, the American minister, invited half a dozen of us to attend the Convention with him to-morrow; which it is supposed will be an interesting day.

"4th.— Breakfasted with Mr. Monroe, and was introduced, with him and several other Americans, by Mr. Rosse, — one of the masters at arms, — to one of the tribunes, which are on the floor of the Convention. The members were very generally there; and the galleries and tribunes were very much crowded. The prisoners were seated behind the president. Their countenances all bespoke the anxiety which must hang on their hearts. Collot spoke first, and Barrère followed, in vindication of their conduct; and they concluded by demanding of the Convention, that the articles of their impeachment, by the Committee of Twenty-one, should be discussed before the Convention, article by article. This introduced very warm debate and most outrageous passion, mixed with personal scurrility. The members who remained of the old Committee of *Salut Public* — to which the four who are now under trial belonged — are very unpleasantly situated, and will make all endeavors to save them, in order that their own conduct may not be investigated; which it is supposed will ensue, if Barrère &c. are condemned. Four of this same committee fell with Robespierre; and, besides those under trial, there are but four remaining. The business of discussion by article was not determined when the Convention adjourned. The bell was rung often, but with little effect; for its sound was drowned by the hundred voices which were raised at the same time. Legendre was one of the principal speakers; and he, with Cambon, and a few others, were alternately in the tribune. Sullidan was one of the Committee of Twenty-one, and had much to say in vindication of that committee, and the principles which guided their inquiries in the business committed to their care.

"Although a decree was passed that no mark of approbation or the reverse should be shown by the Convention, and though it was a decree *nem. con.*, yet there was as much of the one and the other as before, both by the members of the Convention and the audience. The women in the tribunes have been, in general, so unruly, that they were prohibited for a day or two from entering. I see, however, that they have got themselves again introduced. They go for the session, let it be longer or shorter; and all take their dinners in their pockets. I saw a woman there the other day who was very industriously employed in knitting. They are generally women of the lowest class.

"There were not so many patrols out to-day as a few days past. Probably they feel confident of their party.

"5th. — Employed in following up my business, which is shamefully neglected by the members of the Committee of *Salut Public*. All is finished but their signature; which they pretend, at the offices, the members have not time to get.

"The weather now begins to be pleasant; and walking is agreeable. All is quiet in Paris; and there are but few patrols in the streets. It is generally supposed that some time will be taken up in the Convention with the business of Barrère and the others, — more than was at first expected.

"6th. — The weather lowering and unpleasant; which is, however, no proof in Paris that we shall not have a clear day. This day I received letters from Boston, which, though of ancient date, afforded me infinite pleasure, and make me more and more regret the sacrifices I am making of domestic happiness, in being absent from a family and connections dear to me as life itself.

"Madame de La Fayette breakfasted with Mr. Russell and myself this morning. She is much worn down by her misfortunes, which, she says, she fears will know no end but in the grave. Poor woman! she came very near trying the experiment under the reign of Robespierre. She was kept in prison, under every refinement of deprivation of liberty, for fifteen months. By some unaccountable good fortune, she was removed from one prison to another; which she thought at the time the greatest evil that was left for her in life, as it separated her from her friends, who were confined in the same prison, and placed her with strangers. This removal saved her life; for all who were in the room where she was were taken out and executed a few days before the fall of Robespierre. Among them were her father, and some other relations and intimate friends. She has had no letter from M. de La Fayette since he left France, and suffers all the torments which the warmest affection can be supposed to endure under similar circumstances. Her son and two daughters are in France; and I am told that they are fine children.

"7th.—I am this moment told that the people of Paris are reduced to half a pound of bread a day; and that there have been women waiting at the bakers' shops all night, so as to have an opportunity to be served first in the morning. They say that the tavern-keepers do not draw any. I fear this will make trouble. Bread, I am told, is the sole subsistence of thousands of workmen and their families, relished with an anchovy. May the God of plenty make them a speedy visit, and put an end to their distresses, which seem to be many! It is peculiarly unfortunate that the want of bread occurs at this time; for every agitation helps the malcontents of the city, who are said not to be few. As I dine with the American minister to-day, I shall probably hear the opinions of public characters on the subject of the present scarcity.

"Merlin de Thionville, Fréron, Laveaux, Thibaudeau, the late president, and several other members of the Convention, dined with Mr. Monroe; and, in the evening, Tallien came in. I find by their conversation that they are much interested in the question concerning the fate of Barrère and his companions. They do not hesitate to say that the present trial is a decision between Jacobinism with its excesses and the reign of reason and moderation. God send the latter may triumph! They are for cutting off the chiefs, who are those now on trial, and letting their aiders and abettors sink into oblivion. Were the *modérés* to pursue all concerned in the system for which the accused are now on trial, it would be destroying one system of terror by another. Merlin is the representative of the people who so bravely defended Mayence. He is a fine soldier and a great politician. His appearance is manly, and his countenance open. He wears whiskers, which continue from one temple to the other, — making a circle by the corners of his mouth and over his upper lip; and he has sworn not to shave them until Mayence shall be retaken. He speaks with great energy, and has an eye made for command. Fréron is esteemed a man of first-rate abilities, and great powers of oratory. Thibaudeau was the president for the last decade, and fills the chair as well as any one in the assembly. The spirited answer he gave to the workmen, who were instigated by a certain party to come to the Convention and demand bread, and who, in their address to the Assembly, had the audacity to observe that they almost repented the sacrifices they had made for the revolution, — I say, the answer he gave them probably saved an insurrection, for which they were ripe, and which there is little doubt was their intention. The choice of the president of the Convention is for fifteen days, or two weeks; and this is the only instance in which they have reference to old divisions of time.

"I am told by Mr. Rosse, one of the masters at arms in the assembly, that the prisoners appeared to have great spirits, in consequence of the mobs which are gathering round the Convention. At about four o'clock this afternoon, nearly two thousand women crowded round the door of the Assembly, and demanded an entrance to the hall. They were very noisy, and were with difficulty prevented from bursting the door of the Convention; to which they sent a deputation from their body, to represent their distress for want of bread; pleading, that although the Convention had promised them yesterday a pound per diem for each person, yet they had received but half a pound this day. They were assured by the president that it was their own fault if they did not receive more, as it was ready to be delivered half an hour after they left the bakers'. They received some good advice; and were exhorted to behave like good citizens, and return to their families. Some of the most clamorous were taken to prison; which, I presume, will have a good effect. The people of Paris dread a female mob; for that sex has been at the head of, and indeed the principal actors in, some of the most important revolutions of Paris.

"8th.—The weather is overcast and unpleasant. All is quiet to-day. The poor people are to have a substitute of biscuit and rice for their deficiency of bread. This will keep them still. The private houses of people in easy circumstances, and of the restaurateurs, are only supplied with half a pound per person, and that of a quality very inferior. I am anxious to hear of arrivals from America, and other neutral powers, with breadstuffs; without which I fear there will be a famine of bread. We are told that they are in great want in the south of France; and, if that is the case now, what will be their wants three months hence?

"A motion was this day made in the Convention to call the primary assemblies, for the choosing a new Convention, that the constitution of 1793 may be put in force.

"10th. — This is Decadi. As I have not yet been out, I cannot say whether there is more religion on this than on other days. The shops, I observe, are generally shut to-day; though there are some exceptions. In this country, no attention is paid to the new division of time. They stick by old customs; and with them our Sunday is held sacred, and they lay aside their work.

"I went to-day to visit the place where the Bastille stood; and see, from the space it occupied, that it must have been a very large building. The cells are now all filled up; and there is a figure of Liberty placed on the spot. When one contemplates the misery which that place once contained, the blood runs cold in the veins, and the soul is quickened with hatred against tyrants, wherever they are found, — whether they rule in a *body*, or severally. *There have been, unfortunately, a great many Bastilles in France since that one was destroyed.*

"I am told that the Convention are determined to continue the trial of the prisoners, and not make them over to the new Convention which is to be called.

"Dined with a decadi club of Americans, who meet on that day, to the number of fifteen or twenty, and pass a few hours very merrily.

"11th.—Upon calling for breakfast this morning, the landlord informed us that we could not have any bread. The women were in crowds all night at the doors of the bakers; and Russell tells me, that, at a baker's opposite to where he passed the night, they were assembled at eleven o'clock, and that at eight they were still there. There has never been so great a scarcity of bread, since the war, so early in the season; and this is more the case in the south of France than in the middle. All seems to be perfectly quiet. Putting some women, who made a great tumult, into prison, has had a good effect.

"All nature begins to smile. The trees are putting forth, and this day is enchantingly fine. The walks in the Tuileries begin to be crowded; and it is not to be wondered at, for they exceed the imagination of ordinary minds. The difference in numbers between men and women which is seen in the streets is very striking, notwithstanding the great number of men here who are strangers. Whether it is that men are more occupied, and keep at their labor, while the women are sent abroad in search of provisions, I will not undertake to say. I observe that there are none but women at the doors of the butchers and bakers.

"I was this evening at the theatre of the Palais d'Egalité. This appertains to the immense building, all of which was built by that execrable wretch, the Duke of Orleans, whose memory is abhorred by every honest man, and with whom, I presume, the common damned will hold no converse. The building is the handsomest I have yet seen in Paris, and the performance was very respectable: indeed, I have not been so much diverted since I arrived as last evening. It appears to me that the manners of the French must have changed since Mr. Moore was among them. They certainly appear to have less complaisance than was common among those whom I have been acquainted with. They endeavor to imitate republican simplicity; and the fact is, they come short, in many cases, of common civility.

"12th, or, in old style, 1st April, 1795.—This morning looks as fine as yesterday. My friend Russell this day closed the purchase of a house and eighteen acres of land, which cost 200,000 livres in specie, for 232,500 in assignats. A great spec!

"At eleven o'clock, great numbers of people flocked towards the Convention; and, at about two o'clock, the number of people was so great that the Convention were alarmed for their safety; and the *générale* was ordered to be beat, and the tocsin to be sounded. A great number of deputations were sent from the different sections; and they crowded so closely upon the sentinels stationed at the door of the Assembly, that they fell back, and in a moment the Convention was filled with men and women demanding bread, which they said had been promised them, but which they had been disappointed in. Some called for the liberation of the persons who were detained in prison, as they said, for their opinions. They were so tumultuous that the president was obliged to put on his hat; but this was disregarded, and the members were very much afraid for the event. The persons who are spoken of as being so unjustly detained in prison are the partisans of Robespierre; and it is feared, that, were they again at liberty, they would drench the country once more with innocent blood. Thousands of men and women were gathered in the vicinity of the palace; and at least sixty thousand men are under arms this day. In general, the guards are armed mostly with pikes; but to-day they are armed with guns, which are in very good order. In the streets there are nothing but patrols. Every shop is shut up, and all business suspended. The tradesmen forsook their work early this morning, and were determined upon making a business of it. I am astonished to see the immense number of decent women, who are led into that part of the town where the agitation seems to be the most violent merely by motives of curiosity. In the promenade behind the Palace of the Tuileries, and in the whole area in front of the palace, it was almost impossible to pass, on account of the crowds of people. I am in hopes that all will pass over quietly, and that the arrival of flour will calm the public mind, which is very much agitated, and is kept so by the agents of the Jacobin party, who add fuel to the fire. Should the means of subsistence not come in, God only knows what will be the consequence. The people in Paris have always looked to the government of France for bread; and they of course think it their due, and consider a deprivation of it an infringement of their rights.

"13th. — Penières, one of the deputies of the Convention, was last evening stabbed by the malcontents of the section of the *cité*. The ringleader of the mob was taken up, and will probably suffer for his indiscretion.

"From the general fermentation in Paris yesterday, some measures of a decisive nature have been taken. It seems that the opinion of the Convention was the same with my own respecting the agitation; which was, that it was not the want of bread alone that made the tumult so general, but that a certain party had made *bread* the watchword, and the ostensible reason for their enormities. Under this suspicion, seven of the members have been arrested. They were of the party called the 'Mountain.' Their names are Châles, Choudieu, Leonard Bourdon, Amar, Fourdroy, Duhem, and another, whose name I do not know. The people who have been on trial some time are now condemned by the Convention to transportation to an island in the Mediterranean. When they are once gone, I have some hopes that there will be tranquillity in the city.

"The *générale* was again beat this day; and great numbers of men are under arms. Two sections are in revolt; and Gen. Pichegru happening to be in Paris, the Convention gave him the command of the

Parisian Guards, to go against them. About six o'clock, I took a walk, under the sanction of my Americanship, round the Tuileries, and find all Paris in arms. Not a street but is crowded with men bearing muskets. Every one seems occupied in the business; and you do not meet a boy in the street that is not talking of the business of the day. Clarke and I were obliged to take the rounds of a mile at least, before we got liberty to pass. All the bridges are guarded by artillery, as are the avenues into the Tuileries and to the palace. This day, saw the superb building of the Hospital of Invalids, and the Military School: they are magnificent buildings. The Champ de Mars also affords one of the most magnificent prospects in the world.

"The women appear to be more interested, if possible, in the business of the day, than the men. You cannot pass a house where you do not see a woman with a newspaper in her hand, and half a dozen persons round her swallowing her news; and this evening, as we passed the Pont Neuf, we had the curiosity to approach a crowd, where we saw a very fine-looking female reading the news to a large number who stood by. It was in the open air, and by candle-light. This is so very different from the character of our women, that it strikes us with astonishment; at the same time that a Frenchman passes by, and takes no notice of it.

"14th.—The deputies who were denounced yesterday were sent off last night to the Castle of Ham, in Picardy. They were eight in number, and it is supposed will be followed by many more of the same section. Barrère, Collot, and Billaud de Varennes, were also sent off, under a guard, to the south of France; from whence they are to be embarked for the island destined to receive them. The mob stopped the coach, and were determined to put them to death on the spot, but were prevented by the guards.

"The papers this morning tell us that there were fifty thousand men under arms last evening in the vicinity of the Convention; and this is not difficult to believe. The sections which were in insurrection are now quiet. The complement of bread is this day only a quarter of a pound. The Convention have assured the people there will be large supplies in a few days; which I hope to God will be the case.

"Gold, two hundred and twenty to two hundred and fifteen per guinea, falling.. The day before yesterday, they were up to two hundred and fifty.

"This day, dined with Mr. Sabonadaire, the head clerk of the Committee of Public Safety. There was present Madame Vallet, who was patronized by Voltaire, and by him distinguished as the *belle et bonne.* He married her to the Marquis de Vallet; and, from her rank, she was imprisoned under the reign of Robespierre for eleven months. I had the pleasure to meet her once before at Mr. Monroe's, and had my heart almost broken with the recital of her sufferings while in prison. She had a daughter with her, of about six years old. Most of her friends who were confined at the same time with her fell victims to the bloody ferocity of the despotism which reigned at that period. Her time was near at hand; but justice came in to her aid, and saved to the world as fine a woman as I ever knew.

"There were many of the members of the Convention present: they are all in high spirits, and show by their conversation that they are confident they have given the final stroke, the *coup de grace*, to Jacobinism. Isnard, one of the proscribed, was there. He was of the seventy-three deputies who were outlawed; and his crime was having spoken in favor of his friend, whom Robespierre had destined to fall. He was in Paris, confined to his chamber, from October, 1793, until a few weeks since. He is a sprightly man, and has the most piercing eye I ever saw in my life.

"The brother of Rabaud St. Etienne, who was sacrificed, was there too. The President Pelet, and the late President Thibaudeau, were also there; and, as they were all going to the Convention, I accepted an invitation, and took a seat with Mr. Monroe in the tribune lately appropriated to the foreign ministers.

"The sitting was noisy; but it was good-natured, and rather the kind which proceeds from high spirits, than such as we had been accustomed to for some time past in the Assembly.

"Not a word from the Mountain. They are quiet; and I hope have been so completely overcome as to put an end to them.

"All Paris is charmed. A smile of satisfaction is marked in every face, and seems to say, 'We are once more secure in our lives and property.' The first politicians are of opinion that the triumph of the 12th Germinal is only second to the 9th Thermidor; on which day the system of terror was thrown down, and those who planted it sacrificed to the manes of those who were martyrs to it. I think it a very politic thing in the Assembly not to have shed the blood of those who so richly deserved it as Barrère and his colleagues in iniquity. It would have been dangerous to have got the guillotine again in operation. Their blood was loudly demanded by the people, and it was supposed they would not have been able to have got three leagues from Paris without attempts upon their lives; and I yet am of opinion they will be assassinated on the road.

"I observed, in coming from the hall of the Convention last evening (at eleven o'clock), what had before escaped my observation; which was, the standards which have been taken during the present war, and which are preserved there as trophies of the victories gained.

"15th. — Went with Mr. J. Russell this morning to Ablens, which is about three leagues from Paris, to see his purchase of a house, or rather *château*. It is built in an elegant style, has between thirty and forty rooms, and nearly seventeen acres of ground, covered with five thousand trees. The whole is walled in, with stables for thirty horses, an ice-house, and indeed all a man wants in buildings, with very handsome furniture; and, for the whole of this, he is to pay two hundred and thirty-five thousand livres, — equal to about one thousand guineas in gold. Its vicinity to the river, too, gives it great advantages. The ride from Paris to Choisy, where is a palace of Louis, the late king, is as rich as cultivation and a naturally fine country can make it. The Seine, running through a level country sowed with grain, without a hedge or fence to intercept the sight, bounded by a ridge of hills, which are under no less cultivation than the plains, interspersed with *châteaux* at small distances from each other, and rows of trees trimmed with great taste,—all together form as fine a scene as the fancy can paint. The gardener and his little family seem delighted with the prospect of having their new *lord*. This is not to be wondered at; for he has so much openness of countenance, that one need not have studied Lavater to trace the goodness of his heart in his features. Each vied with the other to serve us; and they seemed to be quite as happy as we were. They were entirely ignorant of the late agitations of Paris, and seemed to know of nothing but what had taken place within their garden walls. Happy people! long may you taste the pleasures of contentment! They were not discontented, I dare say, with our visit; and I have no doubt of the sincerity with which they wished the pleasure of seeing us again. The good woman told us, that, if we had no objection, she would improve the opportunity of our carriage to go and see one of her children, who was at a couple of miles' distance. We willingly gave our consent; and she mounted the coach-box beside the driver, happier and more contented than we who were within, if we might judge by her countenance, which I have generally found to be a very good criterion, particularly with persons in her rank of life.

"There are many country-seats to be sold in France, at this moment, for very little more in paper than they were worth in specie a few years since. The riddle is solved when one is told that an assignat is a tender for the payment of debts contracted in specie before the war, or at any time since. The justice of this can only be supported on the same principle with the same fact in the American war, — necessity.

"In coming to town yesterday, we observed with pleasure that all the windmills in the neighborhood were going; which we take for certain evidence of a supply of wheat. In driving through the streets yesterday, I was much distressed to see the crowds of women who surrounded the bakers' shops. They go there in the night, and some of them tarry half the next day, to get the scanty pittance of half, and sometimes a quarter, of a pound of bread. This, to people who were in the habit of eating from two to four pounds of bread per diem, is a great and serious evil. The conception they have of the word 'equality' was evidenced towards us; for, when we were passing the crowds, they several times observed, 'This is equality,' pointing to us. They had an idea that every one was to be put upon a footing in point of fortune, as well as in being governed by equal laws, which a certain class in the community could not trample on with impunity.

"16th. — The morning overcast. This is Sunday; and, if the weather should prove pleasant, I intend going to hear Mass. Great numbers of shops are shut up this day, and many people are going to Mass. Went to see Madame de La Fayette: found her lodged in an obscure hotel, and up three flights of stairs. She seems to be much disturbed in mind by her misfortunes. May He who rewards the virtuous ease her situation, and make her happy!

"17th.—This day, went to see the Pantheon, which is celebrated as one of the first buildings of the kind in Europe. Of this I am no judge: I can only say, that it as far surpasses every thing I have ever seen before as it is possible to conceive. Its height, to the upper part of the dome, is three hundred and eighty French feet; and from its top all Paris is to be seen, and affords one of the most enchanting scenes in nature. This building is entirely of stone: not an inch of wood is there from top to bottom of it. In the vault under it, which runs along the whole extent of the building, are deposited the remains of Rousseau and Voltaire. The monuments which contain them are in wood: they are to be wrought in marble, and will be the finest monuments in the world, we are told. The body of Marat was deposited here by a decree of the National Convention; but it is now taken out, as unworthy of such a place. Le Pelletier was also, by a decree, placed there; but, after Marat was displaced, the friends of Le Pelletier thought fit to remove his ashes also. A late decree of the Convention forbids the placing or raising a monument to the memory of any one there until ten years after his demise. This was occasioned by the error they were led into respecting the character of Marat, which will be handed down in France as disgraceful to humanity. The sculpture in the Pantheon is very fine. There are a great number of workmen now occupied in finishing it; but it will not be completed for several years, although it was begun forty-two years ago.

"Guineas, this day, one hundred and eighty-two to one hundred and eighty-five livres.

"18th. — Bread is getting more plenty than it has been, to the joy of every one. Went this evening and saw the opera of Castor and Pollux. The scenery is superb, and the singing enchanting. The dancing, as usual there, surpassed any thing of the sort in the world. Both Hell and the Elysian Fields are represented in this piece, and come up to one's ideas of both the one and the other. The orchestra was composed this evening of eighty-three performers; and, in the course of the evening, there were between two and three hundred persons on the stage, — as dancers, soldiers, &c.

"20th Decadi. — This day, having no business in town, I went with Russell and Higginson three or four miles out of town to see a country-house which was owned by the Count d'Artois. It is said to have been completed in sixty days from its commencement, upon a wager he laid. It is built in a fanciful and pretty style. The gardens are as romantic as possible; and the view from some parts of the house beautiful, particularly of Mount Calvary, which, from its appearance, seems better entitled to the name of paradise than to the one it bears, — for it is under the highest possible cultivation, — and from its summit must afford a delightful view of Paris and its neighborhood. This seat of the count's is said to have been built by desire of the late queen, and is called 'the queen's bagatelle.' It is, and ever will be, an eternal monument of the depravity of his mind, from the disgraceful figures which are meant to adorn one of the chambers, with which every person not lost to sense of common decency must be exceedingly disgusted.

"The Bois de Boulogne is an immense forest, which extends several miles in circumference, quite to the borders of Paris, and, I am told, is much frequented in summer. The want of fuel last winter, in consequence of the rivers being frozen, and preventing the boats from coming down river, obliged the Convention to cut down a large part of this delightful wood, to keep the poor from suffering.

"21st. — There is not yet an increase of bread; and the peasants are said to occasion the scarcity at Paris by stopping the wagons to supply their own wants. The weather is becoming pleasant in the extreme. This day, received letters from Boston, of date of 7th February. Visited the Hospital of the Invalids, and found it very beautiful. There is an immense dome to the building, in the centre of four smaller ones, all lighted from on high, and decorated with paintings from the first hands. The chapel is magnificent; but its chief ornament, the pulpit, is demolished. The elegant figures and pillars which adorned it are still there,— monuments of what it was. The chapel, which is an immense hall, as well as the floors of the domes, is in marble, elegantly inlaid with beautiful figures. They are occupied in effacing the *fleurs de lis* and other emblems of former times. The inner court of the Invalids is very spacious indeed; the whole on an immense scale. We were shown the tables where the invalids dine. They were kept in very neat order; and the pewter cans shone like silver. When one contemplates the causes which have produced the misfortunes of those people, or of most of them, and traces them to the ambition of kings, or tyrants under other names, he is led to wish that all the world would have the resolution to throw off the yoke, and enlist under a republican government, where all does not depend upon the caprice of a single villain, but upon the voice of the people. The invalids are well clothed, and appear very civil. We were not once attacked for money while we were there; which I thought something surprising.

"I took a walk upon Montmartre, an eminence just outside the Barrière of Paris. It commands one of the richest scenes I ever witnessed. The whole extent of Paris, and the country for leagues round, is open to view. The Seine, with its windings, heightens the beauty of the scene very much. The beauty of the style of cultivation, both in the fields and in the gardens, is enchanting. One of the telegraphs is on the summit of Montmartre; and one more is in plain sight towards the east.

"The preliminaries of peace with Prussia are this

day announced to the Convention, and give pleasure to every one. Spain, too, is said to be doing the same. In consequence of this news, guineas, which were yesterday two hundred and twenty, are this afternoon one hundred and eighty.

"23d. — Continuance of the fine weather. No definite answer respecting our unsettled business; but I am led to hope something, from several claims having been lately settled.

"In passing by one of the telegraphs which is situated on the old Louvre, I found it in operation. It is often used to communicate intelligence to and from the army and the different parts of the Republic. Every different position of the machinery remains stationary until it is taken off by the one next to it, which is on Montmartre, about a mile distant. It is certainly a wonderful invention, and does great credit to the projector. It communicates any event with great rapidity, though not in detail.

"24th. — The morning rainy. We had yesterday the very unpleasant information of a declaration of war by the Emperor of Morocco against the United States of America. This stroke, it appears, is not aimed particularly at the American States, but at all those powers which have not consuls at the court of Morocco, among which we are comprised.

"Paris is quite tranquil. The energy shown by the Convention on the late occasion has awed the lower class of people into respect for them. Strong guards have been sent into the country to escort the teams charged with provisions for Paris, which have been frequently interrupted in the neighborhood, to supply the wants of the inhabitants. The Convention has lately done itself the highest honor in passing a decree for restoring to the heirs of the former owners all the estates of those persons who suffered unjustly during the reign of Robespierre. By this righteous decree, thousands of widows, and children who mourn a murdered father, and many a parent whose heart is rent by the loss of a darling child, are in a degree relieved, not only by the opprobrium being no longer fixed to their memories of having been enemies to liberty, but by their being, on the contrary, now regarded as martyrs for its glorious name. In some instances, families who had the distress of poverty in addition to their other sufferings are now restored to easy circumstances, and in many cases to affluence.

"Exchange for louis two hundred and fourteen.

"25th.—The morning overcast. I dined this day with Mr. Murray, at the Maison de Grange Batellière. This, I think, is more pleasantly situated than any house in Paris which is occupied as a hotel. In walking through the streets of Paris, one would be led to suppose that every foot of ground in the city was covered with buildings. This is, however, far from being the fact; and I was much astonished to find that some houses, which appeared from a front view to have appertaining to each only the land it stood upon, have large and elegant gardens in the rear, laid out with all imaginable taste, and as spacious as one could wish. It is the same with the external appearance of most of the houses. They have very unpromising exteriors; but many which bear this appearance are decorated inside like palaces.

"Several of the National Convention dined with us to-day. Pelet was very inquisitive about our commerce, and seemed anxious to know if it was our opinion that we should be largely connected with the French after the war. This, I have no doubt, will be the fact, and that it will be advantageous to us in a great degree. He tells me that the quantity of wheat raised in France was never equal to its wants; and that, although considerable flour was shipped to their colonies before the war, this was more than counterbalanced by the importations from the States of Barbary and the islands in the Mediterranean; and that wheat, in the best of times, was always worth twelve livres tournois in specie per quintal. This would give a good peace freight from America.

"26th — I have been this day gratified, much beyond the expectation I had formed, in a visit to Versailles. We passed through the beautiful town of St. Cloud, where is one of the most neat palaces in Europe. This was the favorite residence of the queen; and here she expended a great deal of the treasure of the nation. We did not stop to examine this building, or its beautiful cascades and sheets of water, with which, and parks, avenues, statues and other sculpture, it abounds.

"The road to Versailles is paved, and kept in excellent order; and the whole distance to it from Paris, which is about ten miles, was always lighted, under the old government, over night. This expense and unnecessary piece of luxury and extravagance is now dispensed with.

"On every side is seen the labor which has been expended upon this country by its former lords, to accommodate every thing to their convenience. It is very common to see a crossway which must have been raised at the expense of hundreds of thousands, merely to save the descent into a valley, and make the road quite on a level.

"There are several small villages in the route; but none afford any thing very striking in appearance, except the one before mentioned.

"The city of Versailles contained, before the revolution, a hundred thousand inhabitants; by which one may judge of its extent. It takes up, however, much more space than cities of that number of inhabitants in general in France, on account of the great width of the streets, which are all beautifully adorned with rows of trees. There are three streets which terminate in front of the palace. They run in a triangular direction, and have a very pretty effect from the palace. When I say the front, I write as it struck me on first seeing it. Its appearance is majestic, and excites astonishment. After passing half an hour in what I thought the front of the palace, I was undeceived, and told that this was the rear; which, upon going towards the gardens, I soon found to be the case. The stables belonging to the palace are situated between the three roads before mentioned; the centre one of which leads to Paris, and is for a long way broad, and adorned with trees. The extent of the stables is wonderful. They are built (as is the case everywhere in France) of stone. The railing of iron in front of them is a very masterpiece of workmanship; and it has all the appurtenances of a stable, such as curry-combs, shears, whips, halters, &c., interwoven in it in the same metal, and must contain a great quantity of iron. I am astonished to see so much of this metal left untouched. It is certainly a proof of their being not much in want of it for the operations of the war; as they would not have hesitated to appropriate it, as they did that in the Gardens of the Tuileries.

"In the Petites Ecuries there is preparation for six hundred horses; and in the Grandes Ecuries, for fourteen hundred. The distinction of great and small stables has arisen from the addition made by Louis XVI., wherein eight hundred horses more may now be accommodated than there was room for in the old stables. In the Grandes Ecuries there is a riding-school, where the Hussars and other *gens d'armes* practise, riding every day from nine to twelve o'clock. There remain one hundred and twenty horses of the late king, amongst which are some very beautiful ones. There is one of his favorite riding-horses — a dapple-white — yet there. I was a little surprised that Jacobinism had not carried its frenzy even to the destruction of this beast, as it did to many others. The horses are in excellent order. Although they have very little grain, they are in as good case as one could wish. In October, 1792, there were twelve hundred horses in these stables, many of which have died of honorable wounds in the cause of freedom and France.

"In the yards in front of the stables there is room to draw up as many horses in line of battle as the stables will hold. It is finely paved, and kept very neat. Between the stables and the Place d'Armes is an extensive common; and several roads, leading to different cities, cut it at all angles. The Place d'Armes, or large court in rear of the palace, has an iron railing round it, and is large enough to contain several regiments of men drawn up.

"The stairs leading to the queen's apartments are entirely of marble, richly inlaid in various colors, and must astonish every one who contemplates the amazing expense incurred. However, eighty millions sterling will, to be sure, go a great way; and this is the sum said to have been laid out by Louis XIV. only, upon the city of Versailles. The apartments are now in a very wretched state, being deprived of their tapestry and furniture of every kind. The ceilings of the rooms, which still are quite unimpaired, convey to the mind what the whole must have once been, to be on a par with this part of them. Elegant sculpture and paintings from the first hands adorn every one of them.

"You are shown a very beautiful apartment in every fine house in France, which is called the dressing-chamber. This is always lined with looking-glasses, and is the most highly furnished chamber in the house. In one of the palaces of Versailles there is a recess formed to receive a sofa. The sides and back of this recess are entirely in looking-glass; and it is so arranged, that two persons looking into the side-glasses see themselves multiplied one hundred and twenty times. This has given rise to many stories, much to the prejudice of the late queen. The suite of rooms in the king's apartments, known by the names, Hall of War, the Hall of Peace, of Hercules, of Bacchus, &c., are adorned with some of the first paintings the world can now boast of. The grand gallery is the *tout ensemble* of all that is delightful. There are nine large paintings, and eighteen small ones, representing the conquests of Louis XIV. They are done by the first masters of the times; and the likenesses of Louis, Turenne, and the principal actors of the times, are preserved with great nicety. From all these rooms, the views of the gardens surpass what the most lively imagination could paint.

"From this suite we were taken to a beautiful chapel appertaining to the palace. The emblems of royalty are not yet effaced in this place, — the only one where I remember to have seen them remaining in France. The private chapel of the royal family is in the gallery of this chapel. Here they said Mass when ill.

"The Opera House is said to be the first in the world. It has the remains of former magnificence, but is very much injured since the revolution.

"The pile of buildings of the palace with its appurtenances is astonishing. Where the Gardes du Roi were once lodged, are established national workshops in cannon and small-arms.

"To give one an idea of the Gardens of the Palace, and the scale upon which they are laid out, it is enough to say that there are upwards of one thousand of large orange-trees in the greenhouse, some of which, we were assured, are nearly five hundred years old.

"30th. — This day, arrived James Carter from Havre, and handed me a number of letters, which gave comfort to my soul.

"The Convention is said to have discovered a plot, at the head of which were Cambon and the other Jacobins who were of the Convention, and who have done every thing to produce an insurrection and stir up a disturbance in Paris. To effect this, they are said to have taken measures to stop the arrival of grain; and have distributed money amongst the malcontents, to aid them in their deeds of darkness. They intended to have cut off the present ruling members of the Convention; and, that they might bring the royalists into their party, they intended to establish young Capet on the throne. All this has been discovered; and the authors or the heads of the party are called upon to come to the Convention and vindicate themselves, or they are deemed convicted and sentenced to transportation.

"Floreal 1st. — This day I accompanied my friend, J. Russell, to the Croix de Berney, on his way to Havre. The day pleasant. Guineas, two hundred and twenty.

2d. — The day overcast. Exchange, two hundred and thirty. Bread a little more plenty; and it is hoped that it will continue so.

"3d and 4th. — Pleasant weather. All quiet at Paris.

"5th. — The alternate rain and sunshine, which have been in constant succession for some time past, promise an abundant harvest; which will be very necessary for the happiness of the inhabitants of France. It is said that Spain has made a treaty of peace with this Republic; in which case, there remain only England and the Emperor to sustain the coming campaign. James Carter left Paris for Havre this day. Guineas, two hundred and forty to two hundred and thirty-seven.

"6th. — Yesterday was announced to the Convention a peace with a large body of people who have been a long time in insurrection in Normandy and the neighborhood. They were known under the name of Chouans, from their leader's name. This is a very important event. The civil war has cost the Republic oceans of blood and millions of money. The indiscreet decrees respecting religion were the cause of all this mischief; and fanaticism could not bear the shock. Revolt was the consequence; and the malcontents were joined by all the others in the Republic, whether from religious or other motives, and the combined force became very potent. The lower class of Chouans have committed great enormities, — murdering and robbing in every part of the country where they have been. The mails which were obliged to pass in the neighborhood went under a strong escort, and were often attacked. A cockade of the nation was enough to insure death. Those, therefore, who passed the road, took the precaution to leave any thing of the kind behind, and to adopt a cross in the place of this badge. Guineas, two hundred and thirty-seven.

"7th. — The Convention have this day decreed that specie shall be considered as merchandise, and that every one may exchange assignats against it. A few months since, it would have cost a Frenchman his head to have been detected in making a difference between assignats and specie. As this will bring people out who were before afraid of doing any thing in this way, it is supposed that there will be a great call in the market for specie, and that it will rise very much. Another circumstance, which will tend very much to occasion a fall of the paper, is that the Assembly has decreed to pay all specie contracts in paper at the exchange. This will throw a vast quantity of paper into the market; and I should not be astonished if it were refused altogether. Some of our countrymen have half a million of dollars in specie due. This will make a great sum at the present exchange.

"This day, Messrs. Codman, Deblois, and myself went to see the famous manufacture of porcelain at Sèvres, about seven miles from Paris. The building is very large, and surrounded by gardens under the highest cultivation, and magnificent country-seats. The porcelain made at Sèvres has the reputation of being the finest in the world. Some pieces there have no price, particularly two pictures painted on china, which are celebrated as masterpieces of the art. The excellence of this is that their colors can never pass away; and, although these pieces have been painted a number of years, they are as fresh as if the production of yesterday. They are to have a place in the Museum. The great vase is the largest piece of china ever made there, and is immensely valuable. We were shown cups which cost several guineas each in the best of times. For one service of porcelain which was displayed, they asked one hundred and fifty thousand livres; and, as they do not add on these valuable articles more than fifty per cent upon the old prices, this must have been valued at nearly twenty thousand dollars before the revolution.

"We were shown the process; and, indeed, saw the clay moulded, and a plate made in a very short time. We were carried through the rooms where the different parts of the work are completed, and were much amused. There were a great number employed in painting; and in one room there were none but women, who were also painting and burnishing. The manufactory is extensive, and formerly employed a great many people. It was a royal manufactory, and is now national property. The rooms where the china is displayed are extensive, and the care taken of them is great. Codman and I bought a number of trifles. In the route from Paris to Sèvres, there is a bottle manufactory, which made upwards of four thousand bottles per diem. The want of charcoal now stops the business entirely. This evening, guineas are two hundred and fifty to two hundred and sixty, and rising.

"8th. — The morning promises a finer day than we

have had for some time past. This day I visited the celebrated Gobelin manufactory of tapestry, about a mile and a half from the Palais d'Egalité, and within the walls of the city. The buildings that contain these masterpieces of excellence are large and numerous. They have the appearance of great age; and the people we conversed with know nothing about the time when the factory was established, or whether the buildings were originally occupied in the present way. Before the revolution, this was a royal manufactory, and is now national property. The number of people employed there before the present war were one hundred; but that number is now decreased to sixty; and forty, having been of the first requisition, are now on the frontiers, or have gone where they learn war no more. The looms, and indeed the apartments, of this manufactory do not accord with the exquisite delicacy of the employment, but, on the contrary, mark the greatest contrast possible. Overhung with cobwebs, and in other particulars very much neglected, they speak the poverty of the factory. The people employed here have from five to eight livres a day in paper, and nourish themselves. The copies from which the weavers work are among the first paintings in the world, in point of elegance, and the productions of the most celebrated masters. The copy is placed behind the weaver; and, as he manages his colors, he takes the tints of whatever he wishes to imitate with his eye, and makes choice of his silk or worsted in conformity. The most elegant painting does not exceed some of the work now there; and at a little distance cannot be distinguished from it, unless by a very critical eye. Some of the pictures exhibited in the chambers above exceed what the liveliest fancy can imagine. Mr. Trumbull is of opinion that the weaver must have much more merit than the first *copy-painter* can have. There is one kind of this tapestry which is placed horizontally; and, the back of the picture being uppermost, the face is not seen until it is taken out of the loom, which is sometimes four years from its commencement. The colors are all in worsted or silk; the brightest are of the latter; and they are worked in so as not to be distinguishable in the picture. There are several pieces, which are yet unfinished, which were begun before the revolution. They are historical pieces; and, as they contain the figures of Louis XIV. and other monarchs, whose deeds they are meant to record, they have not been worked upon for some time; and I am surprised that they were not destroyed at the time when every thing of the kind, however valuable from its workmanship, and however much it ought to have been respected on account of the arts, was sacrificed by the Vandals who bore the sway under Robespierre. There were no pieces of the tapestry which were within the reach of my purse. In returning from Gobelin, we stopped at the *ci-devant* Jardin du Roi. It is laid out with admirable taste, and is open to every one who pleases to walk there. In the centre is a pond and an enclosure, in which there are a great number of rare birds. We saw here a lion, a tiger, several kinds of monkeys, and two white bears: these last are from Greenland. They are large, and appear ferocious. The lion is perfectly good-humored; but the tiger is all that can be expected from that animal; and my blood chilled as I observed him. One of the monkeys is remarkably large, and is as dangerous as the tiger himself. At this garden (now called the Garden of Plants) there are a great number of natural curiosities, preserved in a long, elegant building, which we had not time to visit, and with which I flatter myself with the prospect of another hour of pleasure before I leave France.

"9th. — Rainy and unpleasant. Assignats depreciating very fast, and reminding us of our old continental paper.

"10th. — Went to the manufacture of porcelain in the Rue du Temple. Saw a great deal of china of most delightful fabric, which led me into some extravagances.

"11th, 12th, 13th, and 14th. — Cloudy and unpleasant weather, which confined me pretty much to the house. Guineas rise to three hundred and forty to three hundred and fifty."

Although a short account has already been given * of the execution of Fouquier Tinville and others, written from memory in the autobiographical sketch dated at Saratoga, in July, 1846, — more than half a century after the occurrence, — the entire description of the scene, given in a diary kept at the time, is here inserted, as the details convey some further in-

* Page 56.

formation in regard to the state of public feeling in Paris.

"17th. — This day the *accusateur-général* under Robespierre, after a trial of nearly three months, was convicted of having caused the death of the innocent and helpless, and was condemned to suffer death, with sixteen of the jury who were partners in his guilt. The public indignation against this man is very great; and I believe, that, had he not been offered up as a sacrifice to appease the multitude, they would have vented their ire somewhere else. Old persons who had passed the hour of conspiracy, and young ones who had not arrived at it, shared the same fate under the judgment of this monster. Women who were far advanced in pregnancy met a smilar fate; and no sex, age, or condition, was respected by this greatest of wretches. The fairness shown in his trial does honor to the tribunal, and is a great contrast to the proceedings at the tribunal where he brought forward his accusations. Fifty to sixty in a day were sacrificed to the malice of this monster, who seemed to delight in the slaughter he was administering. It was expected he would be guillotined at four o'clock this day; and great numbers were out to see him pay the debt due to justice. They were disappointed. To-morrow he dies, so Gen. Menard tells me. I shall be unfeeling enough to visit the place of execution. Louis, three hundred and twenty-five.

"18th. — At ten o'clock this day, Mr. Russell and myself went to the Place de Grève, where there were already some thousands of persons collected to see the execution of the condemned Fouquier Tinville and his *co-accusés*. The fatal instrument was erected; and the windows of every house were thronged with females, who had come to the exhibition; while places in the neighboring houses were in such request, that fifty livres were paid for the privilege of going into a chamber near which was placed the guillotine. The number of women present on such an occasion struck me with disgust, and at the same time commanded my pity, when I reflected upon the cause of the indifference with which exhibitions of the kind are seen at Paris, which undoubtedly has arisen from their frequency. The patrols were many; and the populace were kept at a distance from the guillotine by the *chasseurs*, who were on guard this day. There was scarcely a face that did not wear a smile; and anxiety was marked on the countenance of every one, but of a different kind from what is visible at executions with us; for it seemed to be expressive of a wish that the criminals would arrive, that they might feast upon the sight of blood. Such have been the crimes of those men, and particularly of Fouquier Tinville, who was attorney-general during the horrid executions under the monster Robespierre, that it is not to be wondered at that all France called for their lives to appease the manes of those poor wretches who had been precipitated into eternity with all their sins upon their heads, many without even an accusation, or, if accused, never having an opportunity to defend themselves.

"This same Fouquier was not contented with the sacrifice of a few, but has frequently had condemned and executed from thirty to forty within three hours. Whenever there were any trials to come on in the morning, the guillotine was placed, and the wagons brought, upon the presumption that there would be use for both. Under these circumstances, I say, it is not to be wondered at that the people wished they might expiate their crimes with their lives; but to insult misery is brutal and unfeeling.

"At a quarter before eleven o'clock, the cavalry made its appearance; and soon followed three carts, in which were the prisoners, — all of them seated in the carts. They had their hair cut short, and their hands tied behind them, and were covered with loose great-coats. They were seated with their backs to the horses; and I observed, that, as soon as the carts turned the corner to come into the square, they looked towards the instrument which was to deprive them of life.

"As soon as they appeared, there was a general clap of triumph. For my own part, I expected to have sunk under the oppression which I felt: the reflection upon the fate of thousands, many of whom were as innocent of the crimes with which they were charged as I was, the idea of the misery into which the distressed families of those who had suffered had been precipitated, — all served to depress my spirits, and make me repent my curiosity, and wish myself at my lodgings.

"The present *accusateur-public* of the Revolutionary Tribunal preceded the cavalcade in a coach, which was followed by a very strong guard of horse, and then the wagons which bore the condemned.

"When arrived at the fatal spot, they descended from the carts, some of them with a spring, showing as little concern as if they had come there on a party of pleasure; and some, as they descended, eying the machine for some time, but with great coolness. I was about twenty paces from the stage, and had an opera-glass, which gave me an opportunity to see every feature with great distinctness. The cart which was first unloaded drove up to the side of the stage upon which the guillotine is placed, and a basket about seven feet long was fastened into it. When these arrangements were made, and all the prisoners on the ground, the first victim was Pierre Louis Le Roy, one of the revolutionary jury. He was a *ci-devant* marquis, and had taken the name of Tenth of August. As soon as he had mounted, which was done with a resolute step and a determined look, he began to speak; but the murmurs prevented his being heard; and, the executioners paying no attention to his wishes to speak, he was thrust under the fatal knife, which severed his head in the twinkling of an eye. The inhuman and unfeeling conduct of the executioners is beyond description. One takes the bloody head, and the other handles the mangled corpse, with as little ceremony as one would a beast at a slaughter-house. They are both thrown (not laid) into the large basket; the axe is again hoisted up, and another victim brought forward. The principal part of the number executed were of a middle age. Amongst them were three of the former judges, one president, and eight of the jurors of the Revolutionary Tribunal. The remainder were also subalterns in that fatal tribunal; and, if this prompt machine of death ever did pure justice, it is the general opinion that it did it this day.

"Several of the criminals looked with indignation on the spectators, and uttered something which we could not hear; three, particularly, would not let the executioners hold their heads down, that the axe might have the fairer opportunity of doing its duty without mangling. They looked on each side, as their heads were precipitated through the fatal hole, and seemed to bid defiance to death. They all walked up to the board against which they are tied with great firmness, and looked round with perfect composure.

"Fouquier, as being the most culpable, was kept until the last, and must have suffered a thousand deaths in seeing those suffer who went before him. When he mounted, he had an air of disdain upon his countenance, and seemed to bid defiance to the king of terrors. He also spoke; but I was unable to hear what he said. This sight, which (however vile the criminals) one would suppose could have been seen by no one without emotion, was looked upon by those who were about me with all the indifference imaginable; and the women who were in the chamber where I was, witnessed it with as little feeling as a block of marble would have had. The clap of applause at a moment like this is to my mind disgraceful, and shows the depravity of the minds of those who exhibit such signs of triumph. In fourteen minutes from the time when the first criminal was brought upon the stage, the last head was in the basket; and in this time there were at least two minutes lost in changing the basket, as one was full of bodies, and was drawn off, and another was brought alongside the stage to receive the remainder; so that, if the first basket would have held the whole, this operation upon the sixteen would have been performed in twelve minutes. The expedition with which it is completed is the only thing in which there is the smallest show of humanity. The body does not move; not a spasm can be seen to contract it. The last person is always the one esteemed most culpable; and his head is taken up with the most brutal indifference, and shown to the spectators all round the scaffold. The sight of the mangled corpses, the heads drenched in blood, and the hard-heartedness of the people, make this the most awful spectacle one can imagine. The executioners were as bloody as butchers, and quite as indifferent as our beef-dealers are when cutting up the ox they have slaughtered. Notwithstanding the horror of this sight, I do not repent having been witness to it. I had never thought it possible for people to meet death with so much indifference. It has become so familiar to them that they think nothing of it, even when they are the victims. I tarried until the mob had gone off, and saw the machine washed down, while gallons of blood were streaming from it. It is dangerous to familiarize the public to exhibitions of this kind.

I know this by my own feelings; for certain I am that my emotion decreased with every head that fell.

"19th. — Pleasant weather.

"20th. — This day, went to Ablens sur Seine, to the place bought by Russell and Higginson. The country is becoming charming; the crops promise well; and all nature seems to rejoice.

"Guineas, three hundred and seventy.

"21st. — Very pleasant, and the weather becoming warm. We are told that the infamous Lebon, whose cruelties have exceeded those of Nero himself, is soon to be tried; and his life will end on the Place de Grève, *sans doute.*

"To-morrow I set off for Holland with Messrs. Russell and Jeffrey."

The following extracts from the journal kept by so careful and intelligent an observer, while travelling through a portion of France and Holland, will probably be found interesting. They contain his remarks on the manners of the people there in the last century; on the devastation of war, then recent, with descriptions of fortified places of great strength, though far inferior to that which is now the object of the grand struggle in the Crimea; and on the agriculture and general appearance of the country. They relate further incidents, too, in the suppression of the last struggles for the system which had prevailed in the reign of terror, and which finally expired in one trial and execution of a deeply tragic character, the report of which, by an eye-witness, will be found to confirm the statement of historians: —

"1795. — This 11th of May, left Paris at one o'clock, in company with Mr. J. Russell, of Boston, and Mr. Jeffrey, also of that place, for a journey to Holland. Notwithstanding the many charms which Paris has for people in general, I confess I never took my leave of a place in my life with less regret. . . . The accounts which a stranger has to settle with all about him, when he leaves any place in France where he has resided any considerable time, are not of the most pleasant kind. These are with the *domestiques* of every department, which are not few. They all make up their minds that they ought to receive a certain sum; but, trusting to your generosity that they shall be overpaid if it be left to yourself, they make no direct demand. Now, if one can agree in calculation with the amount they make up to themselves, it will always be best to pay a little over than a sou under it, as by this single action you are to be judged; and should you give them less than the sum they think strictly their due, or even that sum only, all the good actions of your life will not save you from the epithet which you will have applied to you in their minds, of *C'est un misérable.* An acquaintance with this fact has perhaps saved us from coming under this description; and a few livres entitled us to *Ce sont de braves gens*, and a thousand *Dieu vous bénisse*, from all around us.

"From the accounts we have received of the badness of the attendance at the post-houses, we anticipated much trouble in procuring post-horses. And, indeed, we made a bad beginning; for, upon sending to the Post House at Paris, we found we could not have horses there for two days; and we were therefore obliged to take our horses, which we had driven in Paris, out to Bourget, which is three leagues from Paris. I had never passed the Barrière, which takes us out to this place; and, had we not now come this way, I should have lost the view of one of the most beautiful parts of the environs of Paris I have yet seen. The roads are fine; and a short time set us down at the first post, where we were not long detained for post-horses, with which we cantered on to Louvres, which is three leagues from Bourget. At all the places where are the post-houses, there is a small village, — this is every two or three leagues, — in which place are collected the farmers who cultivate the ground in the intermediate space; and for this reason we see no such thing as a farmer's house standing by itself, surrounded by its noble barns and granaries, — a sight which is so frequent and so pleasing in America. These towns, or bourgs, bear a great resemblance to each other, and are poorly built, with very crooked streets, and the evident marks of poverty upon every house. The contrast is to be drawn between this wretched picture and the magnificence of the *château* which you always see in the neighborhood of those villages, and which was formerly occupied by some lord or other nobleman, whose vassals were happy in procuring by the sweat of their brows a scanty subsistence in a life devoted to him. These post-towns resemble each other very much, and give one no very favorable idea of the cleanliness of the inhabitants. No sooner does one alight at those towns than he is surrounded by a certain class of *misérables*, who have claims, and just ones too, upon every one who can afford to ride; and happy the man who has a heart to open his purse-strings to the adjustment of accounts on which so much enjoyment depends. No sooner had we alighted than a group of these *misérables* made a sortie from a wretched bed in the stable, and implored our charity. Their very appearance had anticipated their request; and we got their blessings. And I suspect, from the event, we had the appearance of earning it with a good will; for the good people brought every one they could find who they thought had a claim; and, thank God! we had both will and power to make them all happy for the moment. We find much less difficulty in getting post-horses than one would have expected; and, therefore, were not detained long at this place.

"The postilion is entitled to five livres the post. We pay him eight; which I think accounts for the expedition with which we are served. And this is the most economical practice a man can adopt in France; for, without the aid of the postilion, you are detained in a wretched hovel, where you can take no pleasure, nor find even tolerable accommodation. I therefore recommend to all my friends to keep well with this class of people, in whose power every traveller is obliged to put himself very much. When we stopped *à la Chapelle* three leagues from Louvres, we had scarcely seen the postilion dismount, before the sight of our carriage, which is really very beautiful, attracted the attention of those about; and we saw ourselves surrounded by a dozen or two of good people, who were admiring it. One, whom we afterwards found to be a blacksmith, seemed more particular in his examinations than the rest, and soon found that we had occasion for him in the line of his profession. There were two nuts wanting to the screws, which he said he would furnish. Upon asking him if he had them made, so that we might have them at once, he answered, that, if twenty thousand were wanted, he could furnish them in five minutes. Sterne's bucket of water and the ocean struck me. It was in point; and I placed it to the same account he did, — that the French language is copious, and expresses more than it means or intends. The little claims once settled, we took our leave of the blacksmith and his compatriots, and in an hour reached Senlis, which is a town of some considerable extent, and is surrounded with a wall. It contains about three thousand five hundred inhabitants, is tolerably well built, and has the appearance of having been a place of considerable consequence. There are many very handsome houses here, and two churches. In passing this town, we observed a great number of regular soldiers, who have strong marks of having seen service, and were as good-looking fellows as I ever saw. Our passports were looked at here; and, after a few minutes' detention, we took our leave of this place, and were delighted with its environs, which are charmingly laid out, and surrounded with the most delightful avenues of trees I have yet seen in France. The ruins of a church, perhaps once famous, stand in the neighborhood, and mark the age of the city. . . . We arrived at Gournay at midnight.

"The centre of the road is paved wide enough to admit of two carriages abreast, and the sides kept in pretty good order.

"The beauty of the country we have this day passed through may be equalled, but cannot be excelled, by any in the world. Almost every inch of ground is under cultivation, and promises a good crop. The rows of trees which adorn the roads on each side add very much to the beauty of the country, and, at the same time, would, upon an emergency, supply a vast quantity of timber. They are principally elms, and have a majestic appearance. At the post-houses the masters seem much dissatisfied, and barely give one a civil answer when horses are asked for. They have reason for being out of humor, as the rate which the law gives them is not more than a fourth of what they used to get at the present exchange.

"In riding through some of the villages, we were followed by numbers of children, who threw bouquets into the carriage-window, and trusted to those within for something in return. Nineteen and a half leagues.

"12th. — At six o'clock this morning we set off, and in an hour arrived at Cuvilly, and from there to Couchy les Pots in another. The part of the road we have been travelling this morning is, in appearance, more like America than any other I have seen in France. There are a great many apple-trees, and more pasture-ground than I have observed anywhere else. The only thing wanting to complete the similarity is fences; of which there are none in this country. Indeed, they are not here necessary as with us. We turn our cattle and sheep into a field to feed; and here, a shepherd follows the flock and directs the spot for it. Nothing is more entertaining than to see the surprising manner in which the shepherds' dogs are trained in France. They are making constant circles round the flock; and, if one trespasses the bounds ordered, the dog will walk up and take him by the foot; and in this way they are all kept in a small compass. The life of the shepherd, so much sung of, must be a very idle and vacant one, with nothing to do but see that the dogs, which are the attendants, do their duty, — nothing to exert themselves about. But this must be irksome and disagreeable.

"From Couchy les Pots we were in Roye, a small walled city three leagues from thence, in an hour and a half. The walls of this place are out of repair, and general decay seems to hang upon it. It contains, however, an excellent tavern, called the 'Soleil d'Or,' which afforded a fine breakfast; and we took leave of it, well satisfied with our fare. It contains about three thousand people. There are no manufactories here. From this place we were well driven to Fouches, which is a village where there is an immense post-house and stables, — its proprietor a *ci-devant* lord, who has been fortunate enough to save his head and his property. When we arrived at Marché le Pot, the postmaster made such bitter complaints, that we were induced to give him double fare; and came off, I dare say, in his opinion, dupes and green ones. The fortified city of Peronne is three leagues from Marché le Pot. This place is very well fortified, but in an ancient style. Its entry is through three gates, one within the other some distance, with a ditch, wall, &c., between each, until you come to the wall which surrounds the city. . . . After many manœuvres with the postmaster and *aubergiste*, who had joined their plans to oblige us to tarry all night here, seeing us persist, they gave us horses; and we left Peronne for Fins, which is four leagues, and is only a post establishment. We here got horses without much delay, and had every reason to suppose we should get to Cambrai before the gates were shut. Had we found the people disposed to forward our wishes at Bonaves, three leagues from Fins, we should have got there with all possible ease; but the fact was otherwise. We soon saw they were determined to keep us all night; and as no reasoning will ever change the *menée* of a French postmaster, backed by inclination to get you to tarry any time to spend money in his house, which is generally the case where the postmaster and publican unite in the same person, we put the best grace we could on the thing, and are making the necessary arrangements for passing the night here. The accommodation is bad; and, had we not been fortunate enough to have taken something with us from Roye, we should have been supperless. The pavement on a part of the road between this and the last post is taken up. We suppose this was done to prevent the passing of the cannon of the Austrian army on to Peronne, in case Cambrai were taken. This makes the travelling very unpleasant, and in some places even dangerous.

"All the houses of the farmers, for thirty or forty leagues back, are covered with straw, very neatly laid on, and of a thickness to oppose either water or cold, — it being seldom less than eighteen inches thick; and in some places the sides as well as the top of the house are covered in a way which has, when it is new, a very neat and handsome appearance. The farther we proceed from Paris, the less esteem assignats are held in, and more is demanded for every thing which is had.

"13th. — At eight o'clock, we arrived at Cambrai, which is a fortified town, and I believe has always had a small garrison. Its walls are very high, and the ditches which surround it deep and wide. The *porte* at which we enter has a formidable appearance; and the thickness of the wall I should suppose at least seventy feet. We took a stroll round the town, which has a walk quite round, and shows remarkable strength. The appearance of Cambrai is less disgusting than the towns in general through which we have passed, and the streets are commodiously wide; and, in general, the town is better laid out than those through which I have passed. The town and its environs bear strong marks of its having been the seat of warfare. The houses are in some streets entirely shut up; and in no part of the town is there any appearance of business. This place, which was the famous manufactory of cambrics (from the name of the town), has not now any thing of this kind going on. The people appear entirely unoccupied, and seem not very well content with the continuation of a war which is so injurious as this must be to manufacturing cities. The cathedrals and some other public buildings are very large, and built in a Gothic style. This place was the residence of the Archbishop of Cambrai, and was overrun with monks and other dependants upon the church. We are told this single place contained eight hundred priests before the revolution. What a tax upon the industrious citizens! We were shown a great many buildings which were occupied by this class of people; and which authorized the belief, that there were as many of this sort of gentry as we had been told. This place, as well as almost every other one of consequence in the Republic, has been the scene of the butcheries of the Jacobins and their emissaries. The infamous Lebon had about two hundred persons sent to the Revolutionary Tribunal; which was only a stage towards the guillotine, as they never failed to go from thence to this fatal machine. Riches were cause enough for accusing one of being an aristocrat: as such he fell, and his property was pillaged by those who had caused his downfall. There is one street, the best built in this place, which has not now one of its former owners in it: they have fallen a sacrifice to this vile assassin of the human race. At Arras, about four leagues from hence, he caused six hundred to fall, and, in some instances, in a manner too horrible to relate. . . . The guillotine which was erected on the *place*, in front of the Maison de Ville, was publicly burned some time since. In walking round the ramparts of the city, we find the walls going to decay, and the works generally rather out of order.

"We wished to have got an opportunity to go into the Citadel; but find that no strangers, nor indeed even the inhabitants, are permitted to enter there. It is said to be very strong, and capable of a good defence. It is situated upon the highest ground in the city; and commands the neighboring grounds, which are level for some way round. The only commanding ground within a mile is upon the road we came. The possession of this would be fatal to Cambrai, were it besieged. It must have fallen, had a heavy artillery been placed there. At the time of the siege of Valenciennes by the Duke of York and the Austrian armies, the *avant-gardes* were frequently within a short distance of the gates of the city, and burned the houses in the *faubourg* which is towards that place. They never, however, sat down before Cambrai to besiege it. I should suppose that this place contained, before the revolution, from twelve to fifteen thousand souls. At present, I am told, there are not half that number.

"Upon returning to the tavern, to make the necessary arrangements for getting our horses to go on, we found, to our mortification, that the support of one of the springs of our handsome carriage was broken; and, lest we should be detained where we should find less facility for getting it mended, we concluded, after holding a council on the business, to have it repaired here. We shall therefore be detained a couple of hours longer than we intended; and, as the weather is not very pleasant, we do not much relish the necessity.

"At two o'clock, we left Cambrai for Bouchain. We find many houses on the route razed to the ground, and the country, generally speaking, wearing strong marks of the devastation attendant on war. The roads are cut up, and are unpleasant to travel. From Cambrai to Bouchain is four leagues. We arrived here at about four o'clock. This is a very small place, but strongly fortified, and is capable of holding a long siege. A branch of the Scheld washes the walls of Bouchain, and makes it still stronger than it is from its walls; which are strong in themselves, and well mounted with cannon. We here found a difficulty to get horses; and we had every reason to fear we should be obliged to remain in this place, which is one of the dirtiest I have yet seen in France. The fear of being detained in a most infamous tavern determined us to get horses, if we gave a guinea apiece for them, to carry us to Valenciennes. Our necessities were taken advantage of, and we were obliged to pay eight times the common postage; and, in addition to this, ran the most imminent danger of being upset, and our carriage broken, by the maladroitness of the man who acted as postilion. There is a considerable force kept in all the frontier fortified towns. We are now in the Low Countries, or what are called Les Pays Bas François, which we entered two posts before our arrival at Cambrai. The allied armies sent their scouting parties over all this part of the country, and to the walls of Bouchain; but they never sat down to besiege it. The houses on the road are in heaps of ruins from Bouchain to Valenciennes, and particularly as you approach this last place, at which we arrived at seven o'clock in the evening, very much satisfied with having a whole carriage; as, from the manner in which the fellow behaved, we had but little hopes of reaching here.

"The houses, in general, are built of brick in this part of the country, and covered, as we have found them for a long time back, with straw. The country we are now in is more level than that which we have passed through. We find, by the language of the postmistress, that only specie will get us farther on; and we therefore expect to be pretty well fleeced, as they have been in the habit of receiving large nominal prices, and are not apt to calculate with nicety the difference between paper and silver. After a very indifferent supper at a *table d'hôte*, we went to bed; and were in very good humor, or we should have scolded at the woman for giving us such infamous accommodations.

"14th. — As soon as we had breakfasted, which we did very heartily and upon excellent fare, we requested one of the postilions to procure some one to conduct us round the town of Valenciennes, — an object I have been long desirous of seeing. He soon returned, bringing his daughter, — a girl of about fifteen years of age. She was very intelligent, and gave ready and satisfactory answers to all we asked her. She had been in the city during the siege. The strength of this place, to one who has seen so little of fortifications as myself, is inconceivable. The ditch, which is in one part filled with water, is at least one hundred and twenty feet wide; and the walls all round as much as eighty feet, built of brick, and of a thickness which one would suppose could withstand any thing in nature. We were not permitted to go into the Citadel, which is on the side of the Gate de Cambrai, and opposite to that on which it was attacked by the allied armies. As the ground is higher without the Gate of Cambrai and opposite to the Citadel than anywhere else round the city, the armies which attacked it made an attempt on that quarter; but the heavy metal from the Citadel dismounted their cannon, and obliged them to attack towards the Gate of Mons; to which point they brought the most vigorous exertions. After a continual cannonade for forty-five days, and a bombardment which exceeded any thing that had taken place before, the city capitulated. There were three mines sprung under the works; after the last of which, the general who commanded the city, whose name is Ferrand, capitulated. A breach was effected in the walls; and, indeed, a great range of the wall was entirely battered down. The melancholy destruction which is exhibited in this city is beyond description. Whole streets are laid level with the dust; and all the quarter of the town towards Mons is but one great heap of ashes and ruins.

"There were ten thousand men capable of bearing arms in the garrison when the siege began; and, at the end of the forty-five days, more than one-half had fallen a sacrifice. The army of the allies was one hundred and six thousand men, commanded by the most able generals in the service to which they belonged. This sacrifice of men and property was made to get possession of a place they held about nine months; and then, in their turn, they laid their arms down to Gen. Dampierre, who bravely fell near this city, and who is buried on the heights of Fremas, where there is a monument erected to his memory. Great numbers of people were buried under the ruins of the houses of Valenciennes. The house of the general who defended the city was pointed out to us; and we counted upwards of sixty cannon-shot through its walls. The roof was destroyed by bombs; and it has but the walls now standing. Hard by it is an immense heap of ruins,—the remains of a very large church, which has not one stone left upon another. We entered the court of a large house where there had been great destruction, and were told by a man, who, with his family, was in the cellar during the whole siege, that upwards of one hundred bombs had fallen within the court-yard; and its appearance warranted the belief of the assertion. The rubbish is very much cleared up now; and a great number of the houses which were unroofed are now slated and fitted up. Every part of the town is strongly marked, particularly the steeples of the public buildings. A great proportion of the inhabitants of the city lodged in their cellars, which are always arched and strongly built in fortified towns. The walls of the city quite round are astonishingly battered; and in many places breaches were begun, which are now repaired. The life which the people in this city must have led during the siege is inconceivable. There is but little appearance of business at this place. It was once famous for its cambrics and laces; and, indeed, there are some small manufactories yet at work, but they are inconsiderable. The cambrics were not manufactured in the cities which have the reputation of them; but were woven in the houses of the peasants, and brought to Valenciennes to be bleached and dressed. The lace of this place was more esteemed than that of Brussels. There were, before the revolution, between thirty and forty thousand inhabitants at this place; but they are now reduced to an inconsiderable number, and have little or nothing to do. The number of beggars in every town through which you pass is great; but here they exceed any thing we have before seen; and it was with difficulty we could get through them to our carriage. It is shameful to see the manner in which the churches have been demolished here, and the uses to which they are put. The Cathedral, which is a most superb and magnificent building, serves now as a barn, and is filled with hay. It was appropriated to the reception of horses some time since; and the marble with which it is paved is broken to pieces and destroyed. The sculpture, which is in white marble, and executed in a superior style, is broken to pieces, and the arms and heads of the figures are severed.

In another case, we saw caps, tents, and other articles for the army; and teams had driven into the body of the church, and were loading. There is but a small garrison kept here. We were upon the ramparts of the fortifications; but, as we got there by stealth, we did not remain long. The immense ditch which surrounds the town was in one place filled up by the allied armies, so that it was passable; and an assault was to have been made, if the city had not surrendered. At twelve o'clock, we left Valenciennes, which is the last fortified town in French Flanders, and within two leagues of Austrian Flanders. Before we got to the post, we were stopped, to be searched by the last custom-house of the French, and, a little farther on, at the first of the conquered country.

"The officer proposed searching our baggage; but a few livres quieted his conscience, and he let us pass. You hardly pass the line which divides French and Austrian Flanders before you see a difference in the appearance of the people. The contrast between the post-house where we next changed our horses and those in France is as different as can be conceived. Every thing had Dutch neatness about it, and had the appearance of cleanliness, — which, thus far, we have been little accustomed to. The countenances and dress, too, are entirely changed; and, instead of houses level with the ground, we now see them entered by an ascent of a couple of steps, and less lumbered about the doors with every thing which is uncleanly. The old proverb, that 'money makes the mare go,' was never more verified than with us. In coming through the Republic, we have paid with nothing but paper at the post-houses, and have been received by the masters of them with great indifference. We now pay with specie; and the moment this is known where we descend, you are scarcely out of your carriage before you have your horses put to; and they set off *à grand galop*, as if the De'il himself was at their heels. Our second post was Quaregnon, two leagues from Mons; at which place we arrived at about four o'clock in the afternoon. The country, in approaching Mons, is very beautiful; and the arrangement of trees on each side of the way makes the roads delightful. We now see what we have not before since we left Paris ; that is, delightful meadows, in which are cattle grazing, interspersed with trees, that give an appearance of luxury not to be excelled.

"There is much more wood in this part of the country than is found in France; and as the trees are all taken the greatest care of, and all the under-brush is taken out, they have a very beautiful appearance. There are, in some places in French Flanders, ditches, to partition off the meadows from the tilled grounds where the cattle range; but this is very seldom the case; and you generally see a boy strolling about, wherever you see a cow feeding, who keeps her from trespassing upon sown ground. The sheep, too, are always attended by a shepherd, and a couple of dogs who keep them feeding where the shepherd wishes. The sagacity of these animals is astonishing, and deserves admiration. This country is so perfectly level that you can see to a great extent; and, all around, majestic steeples enliven the already rich scene. I have counted eight steeples at a time, when riding upon a perfect level, and taking but half the circle of the horizon. Were one to travel through this country, or, indeed, through any part of France that I have yet been in, and judge of the population by the number of houses which are seen interspersed amongst the fields, he would be very much deceived, and suppose it nearly desolated, and with but very few inhabitants. The fact is, the cultivators of the soil are not owners of it, but are collected together, every few miles, in a miserable village, in the neighborhood of which lives the lord of the village, who has them all at his command, and holds them as his vassals. I should rather say this *was* the fact, than that it *is*. It all holds good, however, except as it respects the lord of the manor, who is in the background. But the cultivators are not the more masters of the soil: they have but made an exchange of masters. On our arrival at Mons, we found the streets full of people, who had just come from Mass; and numbers of priests in the streets, in their usual habiliments. If we had reason to complain of beggars at the other places which we have passed through, what shall we say of Mons, where we were beset in a most disgraceful manner? We effected our escape into the house, where we intended dining; but our faithful attendants waited for us at the door, to give us a fresh assault as we made a new attempt to get to our carriage. The dinner more than indifferent; and the price demanded, extravagant. We saw here a number of poor devils of Prussians and Germans, who had been liberated by treaty with the King of Prussia, and an exchange of prisoners with the Emperor. They were mostly miserable-looking objects, — meagre, ill-clad, and sickly. Mons is in the situation of all the once fortified towns in Austrian Flanders; that is to say, defenceless. Their fortifications were destroyed by Joseph II., who feared his impositions would be looked upon as they merited, and therefore destroyed all the works; which has proved of infinite service to the French, who, without this facility, would have found much more difficulty in conquering Austrian Flanders. Its situation is more elevated than the towns we have passed in the Low Countries; and it might be made strong from the advantage of a river, which I presume is a part of the Scheld, and circulates round the city. The gates of the city are preserved, and the ramparts are converted into public walks. It is a considerable place; and must contain twelve or fifteen thousand inhabitants, from its size. The country between Mons and Bruxelles is the highest wrought scene we have yet observed. Where the country from nature is unfavorable to roads, art has made up the deficiency; and causeways are carried ten or fifteen feet above the ground, for accommodation. The post from Mons is to Casteau, and from there to Braine le Compte. We were served at both those villages with despatch, and went on to Halle with great speed. A new kind of begging is introduced on this road. The moment carriages appear at a distance, the road is lined with children, who chant their demands upon you for charity, and keep upon a trot alongside the carriage until you give them something. Halle is a very large village, and has a considerable garrison in it. The first question upon our arrival at the post was, 'Do they pay in square or round?' The moment the latter was announced, the horses appeared; and two hours put us safe at the Hôtel d'Angleterre, in the celebrated city of Bruxelles.

"15th. — After we had taken breakfast, we took a guide to show us the city. And, that we might have the better idea of it, our first route was for the Cathedral, where we mounted to the top of the steeple, and were able to see every part of the city with great exactness. It is nearly circular, and I should suppose about four or five miles in circumference. The grounds about it are as charming as can be conceived of; to which the delightful ranges of trees, which appear in every quarter, are no small addition. In many places, on the road from Mons, the tops of the trees meet, and you ride for miles in a perfect arbor.

"In going to the Parc, we saw a small body of troops parade, who looked more shabby than they ought. Gen. Ferrand was on the parade. He is a good-looking man, and one I respect for his brave defence of Valenciennes. . . . 'Tis melancholy to see so fine a city as this so trist as it in fact is. A vast number of the houses are shut up, and the streets appear dead to business. At this place was manufactured the famous lace bearing the name of the city. They still keep this going on in a small degree. I saw a number of women, in the different shops I passed, at work with their bobbins upon lace. . . . That neatness for which the Dutch are so famous is striking in this city, and appears to us in higher and more estimable colors from the contrast with what we have lately been so accustomed to. The prejudices of the people are much against the French quite through the Austrian Flanders; and they have been greatly augmented by the violations of what they call sacred things, — the pictures and ornaments in the churches.

"16th. — The Emperor used frequently to visit Bruxelles, which is the capital of Austrian Flanders; and he had, therefore, a beautiful palace just without the town, near which is a tall pagoda, that has a magnificent appearance.

"Nothing can equal the ride from Bruxelles to Malines, which is half way to Antwerp. A considerable part of the way, you ride on the margin of the canal, which is ornamented with stately trees on both sides; and the country, which is as level as the surface of an untroubled ocean, is under the most luxurious cultivation, principally in meadow, and filled with cattle.

"We were off for Antwerp at ten o'clock; and at one we were set down at the grand Hotel, which is said to be the best tavern in the place. The population is certainly much greater in Austrian Flanders than in any part of France I have passed through. In France, the inhabitants are collected in villages, which are three or four miles distant from each other. In Austrian Flanders, in addition to those villages, which are quite as frequent and populous as those in France, you see the scene highly improved, by houses being interspersed amongst the fields, at small distances, quite through the country. The villages are all nicely paved; and the pavement looks as if it had been washed every morning. The mode of cultivation is as neat, and as much to be admired, as their domestic arrangements. The women, both in France and Flanders, do their share towards the cultivation of the soil. In some places, we observed the women cutting the fields of grass with a crooked knife. They kneel on the ground, and seize a bunch of grass with one hand, which, with the knife that they hold in the other, they cut off close to the roots. There is some saving by it, but I should not suppose enough to pay for the labor.

"The population of America must be very much increased before we can have our grounds in such order as here. Not a stone is to be seen: they have all been picked up, centuries since, and buried some feet below the surface of the earth. After the plough has been used, they go over the field with forks with five prongs; with which they dig the already ploughed ground, break every lump of earth, and lay it in beds the whole length of the field, and about ten or twelve feet wide. The bed is rounded off, which throws the water into a trench which is left between the beds, of three or four inches in width. This gives the fields a more beautiful appearance than if they were perfectly level. I also observed that there were constantly women and children at work in the fields, picking the weeds from among the wheat, which was about ten or twelve inches out of the ground. This is a great improvement; but it can only be done where the population has become very great, and cannot, of course, be expected for a century among us. They put a great quantity of manure on their land; and, in some instances, they do it in a way I was before a stranger to. In some fields, I saw them with a cart, in which was a large cask filled with water, that appeared to be a decoction of the produce of the barn-yard. This was placed with one end hanging over the tail of the cart. A spigot was drawn, which had some obstruction to prevent the water from flowing out in a stream; and it was scattered quite the width of the cart as it proceeded. There are a vast number of trees over the whole face of this country, which are all arranged with perfect symmetry, and, I suppose, mark the boundaries of the estates.

"As soon as we had made our arrangements for dinner, we took a guide, and went upon our usual business of visiting the different parts of the town. The first object was to see its extent and situation, it being entirely under our eyes when we arrived at the top of the steeple of the Cathedral, which is considerably higher than any other building that I was ever upon. Its height is six hundred and twenty-one steps from the ground; and we were not a little fatigued when we arrived at the top; but were fully compensated for the pains we had taken, by the magnificent prospect which lay before us. The town is considerably smaller than Brussels. It has a number of churches, which, with the Town House and India stores, are all the public buildings. From this steeple, you see the windings of the Scheld for several leagues on each side. This river, which has cost Europe so many lives, is about a quarter of a mile wide at Antwerp, and its water in the channel is sixty feet deep. The quays are very convenient; and, at some of them, there are forty feet of water. However, — to mount again to the steeple, — as I before observed, it commands a view the most superlative that can be imagined. There are no less than sixteen cities in sight; among which are Breda, Bergen op Zoom, Malines, and St. Nicholas; besides which, there are an infinity of villages, which, having no large marks to distinguish them, are scarcely any of them distinctly seen. The country is perfectly level, and has not a hill or rising even to enliven the prospect. We were delighted with the view; and descended to the lower part of this immense building, to admire the works of art. They are here in perfection of their kind. The town of Antwerp boasts of having given birth to Rubens, Vandyck, the famous blacksmith of Antwerp, and several others of the finest painters who ever held a pencil. Many of their works remain in this church; but the most valuable of them have met the fate of those at Brussels and Malines. This was a cruel thing to this town; for the circumstance of the pictures having been painted by their fellow-citizens, enhanced their value in the minds of those who possessed them, and makes the loss of them the more regretted. In one of the pieces painted by the blacksmith, he has thrown a very great likeness of himself into the background, which will make his face known for centuries to come. The piece is the taking of the body of Jesus from the cross. It is done in a masterly manner, in my opinion; though my fellow-travellers are not much pleased with it. There is the death of St. Sebastian, which is finer than any I have seen before. The painting on glass is superior to that of Brussels or Malines; and a part of it was presented by one of the Henrys of England. The quantity of marble pillars and carved work in this cathedral is surprising. This church is superior to the one at Brussels in point of decoration, and is, I think, considerably larger. We were fortunate enough to be at this cathedral when the organist was touching the instrument, with which we were all charmed.

"I am not surprised at the enthusiasm with which people, from long habit, view every thing in their churches; and I confess I cannot walk through one of them without respecting every thing about me. There is a constant succession, to and from all the churches we have visited, of people, who are doing away the sins of the day.

"Antwerp, from its situation, ought to be one of the most flourishing towns in Europe. This was once the case; but now it wears the strongest marks of total idleness. It is splendid in its buildings; and its streets are some of them very wide, and all well paved and convenient. It contained, formerly, sixty thousand inhabitants; but it has not now more than forty-five thousand, and they have very little appearance of business. Antwerp is at the head of navigation on the Scheld, — that is to say, for large vessels; and, situated as it is in the heart of a country which is in fact but one great village, with navigation by boats on the river and canals for a considerable way into the country, would be the storehouse of all the Low Countries, had it the use of the advantages which nature has given it, and art has improved.

"It is said the French intend that the navigation of the Scheld shall be free to all the world. How true this is, time alone will determine. It will be saying that Antwerp shall be one of the first commercial cities in Europe."

Thirty years afterwards, as appears in a subsequent journal, Antwerp presented the appearance of more extensive commerce, and great improvement in accommodations for the shipping; but the ascendency which the city once enjoyed has never been regained.

"May 17th. — At five o'clock this morning, we left Antwerp, round which is a charming country for a few miles. Our anticipation has been fine roads from Antwerp to Rotterdam; but we are much disappointed, as we had ridden but four or five miles before we left the pavement, which continues from Paris to this place. The country, for eight leagues, is the worst I ever travelled through: the roads are sand,

and the whole face of the country the most barren I ever saw. Although we had four horses, they went upon little more than a walk the whole way. Within two leagues of the Mordyke, the scene was changed, and Nature looked smiling on every side. We here arrived at the diked country, and see the finest pasture grounds in all Europe, and the fields stocked with cattle without number. We pass the Waal at Mordyke, which is a ferry about three miles wide, well attended, and the boats excellent. The roads are pleasant through Holland, lying upon the top of the dike, but unfortunately too narrow, leaving barely room for two carriages to pass; and of course making it very dangerous for them to meet, as both must approach so near the edge of the dike as to stand a very tolerable chance, in case of any accident, of being canted into the canal, which is at the foot of the dike.

"We passed through a number of villages; to describe the neatness of which, would be impossible. The number of trees spread all over this country makes its appearance very beautiful. This is heightened extremely by the vast herds of cattle which are feeding in the fields. The horses are famed in this part of Holland, and deservedly so. At ten o'clock in the evening, we crossed the Meuse, and landed safely at Rotterdam. We take our lodgings at the Maréchal de Turenne.

"18th. — Busily employed in viewing a town which is beautiful to a great degree, and is in a very fine situation for business.

"19th. — From the top of the highest steeple in Rotterdam, we saw thirty odd villages, and were much pleased with the prospect. The windmills, of which there are great numbers round Rotterdam, are built of stone; and some of them I judge to be between seventy and eighty feet high. Capt. George Lane tells me that some of them are sawmills, and that he was in one which carried forty saws at a time. They are also used to throw out the water from the canals into the rivers when the former get too full. The canals in this place admit vessels to your store door, and make the doing business very convenient. The buildings are all plain and good, some of them handsome; the India House and Exchange the only public buildings which are remarkable.

"We find them very busy here; a treaty having just been signed between France and Holland, offensive and defensive, and, the Hollanders say, upon mutual advantages. This remains to be proved. I most sincerely hope the event may prove this to be the fact. We this day dined with Mr. Buldemaker; whom we find a very pleasing man, and who has a charming family. On the morrow, we leave for Amsterdam.

"20th. — The day fine, and promising us a pleasant journey. At half-past ten o'clock, we left Rotterdam; and, at seven in the evening, we were at the Arms of Amsterdam. The road from Rotterdam is generally good; though, like all the roads I have yet seen in Holland, very much cramped for width, two carriages being scarce able to pass without danger of being thrown off the dike. The dikes, in general, are adorned with trees; and on each side are ditches, filled with water, in all directions. Almost every house has a boat, which is used to transport any thing they may wish from one place to another. This makes carts quite unnecessary amongst the farmers; and I do not recollect to have seen one on the road. This part of Holland is entirely appropriated to the feeding of cattle; the whole country being in meadow, and filled with cows. We have not seen one field of grain since we left Rotterdam. The back provinces are entirely cultivated in grain, which is brought down; and the cheese of the Low Countries, and other productions, such as butter and stock, are taken for pay.

"There is nothing in Holland which looks like wretchedness; and you meet but seldom with people who ask for charity, in comparison with the demands of this kind made in France. Their huts all appear clean and comfortable; and those about them look contented. The contrast between this and what we have left in the great Republic is striking.

"The communication between the great mercantile towns in Holland is by the canals, upon which there are convenient boats for passengers; and there are also the finest boats I ever saw, for the transportation of merchandise. The one and the other are drawn by horses, which travel on the margin of the river; or sailed, when the wind will admit.

"The neighborhood of Rotterdam and of this city (Amsterdam) has many country-seats, the style of which does not altogether correspond with our ideas of beauty. The gardens are perfection in neatness, but too stiff and labored to please an American. The canals are filled with fish; and fishing and smoking seem to be the chief amusements sought in this country.

"The height of the water above the land, within the dikes, is very considerable, and in some instances astonishing. At a country-seat of Mr. Vanstaphort's, about three miles from town, the canal, which is parallel with the house, is forty feet above the garden; and, if the sea should once make a breach in the dike, the neighboring country must suffer exceedingly. The canals which lead up into the town are only deep enough to admit of boats coming up; whereas, in Rotterdam, vessels of two hundred tons come to the very doors of the houses in the centre of the town.

"There is a particular quarter appropriated for the residence of Jews, whose number is said to be between forty and fifty thousand. This sect are deprived of many of the privileges that other citizens have; which makes it astonishing to me that they are opposed to the present revolution, which will unquestionably place them upon the same footing with the other inhabitants. Their funds in the British coffers, which are great, I suspect may be looked to as the cause of this disaffection; as they fear, and with reason, considerable injury from the present arrangement. We visited two synagogues; but as there was no singing, which was the only entertainment we promised ourselves, we made but a short stay. There was a general confused noise, — some talking of business, and others saying their Hebrew prayers. The synagogues are good buildings, and always, I am told, frequented by great numbers of Jews.

"Sunday, May 24th. — This day we appropriated to visiting North Holland. We crossed over to a small village, where we took a carriage for Brock, a village very much distinguished for its excess of neatness. Our expectations had been very much raised, and we had formed to ourselves an improvement upon the general cleanliness which pervades all Holland; but our ideas had fallen far short of the reality. The houses in this town are perfect patterns of every thing that is nice. They do not permit the entrance of a horse into the town. The streets are as nice as a parlor; and are sanded every morning, in serpentine lines.

"The houses are painted green and white; and have small gardens in front of them, with box cut into the shape of different animals. The gardens are decorated with stones of various colors. We were conducted to the house of an old gentleman by the name of Claas Ploeger, who has been very curious to collect what curiosities he could from the captains he has employed; and he is very proud of showing to strangers his little museum, which is decorated with a great number of birds and beasts, many stones, and other things, which are rare of their kind. His house, however, we found to be the greatest curiosity he had to show us. At the door where we entered was spread a white napkin to wipe our feet upon, and one of the same kind at each door we entered. We were carried through the different departments, and found every thing to correspond to this excess of neatness. We happened to be at this place just at dinner-time, the cook-maid having taken the pot in which the dinner was cooked from the fire, and the iron back of the chimney-place was as bright as silver. Mr. Russell and myself had the curiosity to wipe it with our cambric handkerchiefs, without their being in the smallest degree soiled. This is a fact which I should not dare to commit but to the eye of friendship, it has the appearance so much of a travelling story; and, had there not been witnesses to it besides myself, I should not have dared even to note it. I promised the old man some curiosities; at which he seemed highly gratified.

"This place is mostly inhabited by underwriters on vessels, who have their agents in town, or go there occasionally. The women in North Holland dress their heads in a very peculiar manner; and I am sure, that, if all the women would make patriotic gifts of the gold they wear upon their heads to their country, the debt of one hundred millions to the French would be easily paid.

"In the houses of North Holland, there is a door which is never opened but to receive the bride on the day of marriage, and at funerals. This town appeared perfectly dull and unpleasant. The inhabitants seem to have no occupation but that of keeping the town clean. The small bridges which are thrown over the canals are neat, and kept in good order.

"From Brock we went to Saardam, — a town made famous from its being the place where Peter the Great served his time at the ship-carpenter's trade. We were shown the house where he lived; which is an obscure hovel, bearing the marks of antiquity about it. This place was once very much distinguished for its ship-yards; but there is now little doing in that way. The number of mills, all of which are carried by wind, is upwards of eight hundred. The town is like all the towns of Holland, — perfect symmetry, and perfection on the score of cleanliness. There is one custom throughout Holland that is very surprising to strangers who visit the country; which is, that of giving to the servant at the house where you dine a guilder. Upon this principle, the servant, when he enters into the service of any one, inquires if he has much company; and his wages are in proportion. They generally keep possession of your hat, so that you cannot escape them; and, when they find you are about going, do not forget to attend you to the door. . . . .

"31st. — We crossed the Rhine a mile from Leyden; and, at eight o'clock, arrived at the Hague. The country from Amsterdam to this place is principally pasturing, though there are some fields of wheat now and then interspersed.

"June 1st. — As soon as we had made our toilets, we called upon Mr. Adams, the American minister at the Hague; who was very friendly in his attentions, and asked us to dine on that day. We traversed the town, and find it very beautiful: indeed, it has the reputation of being the handsomest city in Holland. The garden of the Prince of Orange is very well suited to the Dutch taste, which consists in perfect symmetry of arrangement. They are so fond of this, that they will not suffer a tree to grow as Nature would have it, let its shape be ever so fine; but it must be tortured to meet their wishes. The canals are broad, and the avenues of trees are many and beautiful. This place is still the residence of the states-general and the foreign ambassadors; and the inhabitants are of that class which were always dependent on the court for a living. There are no manufactories here, as in most of the towns of Holland, except such as produce objects of luxury. The public squares and walks are quite beautiful. We saw a parade of Dutch and French troops on the same square: the former looked as if they were just out of a bandbox, as stiff as the musket they bore on their shoulders; the latter were dirty and ragged as you please, but with an air of vivacity and content in their faces that bespoke cheerful hearts. It is an object of no small wonder to see men, who were a few months since cutting the throats of each other, now friends, and uniting their efforts against the other powers which were leagued with the Dutch in the first of the revolution.

"Rotterdam, 2d. — The weather more pleasant than it has been before. Upon the whole, I like this place more than any other I have seen in Holland. The houses on the river are particularly beautiful, and pleasantly situated.

"4th. — This morning, at five o'clock, we left Rotterdam, and, at ten o'clock, arrived at the Mordyke, where we now are, and where we find we shall be detained five or six hours on account of the tide and little wind. This is unpleasant; but, as we are determined not to fret about things we cannot help, we are quietly waiting the moving of the waters.

"At twelve o'clock, our boat made an attempt; and, at half-past one, we were on the other side of the Meuse.

"We were obliged to wait some time, after crossing the Mordyke, for horses, — all of which had been taken into requisition for the transportation of artillery.

"It was two o'clock before we set off; and, to our great mortification, we find, upon our arrival at the place where I am now writing, that there are no horses; and we are obliged to wait until return horses come from Antwerp or the Mordyke. The reflection which cheers my spirits under every cross accident, and which I call constantly to my aid when things go wrong, is that I am on my way to meet those in the society of whom alone I am or can be happy. May the God of heaven be propitious to my wishes, and land me safe in a country which has, in my opinion, the means of happiness much more within the reach of all classes of people than any I have yet seen!

"This country is visited every year by large numbers of storks. They are of the size of a very large crane; perfectly white, except the ends of the wings, which are black. The Hollanders have a tradition, that this bird will only live in republics. Whether it is for this or some other reason, I know not; but they are looked upon as something above the feathered race in general, and the utmost care is taken to prevent any injury coming to them; for the sin of hurting one of these birds is very great. There is no fear of any thing of this kind happening from the inhabitants, who have a religious respect for the bird; but from those who consider the fowls of the air as common stock, and the property of those who can possess themselves of them. These birds build upon the corners of the houses; and, in some instances, I have seen their nests upon places erected expressly for them. Their nests are made of sticks, and are larger in circumference than the head of a barrel. They live upon insects, which the low grounds about here furnish in great plenty. They are birds of passage, and, in autumn, assemble in large flocks, and rove about for several days together in societies of this kind previous to their departure; when they take an amazing height, and disappear until the coming spring calls them to take possession of their old habitations. It is unknown to what country they emigrate. Thomson, in his 'Seasons,' thus speaks of this domestic, affectionate bird:—

'Where the Rhine loses his majestic force
In Belgian plains, won from the raging deep
By diligence amazing, and the strong,
Unconquerable hand of Liberty,
The stork-assembly meets; for many a day
Consulting deep, and various, ere they take
Their arduous voyage through the liquid sky.

And now, their route designed, their leaders chose,
Their tribes adjusted, cleaned their vigorous wings,
And many a circle, many a short essay,
Wheeled round and round, in congregation full
The figured flight ascends, and, riding high
The aerial billows, mixes with the clouds.' *

"The country, in general, looks more smiling than when we went on. The flax, which was then not out of the ground, forms a pretty contrast to the numberless shades of green with which the meadows are clothed. I confess it is with pleasure I am about to leave this country. It has been observed, by an English traveller, 'that (speaking of Holland) it is a country where the earth is better than the air, and profit more in request than honor; where there is more sense than wit, more good-nature than good-humor, and more wealth than pleasure; where a man would choose rather to travel than to live, — would find more things to observe than to desire, and more persons to esteem than to love.'

"5th, Antwerp. — At eight o'clock, we arrived at this place, having ridden all the night. When we were going to Rotterdam, over the same road we passed last evening, it was in the daytime; and we observed, that it would be impossible to go over it at night without being upset. We little thought that we should make the trial on our return; but this was the fact; and we were so fortunate as not to realize what we had great reason to fear. Although I was extremely disposed to sleep, yet the beauty of the evening, and the melody of the nightingales,

* It is ascertained that the stork migrates to North Africa.

which serenaded us the night long, kept me awake; and I scarce ever remember to have passed a more pleasant night. We find that we cannot cross the ferry which passes the Scheld until slack tide, which is twelve o'clock; so that we shall not be able to get any farther than Ghent (or Gand, as the French call it) this night.

"The few houses which are left (after the devastation of war) between Courtray and Menin speak our approach to the territory of France. That neatness so conspicuous in the houses in Holland and Austrian Flanders is taking its leave of us; and more urbanity and good-humor, with less attention to cleanliness, is visible.

"The line between Austrian and French Flanders is about a mile from Menin; and here is established a custom-house, where we were stopped to report our luggage and destination, as well as place of departure; which being done to the satisfaction of the officer who made the inquiries, he suffered us to go on without examining our baggage. All the houses round Menin have been destroyed; and every thing speaks the distress that must have existed here the last year. The road is almost impassable, from the pavement having been torn up by the heavy cannon and wagons which have passed over it. There are outworks all round this city, which tell the regular approaches of the French when they besieged it.

"The first village we passed, after leaving French Flanders, was one of the most wretched places I remember to have ever seen. Mud-houses, covered with straw, hold a set of beings whose general appearance corresponds to their habitations.

"Lisle, June 6th, 1795. — We arrived at this place at seven o'clock this evening; and, as soon as we had made ourselves up a little, we went to the Comedy; where we were much amused, and found better acting than we had anticipated. The house is very handsome within; and the style without is that of the Italian Opera at Paris, which is thought as well of as any theatre in the city.

"We took up our quarters at the Hôtel de Bourbon. I was surprised to hear this hotel called by its *ci-devant* name by the postilion who conducted us there. The fact is, that it is now thought less enormous to call places by the names which they have borne for centuries than it was a short time since. At the *table d'hôte*, we saw two gentlemen who had just arrived from Paris. They tell us of the difficulty of procuring horses; and would make us suppose that they have worked wonders, in surmounting all the impediments they have had to encounter. We have been used to this kind of story; and therefore they give us no uneasiness. We find our fellow-travellers, too, have had their 'hair-breadth 'scapes' in the late insurrection of the *faubourgs* of Paris. We are told that there are several deputies of the Convention decreed of accusation; that is, in other words, destined to lose their lives on the scaffold. Great God! when will the vengeance of party-spirit subside, and the calm effects of reason take its place? My eyes are tired of seeing, and my ears of hearing, of the sacrifice of the advocates of opposing principles to the unforgiving spirit of that party which may be at the head, and take the lead, for the time being.

"In the great square in front of our hotel, they are erecting an altar, where will be celebrated the triumph of Liberty over Jacobinism in the late business in Paris. A funebrial *fête* is ordered for to-morrow throughout the Republic, on account of the death of the member Féraud, who was assassinated in the Convention.

"The gentlemen from Paris tell us that the man who shot the deputy, and the one who afterwards carried the bleeding head on a pike, in exultation, to the Convention, have both been taken up and guillotined, with about twenty *gens d'armes*, who were convicted of aiding and abetting the late affair. There have been strong suspicions for some time respecting the good disposition of the *gens d'armes* towards the Convention; but there is now no doubt of their being inimical; and they are ordered out of Paris. Troops of the line are now the guards of the Convention and of Paris. It is melancholy that this same guillotine should have got into such quick motion again. It is to be feared that ill use will be made of it.

"7th. — Lisle is esteemed one of the most considerable cities in France. Its numbers are not so large as I expected: they are not more than seventy-five thousand. The streets are well paved; wider and straighter, generally speaking, than those of any other place I have visited in France; and, were they kept clean, they would certainly appear to still greater advantage. The fact is, they are like all the towns in France that I have seen, — overflowed with filth of one kind and another. I am a little surprised that their proximity to Austrian Flanders has not improved them on this score. Old habits are not easily dispensed with: they will, therefore, live as they always have lived, — a gay, laughing, unthinking, dirty people. I mean dirty as it respects their houses and streets. As to their clothes and persons, they have infinitely the advantage of their neighbors.

"We are told that there never was more business done in Lisle than at this moment. The truth is, that the Parisians, who are losing all confidence in paper-money, are throwing all they have into those towns which have goods to dispose of: and the event must be ruinous to the manufacturers, whose goods are estimated according to the rate at which the materials cost them; which it will be impossible for them to replace at treble the price they paid for the present stock. Were a person to travel through this place unacquainted with the situation of France, and the great distress that a very destructive war has occasioned to the country at large, the last thing which would present itself to his imagination would be, that the country was in any other situation than that of peace and happiness. All is gayety and pleasure; and not a frown seems to sit upon the brow of any person I have met.

"The cannonade of this place lasted nine days and nights without ceasing; when, finding that, from its natural and acquired advantages, it could be taken only with infinite difficulty, and, when taken, could not be held, on account of the Citadel, the enemy abandoned their enterprise, after having committed this cruel devastation. The Archduchess of Austria touched several mortars which were fired into Lisle; by which her name will be handed down to infamy.

"This place was fortified by the famous Vauban in the time of Louis IV., and is esteemed his *chef-d'œuvre.*

"The Citadel is esteemed the finest in Europe; and, although we were assured that no person could gain admittance, our curiosity urged us to the attempt; which was attended with success, and the highest degree of gratification. When we asked admittance of the sentinel who was at the outer gate of the Citadel, our cards of admittance were demanded; and the soldier was surprised to find we were not furnished with any, and told us we could not repass without them. We were conducted to the commandant, who received us with a great deal of politeness. We told him that we were Americans, and showed him our passports, saying that we were desirous of seeing this fortress, celebrated throughout the world as the *chef-d'œuvre* of Vauban. He said he would gratify us; and immediately sent the secretary with us, and told him to show us every thing that was curious. We were flattered very much by this civility, which was what we had no right to expect. The young man who conducted us explained every part of the works to us, and showed us all that was to be seen.

The Citadel, when completely garrisoned, is capable of holding eight thousand men; for which number there are complete accommodations. All the barracks and magazines are built in brick and stone; and are very neat, and well constructed. There are also subterraneous barracks and hospitals, equal to the accommodation of the complete garrison, in case the barracks should be destroyed. All parts of the works are mined; and the fortifications are so constructed, that, in case the city is taken, there cannot be a single piece of artillery brought to bear upon the Citadel; whereas the strongest works of this fortress are opposed to the city; and it would not be possible for the enemy to keep possession of it three hours, if the batteries from the Citadel were opened upon them.

"After we had taken a very particular survey of the Citadel, the gentleman told us that we had seen every thing there which was worthy of notice; and he observed, that we could now say we had seen the finest piece of workmanship, of the kind, that genius and art had to boast of. We returned on the same route by which we had entered, and went immediately to our lodgings, not a little fatigued with our ramble, and disposed to breakfast. It was ten o'clock when we got home, and we had set off at six; so that we had been about four hours without any respite from walking.

"At eleven o'clock, we left Lisle, after being obliged to hire private horses to take us to the first post. Through the first post, the road was entirely torn up by the cannon and heavy wagons which had passed over the pavement during the siege, and made it difficult to pass. We, however, got on to Carvin without any accident. This is a small village; the houses miserable huts, filled in with mud, and covered with straw. The postilion, in expectation of being well paid for his services, drove off, with a crack of his whip, at full gallop; and an hour saw us at the Post House at Lens. I was surprised to see the people on the road and in the village so well dressed; and, upon inquiry, found it was for Sunday. This is a great proof of their disapprobation of the new division of time adopted in France, and is a sign of its falling off altogether. I asked some of the good folks if they went to Mass; and they answered, that any one who wished to say Mass did it how or where he pleased. The churches are not yet opened; but it is expected that they shortly will be so universally. I asked a young woman, who was standing at the door of the Post House, if she had been to church. She answered, that she was too good a republican to go to places of that kind. She appeared to be about sixteen years of age! I do not think, however, that the system of Robespierre has had this effect generally. Like persecutions of every kind, it rather attached those who thought it an oppression to the object of it than weaned them from it; and the women, in particular, were made enemies of the revolution by this most impolitic measure of restraining people in their mode of worship. With those who have any religion, all the laws that man can enact will not succeed in changing their minds. The unhappy effect was on those who had hearts to commit bad actions, but who were kept within bounds by the fear of a day of reckoning; so that, when all fear of this kind was removed, they gave way to the commission of crimes which blacken the history of this country.

"We set off for Arras. Our last postilion having made a good report of our liberality, we had nothing to complain of. We had but poor horses; but the driver had all the disposition to get them on in the world.

"There is a kind of grass very common here, which is called *sain foin*, or, in English, *wholesome hay*, which looks very beautifully in the fields. It has more likeness, when at a distance, to clover than to any other herb I know; but, when near, it is quite different. Its color is a bright murrey; and its quality is much more esteemed than even clover. It is sold at nearly twice the price of any other hay which is grown in the country.

"At about half the distance from Lens to Arras, there is a hill, over which the highway runs, which affords one of the most superb prospects I ever saw. From this eminence, we came in sight of Arras; and we were petrified at the thought of all the horrors of which this place has been the theatre. Robespierre was born in this place; and most unnaturally doomed it to destruction, by sending Lebon to reside here as representative of the people. The unlimited power which has been annexed to this appointment has caused thousands of sacrifices in this devoted country. Had the judges and juries which composed the revolutionary tribunals been chosen indiscriminately from among the people, it is to be presumed that thousands would have been spared who had no crimes to be charged with but that of being virtuous, and having spoken against some of the sanguinary measures of the bloodthirsty men who held the bloody axe over the heads of their unhappy countrymen. The fact was otherwise: they were, in all instances, the creatures of the representative who was in commission where the tribunal was held; and they generally proved themselves faithful servants of their hellish masters.

"Perhaps there never was a situation in which people were more at a loss how to act than those who had nothing to do with government affairs, at a certain period, throughout the Republic. A smile has been construed as an indication of the probable success of a premeditated plot; and he who wore it paid the forfeit with his life. A pensive countenance was construed into a design in contemplation against the state; and, if a person staid at home to avoid so critical a situation as hazard might have thrown him into while mixing with the crowd, it was observed by one of the thousand emissaries employed by those who sought for blood; and an accusation was brought against him, as brooding over mischief at home, and threatening the unity and indivisibility of the Republic. These are among the many crimes charged against Lebon, and from which he cannot clear himself before his judges. As the appointment of the tribunal was by the representative, he had also the power of changing its members as often as he pleased, or as frequently as they did not carry into effect his sanguinary measures. An old man was devoted by Lebon to death on the scaffold, and was sent to trial by those judges, from whom few escaped but by the gate of death. His virtues were many, his character unimpeachable; no charge against him had the smallest degree of support; and he was dismissed, and, to the joy of his friends and family, returned as from the grave. He was very rich, and was an object of the avarice of this monster; who no sooner heard that the man whom he had doomed to death had been spared, than he sent for the judges, and demanded how it came to pass that he was not condemned. They answered, that there was not the smallest shadow of support to the charges; and that, without some show of reason, they could not condemn one who was of so fair a character; and they had therefore cleared him. He dismissed them from his presence in a rage, broke them all, and named new judges; and had the innocent citizen, who supposed himself now secure (having passed the fiery ordeal), once more torn from his friends, and sent to the tribunal. The same afternoon, he was beheaded on the scaffold; his property was confiscated, and his wretched family thrown into prison.

"It is not surprising that every one is exasperated against Lebon, to a great degree, in this city and the neighborhood. I had always supposed that the rich alone had been the sufferers in the excesses that have been committed in France; but I now find that this is not the fact. The principle was to spread terror throughout all classes of citizens; and therefore the farmer and artisan, as well as the merchant and nobleman, were involved in the general calamity. It would be dangerous to commit such power to the most virtuous of the community as was put into the hands of the representatives on mission.

"I am informed, on good authority, that the wife of Lebon was, if possible, more inhuman than he himself; and that once, when only three or four persons were to be guillotined, upon being told of it, that she might attend, as was her usual custom, she observed that it was no object to see so sorry a spectacle as only three or four would make. I think the horrid passion of this woman may be traced to avarice, which was fed by the death of so many unfortunate persons, who all contributed to fill the coffers of her husband; while her person was adorned with jewels rifled from their widows and orphans. There remained a vast number of persons in prison, at the time of the overthrow of Robespierre, in almost every part of the Republic. His death gave them their liberty; and their places are now occupied by their persecutors. When this system of retaliation will cease, God only knows.

"8th.—We were off at six o'clock; and intended to breakfast at Doulens, which is a post and a half from where we lodged: but the Post House did not afford any thing eatable; and we were, therefore, obliged to have recourse to our wine and bread, in place of a more agreeable repast. We found the post-horses at Doulens the worst we had met on the road; and, although it is but six leagues to Amiens, we fear we shall get there at a late dining-hour.

"The province of Picardy, of which Amiens is the capital, is very highly cultivated in grain and pasturage, and abounds with fruit; but has not the fine hills and vales, interspersed with extensive woods, which delight the eye in the province of Artois, of which Arras is the seat of government. To supply the place of wood, turf is the general fuel of the province.

"We got on to Amiens by two o'clock, where we found a *table d'hôte* prepared. This place has the appearance of great antiquity. The buildings are mostly in a decaying state. The streets seem to be abandoned, except by beggars; by whom our carriage was surrounded, as soon as we halted at the door of the *auberge*. We felt too much inclined to get something to satisfy our hunger to make the accustomed settlement with this class of *misérables*; and could not have passed them without harsh usage, had we not promised them something when we should be about to depart. This had the effect which was to be expected; and, when we were ready to return to our carriage, we found the court-yard full of the halt and the blind. They had sounded the alarm, and were re-enforced from all quarters. Having made a provision of small bills, we sallied forth, and were astonished to see the number of poor creatures who were collected to ask for something in the name of God. There were always a great number of beggars in France; but the number must have necessarily very much increased with the distresses of the country in general. Many, who were once supported by a son who has been sent into the army, or by a husband who has been dragged to slaughter, are now reduced to this melancholy alternative for the support of a miserable existence.

"We met with an inhabitant of Arras at the *table d'hôte* who was once destined as a victim by the bloody mandate of Lebon; and would have shortly had his trial, had not the Jacobin party fallen. Among a variety of facts which mark Lebon as the Nero of his age, at least in cruelty, this gentleman told us of one, which shows that he took pleasure in refining on the principle he had laid down. On a day in which several persons were to be executed, and when one was already tied, and the axe was on the point of falling, he cried to the executioner to stop. The unhappy man was raised, and stood in a state of awful suspense. As he was conscious of his innocence, he had a momentary gleam of hope that his rectitude had been made to appear, and that the paper which Lebon held in his hand was his pardon. When all was silence, Lebon read an account of a victory of small importance, which he had just received tidings of from Paris; having finished which, he told the executioner to proceed in the business of death. The person who gave us the account of this incident, said he was present when it occurred. It is astonishing that the great majority of the people of this country should have remained so long torpid under such a state of tyranny. The fact is, that all classes of people were petrified; and no one dared to communicate with his friends, much less with people in general, respecting the evil that every one felt. Terror hung over the nation; and no one dared to show the way to opposition, lest what was the effect of a principle of self-defence should be construed as the result of a counter-revolutionary principle. This has been the watchword for all the horrors that have blackened the history of the country. A word, and sometimes a look, was taken for incivism; and immolation was the consequence. There was an unparalleled activity in those bloodthirsty men, which did not give time to those, who had courage to contemplate a plan of opposing the bloodsuckers of the country, to put their wishes in practice. The excesses of Carrier in Nantes and its vicinity ended in an open war in that part of the country, which has caused the Republic the loss of more than three hundred thousand men,—or rather inhabitants; for there was no distinction of age or sex: all fell before the victors, whether rebels or republicans. The sanguinary disposition of Carrier was not contented with the tardy mode of execution which the guillotine offered: so he had boats constructed, into which he plunged indiscriminately men, women, and children; and, merely opening a valve which was in the bottom, the boat sunk with the unhappy passengers. . . .

"Paris, 16th.—The weather is becoming extremely pleasant, and entices one from the walls of Paris; which, as the season advances, is becoming very disagreeable from the heat and filth.

"We are informed this day that the trial of the eight deputies of the National Convention, who were decreed of accusation by their colleagues, as promoters of the disturbances of the 1st of Prairial, is to come on before the Military Commission. This court has been established since the Revolutionary Tribunal was abolished. It is neither more nor less than a court-martial, and is composed of eight officers of rank. They have had the trial of all those persons who have been arrested as concerned in the attempt against the Convention, many of whom they have sent to expiate their crime at the guillotine.

"The name of the Revolutionary Tribunal has been detested throughout this country; for it has condemned all the martyrs who have suffered in the cause of liberty through the influence of Robespierre; and, indeed, all who suffered by the guillotine had their mock-trial at this bar. The last trials before this tribunal were those of its former judges, jurors, and attorney-general; who were tried for the crimes they had committed while in office, and condemned to die for their unheard-of cruelties by the same machine to which they had condemned thousands. This was esteemed the most just thing that was ever done by this tribunal; and with it ended its existence, a short time previous to the insurrection of the *faubourgs*. As there was no criminal court established, the Military Commission was created, for the purpose of trying those concerned in that affair. It is held in the house of an emigrant, which can hold but few persons. We found a large body of people waiting, and very much feared we should not gain admittance; but Mr. Russell, having an ambassador's ticket of entrance to the National Assembly, obtained permission for us to enter. We were introduced into the room where the court sat, which was capable of holding about sixty or seventy spectators. The names of the members who were accused were Bourbotte, Rhull, Romme, Goujon, Du Roy, Forestier, Dusquesnoy, Soubrany, and Peyssard. Rhull, unable to undergo a trial which he supposed would be but a prelude to his death on the scaffold, put an end to his existence the day before yesterday. When we entered, we found Bourbotte before the court. He was seated in the centre of that part of the room occupied by the court, and was guarded on each side by a soldier, who held a drawn sword in his hand. The judges were dressed in their regimentals. Three or four of them showed by their uniform that they were general officers; and seemed, from their conduct, to have some fellow-feeling for the unfortunate men who were arraigned before them. There were eight sentinels in the room; and every thing looked martial. There was also a body of troops in the court-yard below. Bourbotte is a very handsome, well-made man, of about thirty-five years of age. He was accused of being one of the members of the Convention, who, on the night of the 1st of Prairial (or 22d of May last), made some of the motions upon which certain decrees were passed by the few members who remained in the hall of the Convention. One of his motions is said to have been for the immediate arrest of the members of the Committee of Public Safety and General Surety. He denies this; but there is a person who has proved that he was in one of the tribunes, and that he himself heard him make the motion, and second others equally *anti-modéré.* He was asked by the president of the court-martial if he had any observations to make upon the evidence of the person who had been giving his deposition; and answered, that he had nothing more to say than he had before said in answer to the interrogations which had been put to him. Every thing that is deposed by a witness, or answered in defence by the prisoner, is taken down by a secretary, as the one or the other speaks; so that the prisoner speaks as many words as he supposes the secretary can remember, who writes them down, and then goes on with all he has to say. When the prisoner has finished, it is read to him, that he may agree to its being what he uttered; after which, he signs it, as confirmation of its validity. I should have supposed, that, uttering in this way perhaps half a sentence at a time, one would lose the thread of the defence, and would labor under a great disadvantage. This, however, was not the case in any instance this day, that I remember, as respected those on trial. The witnesses appeared much less cool and collected than those whom they accused, and made several mistakes in keeping the thread of their testimony. The prisoner had his snuff-box, which he carelessly twirled betwixt his thumb and finger, occasionally taking from it a pinch of snuff. He showed not the smallest signs of fear; although he must be sensible, and undoubtedly is so, that, in three or four days, the thread of his existence will be cut. The evidence is very full against him, and nothing can save him.

"The witness deposed, among other things, that he heard the prisoner say that he had just come from a coffee-house in the neighborhood, and that he had taken there several glasses of wine; and, from the warmth of his expressions, he (the witness) supposed him to be intoxicated. The prisoner smiled, but answered nothing.

"Forestier is an old man, and the charges against him are light; and I am of opinion that he will not be found guilty.

"The witness who was examined respecting Du Roy, Romme, and Goujon, testified that he saw three of the members (describing them according to their dress and appearance) very warmly taking a part in the Convention in forming the decrees which were made on that memorable night. The prisoners were severally called in; and the witness said they were the persons he alluded to. They observed, that, in such a situation as the witness was in, and in the tumults of that night, it could not be possible for him to be certain of the identity of their persons. This idea seemed to me to be rational enough; but the rest of the audience smiled at the idea. They all answered, upon being asked if they had any further defence to make, that their answers to the interrogatories put by the court were their defence; and they said not much to the witnesses who were examined.

"These members are all of what is called the Mountain party in the Convention. This is another name for Jacobin; and therefore all Paris is against them, since the Convention (that is to say, the *Modérés*) have got the day. How it would have been, had the *faubourgs* got the upper hand, there is no knowing. Goujon is quite a young man. One of the witnesses deposed that he heard him speak with a great deal of warmth on the night of the 1st; on hearing which, Goujon asked, with a smile of indignation, what member of sensibility there was who would not show warmth on such a night as that. He seems a very intelligent young man, of about twenty-six or twenty-eight. If his fate is to be a guillotine, Mr. Russell and I are of opinion he will meet it like a man. Indeed, they all show an astonishing degree of coolness and reconciliation to the fate that awaits them, particularly Bourbotte, who, as he left the room, bowed and smiled upon several persons, who were, I suppose, some of his acquaintance. There is one thing respecting this trial which I cannot think quite right. When these men were decreed of accusation, and ordered to be tried by the Military Commission, they called upon several members of the Convention as witnesses in their favor. The court referred the propriety of calling the members of that body, who had been their accusers, as witnesses; and the Convention, after discussing the point, agreed that the court were competent to determine every thing of that kind, and passed to the order of the day. The fact is, the members were not called! Had there been a question of calling any of the members of that body, who accused the prisoners, in behalf of the government, it would not have been right; but that they should deny this privilege to the accused, seems to me extraordinary. The judge informed us, at about half-past three, that the court would be opened again the next day at twelve o'clock. As I was going out, the officer who conducted us to the chamber told me, that, if I wished to see them receive sentence, I must come by eleven o'clock to-morrow. There seems to be no doubt in the minds of the people how this business will terminate; and I dare say they would not be insured from the axe of the law for ninety-nine per cent. Romme appeared to me to be the only one who had fear marked upon his countenance. He is very obnoxious to the reigning party; and they will rejoice at his fate, should it be execution on the Place de la Révolution. If possible, I shall go to the commission to-morrow.

"Exchange this day rather better than for some days past. I am told that guineas have been sold for five hundred and fifty to-day. They were eight hundred yesterday. There is a report about finance once more coming forward, which occasions this.

"17th.—Mr. Russell and myself having business to attend to until one o'clock, we did not go out as we intended. We then went into the Rue St. Honoré to call on Mr. Pearsall, where we heard that judgment had been pronounced upon six of the eight deputies, and that they were to be executed immediately. We felt anxious to see the conduct of men, who had smiled at death at a distance, upon a nearer and more certain approach of the king of terrors. We took a stand in the street which leads into the Place de la Révolution, where the guillotine was already erected, although the prisoners had not been condemned above an hour. We had not waited long before we saw the horse-guards approach; and, soon after, the prisoners, upon a cart. We found there were but three of them in the cart, whom we recognized as Bourbotte, Du Roy, and Soubrany. The first was sitting erect in the cart, and the others were lying upon their backs. We did not know how to account for this, until we saw they were all weltering in their blood; and we soon heard that they had all attempted to take their own lives as soon as they were remanded to prison. Bourbotte looked very pale from the loss of blood; but his appearance was as placid and as little agitated as if he were taking an airing in a coach; and he looked round with a smile upon us barbarians who were assembled to see him die. The guards were very strong, and were all troops of the line. When the cart arrived at the guillotine, Soubrany was lifted out, and laid upon the plank without being tied. There was very little life remaining in him; and a few hours must have relieved him, had the execution of the sentence been procrastinated. It is common for all the prisoners to descend from the cart upon their arrival at their place of execution; and they are placed in such a manner that they do not see the sentence performed upon their fellow-sufferers. On this occasion, it was otherwise. The situation of Soubrany was such that he could not support himself; and Du Roy was little better: and they therefore backed the cart to the scaffold, which was then about upon a level with it, that those who were unable to help themselves might be the more easily conducted to the machine. In this situation, Bourbotte saw the operation performed upon his fellow-sufferers without an emotion. The two first had lost their senses, and were laid on the plank without a motion which showed sensibility. It now remained for us to see such fortitude as has not been witnessed since the revolution. It has been the wonder of every one, who has witnessed the executions in France, to see the fortitude displayed almost without exception. The high pitch of enthusiasm to which the minds of the people in France is wound up will carry them through any suffering, I imagine, provided their natural strength is left to them; but I had supposed, that, when that was destroyed, this noble constancy would forsake them. Bourbotte was a strong proof to the contrary. His wound was in the side; and his face bespoke, by its paleness, the great loss of blood he had suffered: yet, notwithstanding this, he raised himself from the cart, and, I imagine, requested to have his hands untied; which was done. He looked round upon the crowd with a smile upon his countenance, and bowed his head with a grace which spoke the softness of his manners. His voice had so much failed him that I could not hear what he said. He was not tied upon the plank, but simply laid down; and the executioner was precipitating his head under the fatal axe, when, to the astonishment of every one, and the execration of the butcher who was thus employed, it was perceived that the head of Bourbotte struck the top of the axe, which had not been raised, as is common, after the last head was off. The prisoner was therefore raised up again on the scaffold while the axe was placed. He still smiled; and it was not a smile of annoyance, but of complaisance; and my friend Mr. Russell, who was rather nearer to the stage than I was, heard him say, 'Farewell, my friends! Long live the Republic!' After which, he pushed down the collar of his coat, laid himself down a second time, and, in a second, was ushered into eternity. Never was there more fortitude shown than on this occasion; and the manner in which this man died convinces me — although it is the general opinion that his intention was to make a revolution in the present state of affairs, and of course he deserved the death he met — that he thought himself in the right, and felt a conscious rectitude, which supported him to this great degree under his sufferings.

"18th. — Yesterday afternoon, I left Paris to pass Decadi at the *château* of my friend Russell.

"We have to-day the journal of yesterday afternoon, which tells us that Romme, Goujon, and Dusquesnoy, as soon as they were remanded to the prison, after receiving the fatal sentence, stabbed themselves to the heart, and died instantaneously. Bourbotte, Du Roy, and Soubrany, were less successful in their attempt upon their lives. Their wounds were undoubtedly mortal; but their object was not completed, which was to avoid dying on the scaffold. It distresses me to learn that several of these unfortunate men leave families. As soon as the judge had pronounced the sentence of death, Goujon handed his miniature picture to him, and requested that it might be given to his wife. Dusquesnoy also gave a letter to the judge, which he said contained his last adieu to his wife and other friends, and observed that he hoped that his was the last innocent blood which would be shed in the Republic. 'May it,' said he, 'serve to consolidate the Republic!' and added, 'Long live the Republic!' Bourbotte said to the commission, that it was the enemies of liberty alone who had wished that his blood should be shed. 'My last wish, my last sigh,' said he, 'shall be for my country.' All those who were condemned then gave their pocket-books, letters, and a number of other articles, to the judge, for their friends; after which, they were reconducted to prison, where they immediately attempted their own lives. Forestier and Peyssard were condemned, — the first to imprisonment, and the second to transportation. When the prisoners were put into the cart, Du Roy burst forth into exclamations against those around them; and, among other things, he said, 'Great God! were these hands made to be tied by executioners? How unhappy am I, to have failed in my attempt on my life!' Soubrany breathed a wish that they would leave him to die. Bourbotte did not utter a sentence, but looked about him with the same coolness that he had preserved during his trial. It is a pity such men could not have died in a better cause. There seems to be no doubt, that, had they succeeded in their object on the 1st Prairial, hundreds must have gone for every one at this time.

"The sisters of young Goujon demanded admittance to the bar of the Assembly, but were refused. Their object undoubtedly was to ask the life of their unfortunate brother. They were referred to the Committee of *Sureté Générale;* and I did not hear what answer they got to their intercessions. The fact is that their brother was dead by the time they could have got to the committee.*

* To those who do not remember the decisive effect of this execution, which extinguished *Sans-culottism*, it may be convenient to be reminded of the course of events in the French revolution. When the king was beheaded, in January, 1793, the party in the ascendant was that of the Girondists, aiming at the total subversion of monarchy and the construction of government in a new form, but showing no inclination for rapine or wanton cruelty. They were, however, unable to direct the storm which had been raised. A few months afterwards, they were overpowered and guillotined, or dispersed, by the *Sans-culottes*, or the party called "the Mountain," of whom Robespierre was the leader. From the terrible destruction which followed, the time while he was in power was denominated "the reign of terror." It ended in July, 1794, when he in turn was guillotined, chiefly through the influence of those who had been his adherents. They found that he was planning their own destruction, as his jealousy had led him to effect that of his former associate, Danton. They were not, however, averse to his sanguinary measures: they meant to continue them. But the terror was over as soon as his death was announced. The executions were stopped, and most of those in prison released. The agitations in Paris during the year that followed were, for the most part, caused by the struggles of "the Mountain" to regain the ascendency. The foregoing diary, written on the spot, and giving the daily events for a portion of that year as they transpired, may be useful to those who wish to inquire further. The last effort of the party was that of Bourbotte and his associates. Their execution was followed by the establishment of the Directory, under whose auspices Napoleon soon commenced his career. It is to be regretted that the diary was not continued for a few weeks longer in Paris, as it would then probably have contained a graphic description of his first essay there with the mob, on the 13th Vendémiaire.

The following statement of the number of those who lost their lives in the French revolution will serve to meet some very natural inquiries on that subject. Precise accuracy is hardly to be expected in such a case; but this has been cited as an approximation to the truth, with the remark, however, that there are still some omissions in it: —

Guillotined by sentence of the Revolutionary Tribunal: —

Nobles	1,278	
Noble women	750	
Wives of laborers and artisans	1,467	
Religieuses	350	
Priests	1,135	
Common persons, not noble	13,623	
		18,603
Women died of premature childbirth		3,400
Women died in childbirth from grief		348
Women killed in La Vendée		15,000
Children killed in La Vendée		22,000
Men slain in La Vendée		900,000
Victims under Carrier, at Nantes		32,000
Victims at Lyons		31,000
		1,022,351

"We have this day the melancholy news of the death of that brave man and great general, Pichegru. The paper of this morning announces his fall on the field of honor before Mayence. France could not have lost a braver man, or a better friend to the liberty of his country. His memory will never die in the breast of any one who admires great talents and tried virtue. Every one speaks with affection of this brave officer, and seems ready to pay to his memory all possible honors.

"Ten o'clock in the evening. — The report of the death of Pichegru is officially contradicted by the Committee of Public Safety. This rejoices every heart;

It appears from this, that about nine-tenths of those who perished were killed in the civil war of La Vendée. The number of nobles beheaded appears small, — most of that order having fled from France. It has been supposed that the atrocities which followed are in some measure to be attributed to this general emigration of the *noblesse*, — there being no class left who were capable of withstanding the influence and outrages of demagogues; whereas if more of them had remained at home, as had been the case with the nobility of England in the revolution of the preceding century, although there might have been as great loss of life, it would probably have been in warfare rather than by murder. The proportion of common people, artisans, and mechanics, was surprisingly large for a revolution against the higher orders.

Some statements that have been made of the whole number executed in Paris appear incredibly small, after the terrible exhibitions there, unless it be remembered that the duration of the reign of terror was little more than a year; that there was but one place of execution there at a time, with but one guillotine for the city; and that one exhibition daily was sufficient in most cases, probably, to satisfy the desire for the sight of blood; though, being described by hundreds of witnesses, it might be so reported as to be mistaken for several occurrences of the same kind, and to represent tenfold the actual numbers.

Estimates have been made, for comparison, in regard to number, to cruelty in execution, and extensive consequences to relatives, between the victims in the revolution and the Huguenots destroyed in the massacre of St. Bartholomew's under Charles IX., the latter being variously rated at thirty thousand up to one hundred thousand or more. With great uncertainty in results, enough is ascertained to show that the spirit of bigotry, whether stirred in support of dogmas under the gospel of charity and peace, of despotic power, or of unlicensed freedom, can easily justify itself, in its own view, for the use of torture and murder as its weapons, without regard to age or sex, and without limit in number.

The remarks on the former mode of agriculture in France that have been given in the foregoing pages suggest some interesting comparisons with the present state of things. For a hundred thousand land-holders there before the revolution, there are now several millions. An English writer has spoken of the whole product of the country as greatly diminished by and joy takes the place of grief, with which every one was affected after hearing this morning's report.

"The Commission of Twenty-one, who were appointed to examine the charges of accusation against Joseph Lebon, have reported to the Convention, that, after examining two thousand nine hundred charges and vindications concerning the said Joseph, they are of unanimous opinion that there is reason of accusation against him. For the credit of human nature, I am happy to hear that there is no support to the charge which has been reported against this man, — of his having made the prostitution of a wife the price of a pardon for the husband, and caused him to be executed, after all, in her presence.* It is wished that

the subdivision of property in land that has followed the radical change in the laws of inheritance, which he thinks is shown by the falling off in exports. The late Mr. Colman, who went from Boston to write agricultural reports from Europe, gave it as the result of his observation, after witnessing the wretchedness of the agricultural population in England, that this general division had produced the happiest effect in France. It seems probable that the falling off indicated by commercial returns may be fully accounted for by the fact, that the laborer, having now a larger share in the product of the soil, instead of being fed on those parts of it which are not fit for export, retains the better portion for his own use. In reference to errors arising from false deductions in statistics, it was recently urged with great force by a distinguished *savant*, before the French Academy, that France affords a striking instance of this nature, not being herself a commercial country, and her exports having rather declined from causes that have vastly increased and diffused her internal wealth. The result of the application for a public loan there is a striking fact in this connection. It was all readily furnished, and chiefly in small sums; thousands joining in it, and becoming creditors of the government, who, but for that division, would doubtless be inhabitants of those miserable villages described in the text as appendant to the *châteaux*, and barely subsisting on the *rebut*, or, as we should call it, the refuse, of the harvest.

It was sagaciously remarked by a distinguished clergyman, in reference to the late renewal and failure of the attempt at a republic, that a century at least must elapse, with frequent political convulsions, before it can be expected that the great changes caused by the revolution shall have had their full effect, and France shall settle tranquilly down under the system of government that will be found best suited to the change of habits in her people.

* In a former part of the diary, this conduct, in all its atrocity, is imputed to Lebon; and the admission here made, when his trial was approaching and he was abandoned to his fate, that the imputation could not be sustained, carries with it some historical interest, because the same charge against this man has recently been renewed in Alison's "History of Europe."

his execution may be at Arras. I find I speak of execution before the man is tried: it is as certain in my mind as his trial. Arras was the seat of the greatest of this man's villanies. Upwards of a hundred persons fell here during his reign; and a visit to Cambrai, which is at about eight leagues' distance, cost that ill-fated city two hundred and sixteen of its best citizens. Whole streets cry for the blood of Lebon, and cry aloud.*

"25th. — Dull weather. The committee chosen to frame a constitution for this Republic made their report yesterday. Boissy d'Anglas read the report; which was much approved of, and promises to put the country, which has been so torn up by the roots by dissensions of every kind, under a lasting and good government. The principles are much the same as those upon which our government is founded. The executive, however, is vested in five, in lieu of one as with us; and, as it appears, has nothing to do with the deliberations of the Senate and House of Representatives, or, as they are called here, the Council of the Ancients and the Council of Five Hundred. They have no negative upon their decrees; nor is it necessary to have any other confirmation of the laws proposed by the Council of Five Hundred than that of the Council of the Ancients.

* Lebon was condemned, but not executed. He seems to have maintained, with some effect, that he could show authority for what he had done from those who were allowed to act in the name of the Convention. He is said even to have been severely reproached at first for moderation, and to have advanced rather slowly to the frightful excess of his cruelty. When the red shirt was brought him, as the signal for execution, he desired that it might be taken to the National Convention, who deserved it even more than he; and the writer who prepared a notice of his life appears to think that, so far, he was nearly right. He escaped under the decree of amnesty which followed soon after.

"The Executive Council has the same powers as the present Committee of *Salut Public.* They are to have respectable guards, and to live in a style equal to what is expected from the executive of a great nation. I should have liked it still better if the Council of Five had been vested with the negative which the President of the United States has. That it may answer the most sanguine expectations of the warmest friends of the Republic, is my heartfelt wish.

"7th.—This morning, about eight o'clock, left Paris in a coach, in company with Mr. Pearsall and Mr. Sands, on a visit to Chantilly.

"8th.—At eleven o'clock, left Chantilly by a cross-road, to go to Erménonville, which was the last residence of J. J. Rousseau, and the place where, at his request, he was laid after his decease.

"The road from Chantilly to Erménonville is principally through the woods which composed the park of the Prince de Condé, and is as pleasant a ride as can be wished. The road is in some places bad, the soil being poor; and, for a considerable distance, the sand is as deep as on Cape Cod in America. We had six horses; and therefore had not much difficulty in getting along, though we were longer in going than we expected. The distance is five leagues from Chantilly, and the same from Paris as from this castle. We arrived at Erménonville at two o'clock. What makes this place particularly interesting is its having seen the last days of this celebrated man. The village is very small, and miserably poor. The *château* is now the property of the Marquis de Girardin, who was the particular patron of Rousseau, and whose bounties he shared until his death. The *château* is a Gothic building, and has nothing in itself to attract attention but its situation, which is charming. It was one of the hunting-places of Henry IV. and, from its contiguity to a very extensive wood, was well situated for the purpose.

"We no sooner arrived than a book was offered for sale, with representations of the place in twenty-five cuts. They are well done, and are very serviceable to one going over the grounds, as they point out the most remarkable things, some of which might pass unnoticed without it. A part of the waters which make one of the beauties of this place are cut off; and the Island of Poplars, as it is described, has now no water about it, and therefore loses a part of its beauty.

"The day has been remarkably fine; and we saw this delightful place under every possible advantage. Romance cannot picture any thing more attractive than Nature and Art combined have produced here. The grounds are well situated for the kind of improvements which have been made; and the united taste of Rousseau and Girardin has taken advantage of them. If there is a grot or a winding stream, you would say the hand of Nature, not Art, had placed them there; and the disposition of every thing is as near the works of that goddess as possible. The useful and the agreeable are wonderfully united. The extent of the grounds is about eight hundred acres; and you can walk over no part of it which is not extremely pleasant and interesting.

"A melancholy event took place here a few years since, which is not mentioned in the book I purchased, and therefore I shall note it. In keeping this memorandum-book, my object is not to describe the places I see, but merely to mention my having seen them, that I may have my recollection refreshed at a future day, and have it in my power to point out to those of my immediate connection such places as in my opinion may be worth their attention. I therefore do not pretend to particularize what those who go over the same places would have an opportunity of seeing, but merely what may have fallen in my way by accident, and what, without a note, might escape them. It was the custom of M. Girardin to request the names of those persons who visited his grounds, that, in case any person of distinction was at Ermé-nonville, he might have an opportunity of showing him civilities which he would not otherwise receive; therefore the conductor was always ordered to ask the name and quality of those whom he was about to take over the place, and report them to the marquis. A gentleman, whose appearance was very much that of a person of distinction, wishing to see the place, the man whose business it was to show the grounds asked him his name, condition, &c. He answered, that he was without fortune, title, or name; and therefore requested that he might be excused from waiting on Monsieur Girardin, who, from his appearance, had been led to suppose he was a person of some note, and had therefore desired to offer him some attention. He walked over every part of the gardens and woods, and passed several hours in contemplating the beauties of the place. He then returned to the house, and took his leave. Four days afterwards, he returned to Erménonville, and retired to a very romantic spot in the woods, where he ended his days with a pistol. He left in his pocket a note to M. Girardin, begging his forgiveness for the outrage he had committed upon his territory, but not mentioning the cause of it. The man who told me the story was the person who was with him the first time in the wood, and who has indeed, for twenty years, filled the same office he now does. He represents him as being about thirty years of age, and of a beautiful and engaging appearance. He spoke French well, though he was not a native of this country, but had more the appearance of being an Englishman than of any other nation; and, from his end, I think it quite probable he was so. It is rather singular that they could never trace the place he came from, and to this day are uninformed as to every other circumstance respecting him save his exit. M. Girardin has raised a very decent stone to mark the place where he lies, with this inscription, which I copied on the spot:—

> '4 Juin, 1791.
> Hélas, pauvre inconnu ! si tu tiens de l'amour
> Une obscure naissance et ta noble figure,
> Devois-tu, dans ces lieux, outrager la nature
> Comme un autre Werther, en t'y privant du jour ?'

"As it was the particular wish of M. Rousseau that his remains should rest where he had passed so many pleasant hours, it seems an outrage upon his ashes to take them from the place where they reposed, even to do them the honors of the Panthéon, where they now are, particularly as he is laid beside Voltaire, with whom he was on very bad terms, and between whom and himself there was no love lost. The monument which held this remarkable man still remains in the Island of Poplars. The only inscription which was marked on the stone before the remains of Rousseau were removed was —

'Ici repose l'homme de la nature et de la vérité.'

It is now changed to —

'Ici reposa l'homme de la nature et de la vérité.'

"I never remember to have been more highly gratified than on this day. From what I had heard of the place from some countrymen of mine who had visited it a few days before, I was not in the expectation of being much pleased, and, perhaps from the disappointment, enjoyed it the more.

"The water, woods, the vast number of beautiful poplars, and indeed every thing, serve to make it as romantic as one can imagine. We passed four hours at this place, and then set off for Paris. The ride through the park is fine, and indeed very interesting quite to Louvres, where we arrived about eight o'clock; and, finding we could not get post-horses that night, we made the best of it, and quietly went to rest.

"We felt much gratified by our tour, and recommend every one who has a little spare time to make the same. M. Girardin still resides at Erménonville, though he did not happen to be there when we visited his place. He was under arrest in the reign of terror; and would probably have shared the same fate with thousands of innocent persons, had Robespierre lived longer. Upon his exit, M. Girardin was liberated. He has the character of a very benevolent man, and is said to be much beloved by the village. He had built a house on purpose for Rousseau, which he never inhabited. He lived and died in a building contiguous to the *château.*

"Rousseau died in 1778. His wife is still living in the neighborhood; but, as she and her husband were not on good terms for years before his death, she is not taken any notice of by M. Girardin. As every one loved her husband, it is not unnatural that her ill conduct towards him should have caused her enemies."

The diary is continued in England; and in these times, when travellers approach London and leave it by railroads, it may be a curiosity to see the remarks of a traveller made at the time when it was necessary to prepare for an attack of highwaymen, if crossing Blackheath in a post-chaise after dark; and when it took the better part of a day, on leaving London, to go fifty-five miles to Oxford. Mr. Perkins was never robbed in England; but he avoided it one night by threatening to shoot the driver, who seemed to linger, and, as was afterwards ascertained, was in league with some "gentlemen of the road."

"26th July, 1794. — This morning, I left Paris for Havre de Grace, with a light heart at the idea of once more bending my course towards my native country.

"27th. — This day is the anniversary of the overthrow of Robespierre and his party, and is ordered to be celebrated throughout the Republic as a *fête*. The Convention is to be dressed in its robes, and an oration to be delivered. We have seen no parade on the road on account of the day.

"28th. — We find the packet, which is to take us across the Channel, will not sail until two days hence.

"I have taken a very general survey of Havre de Grace and its harbor and basins this day, and find the latter very well worthy of attention. The city of Havre is built principally of stone and brick; and the houses covered more with slate than tile, as in other towns in France. The streets are tolerably regular, but narrow and dirty in the extreme. The situation of this place for business is excellent: within twelve hours' sail of England, and so near the sea, with the advantage of being the port through which Rouen and Paris, with all the manufacturing towns in their neighborhood, must be supplied, — advantages which are but rarely combined. The town is much smaller than I had imagined, — containing but about eighteen thousand inhabitants. The basins, which have been dug out for the admission of shipping, are competent to contain several hundred vessels; and they are now at work upon another, larger than the two at present in use, and which I am told will, when complete, contain five hundred sail of vessels. They are all lined with brown stone; and vessels of a thousand tons lie afloat constantly. They are extremely severe as to the execution of the laws to be observed in this harbor, or dock, respecting fires and candles; which is undoubtedly very necessary, as the consequence would be fatal to most of the fleet, should one vessel take fire. There are two frigates now lying in the basins, fitting for a cruise.

"Before the war, there was a large number of vessels engaged in the Guinea trade from this place. This, and indeed all other navigation belonging to the inhabitants, is at an end, excepting that with neutrals, which is considerable.

"29th. — The captain who is to take us over is not yet ready to sail; and I must murder this, and I fear another, day here.

"I forgot to mention a peculiarity in the dress of the women's heads, which strikes a stranger as very odd. The head-dress consists of a cap, of which the fore part is drawn closely over the fore part of the head, and only shows the lower part of the hair on the forehead, which is smoothed down with pomatum as close as possible. The cap is made of muslin, and runs up to a peak; which in some instances is, I am sure, half a yard high. From this peak are pendent two lappets, extending to the shoulder; which altogether form a very curious, and to my mind a very ridiculous, dress.

"August 1st, Margate. — We made the land last evening about six o'clock, and saw an immense fleet of vessels passing and repassing. We were shown to a very elegant hotel, where we breakfasted; and, at eleven o'clock, jumped into a post-chaise for London.

"2d.—The difference between travelling in France and England is very striking. Bad horses, and still more badly harnessed; a ragged postilion, with a pair of jack-boots of about his own weight; wretched inns, if they deserve that name at all; and unaccommodating post-masters and inn-keepers, we have changed for horses that would grace the carriage of any one; a postilion neatly dressed and complaisant; inns where one can be as well accommodated as possible, and half a dozen powdered beaux to receive you when you alight from your carriage. These items, to say nothing of a difference in point of price of about one hundred per cent, make up this difference. The roads, though not paved as in France, are remarkably good, and only want width to make them excellent. The number of carriages we met upon the road this day is surprising, and speaks the luxury of the inhabitants of the country. The country through which we have passed is admirably fine, and under high cultivation. The hedge fences which separate the grounds are highly ornamental, and serve very much to beautify the country.

On our arrival at Dartford, we did not feel altogether satisfied with taking with us what articles of value we were possessed of; and therefore made up a package, and sent them by the mail-coach. There are but few post-chaises that take the risk of crossing Blackheath after dark, particularly if not armed;

but we were anxious to get to town, and therefore undertook it, and happily passed Shooter's Hill and Blackheath without any interruption; and, at twelve o'clock, were set down at the London Coffee House, Ludgate Hill. . . . .

"12th. — To-day, fell in with a number of gentlemen who were going to visit Newgate; and, as I had a curiosity to gratify as well as they, I was admitted as one of the party. Our introduction was through the sheriff; and without this, or an acquaintance with the superintendent, it is difficult to get a view of this celebrated prison. To look at the walls of Newgate, one would suppose it was capable of standing a regular siege; but experience proves to us that a London mob is capable of overcoming the enormous strength even of this place, which was attacked at the time of the Gordon riots, and every part of the interior which was combustible was set on fire, and consumed.

"The overseer of Newgate at this time is a man of much respectability, and appears to be as humane a being as is generally to be met with; and there was not a prisoner whose rooms we visited whose eyes did not bless him as he passed. There are as many as eight different yards within the walls of the prison, where the prisoners can walk; but, as it would not do to let them mix together, they are there separated in the day by walls of an immense height, and at night locked in their several rooms. This amelioration of the lot of misery of those whose misfortunes have placed them there has taken place within a few years;

and the police of the prison is now in conformity with the recommendations of the philanthropic Dr. Howard. The cleanliness of every apartment is very striking.

"After we had visited the several parts of the felons' departments, and also those of debtors of a certain class, we were introduced to the chamber of a Mr. Lloyd, who, in the year 1793, was charged and convicted of a seditious libel against the king and constitution of England, and condemned to an hour's exposition in the pillory, three years' imprisonment, and to find sureties for his good behavior for five years for one thousand pounds. He has about six months still to suffer; which, in comparison with what he has undergone, seems but a short time. He calls himself an American; and though he is not so by birth, yet he is truly so by residence, having taken the oaths necessary to qualify him as such. He complains loudly of our government not having interfered for him; but cannot, in my opinion, reasonably expect it. When a man will live under a government which he does not call his own, of which he pays not for the support, and has nothing to do with except to receive its protection from violence, he ought, most certainly, not to make himself busy with what he thinks the weak parts of it. It is enough for those who live under the government as citizens to find fault in public; and Mr. Lloyd's fate, though a hard one, he very richly deserved, in my opinion.

"The celebrated Major Semple we also saw. He is now under sentence of transportation to Botany Bay for seven years. This extraordinary man was in America three years of the last war, and was wounded in the engagement of Bunker's Hill. Being entirely disabled by a ball in his groin, he returned to this country in 1778, and since that period has lived by his talents, by which, had they been turned to virtue instead of vice, he might have become one of the brightest gems of society. His understanding is very much refined and cultivated in various branches of literature; and his appearance and manners are those of a perfect gentleman, and give him great advantages in deceiving those he may have a design upon. His principal crime has been swindling, of which he was master to as great a degree as was ever known. One pleasant story is told of him; and I am afraid it is a fact. Being at two hundred miles' distance from London, and very anxious to get there, where his talents were at the best market, he pitched upon a mode which succeeded to a charm. Having accidentally heard that a gentleman, who was at a neighboring tavern, was about to set off for London alone, he threw himself in his way, and was cursing his ill stars that he was under the necessity of taking a journey of two hundred miles alone in a solitary post-chaise. The gentleman immediately inquired which way his route lay; when he informed him that he was going to London. The other said he esteemed himself very fortunate in having met him; for he was about to take the same journey, and should have been under the necessity of going alone, if his good fortune had not thrown a companion in his way. When they arrived at the first post-house, Semple was going to pay his half the post-hire; but, returning his money to his pocket, observed that it was best that one should pay the whole of the expense, and that he would discharge his half upon their arrival at London. This was readily assented to. Semple called for the best the houses on the road afforded; and, upon their arrival in London, they drove to a tavern, and were to settle their accounts in the morning; but, to the surprise and confusion of the dupe, Mr. Semple had taken himself off, and left him to put up with the loss of his money, and the reflection of having travelled as the friend of a man of this description. A few weeks after this elopement, Semple called upon the gentleman whom he had thus injured, and apologized to him by saying that he was without a farthing; that his good stars had not smiled upon him since, for that he was now penniless: and he finished by requesting the loan of five guineas; which was given him for his ingenuity. The appearance of Semple warrants this story; and I am convinced I should have fallen a sacrifice to him in the same way, under similar circumstances.

"The crime for which he is now to be transported is for borrowing a shirt under some feigned name, and not returning it. This would not have sent him out of the country, had he not been before transported. I am told he is very eloquent in his defence, and astonishes all who see and hear him. His age I should suppose forty, and his general appearance as much that of a gentleman as can be imagined.

"Among others, we had pointed out to us a man who has had the epithet of *savage* affixed to him for his peculiar malice of disposition. He, for some time before his detection, stabbed women in the street with a knife he had made for the purpose. His habit was to get into a crowd, and then cut them across the hands or bosom; and his object seemed no other than to injure their persons, as no attempt was made to take their property. What his fate is I know not; what he merits I can conceive.

"I was the other day informed of a fact I had little idea of; which is, that the horses in England consume nearly half the whole produce of the soil. This, at first blush, will appear incredible; but, when it is known that there is a horse to every six persons in the kingdom, this astonishment will decrease. It is said that the three kingdoms of England, Ireland, and Scotland, contain twelve millions of souls; of which England numbers seven, Ireland three, and Scotland two; so that England must, according to the calculation above, contain 1,166,666 horses. And, as the estimation is that a horse will consume as much as six persons (of all ages), the assertion above, that the horses eat one-half of the produce of the earth, will appear undoubted. There have been several attempts to reduce the number, and horses are taxed very high; but the wealth of those who possess them is sufficient to surmount this difficulty. The tax upon a single horse is light; that upon two, higher; and it advances to a considerable sum upon the eighth or tenth horse. The number of horses which are daily seen in London is almost incredible. I have observed some of the town-carts numbered as high as fifty-seven thousand; and I am told they amount to sixty thousand. There are also twelve hundred hackney-coaches always on the stands in and about London. These make but an inconsiderable part of the number of horses belonging to private persons, public post-chaises, mail and stage coaches, riding-horses, &c. Besides the numbered carts, there are thousands not numbered; and the immense number of brewers' carts is not included. In some of the great avenues, the number of carriages is sometimes so great that one cannot cross the street for a long time together.

"There is, perhaps, no place where a man may travel more at his ease than in England, or where he will pay more heavily for it. There is no part of the country a man can be in where he cannot have a post-chaise, for any distance, in five minutes from the time he calls for it; and the despatch in going over the ground is as great as in preparing for it. Eight miles is the rate at which they commonly drive; but they will, for a sixpence, add two more to it. . . . .

"13th. — I yesterday dined with Mr. Deas, the American *chargé d'affaires*, where I met with a young gentleman of the name of Huger, from South Carolina, who has just returned from Germany. While on the continent, he met with a particular friend of the Marquis de La Fayette, who was at that time digesting a plan for effecting the escape of the marquis, and in which he engaged our countryman to embark with him.

"As the marquis had feigned illness, and had permission to ride out under a guard of two men, the plan was that our adventurers should attack the guards, having first furnished horses at an appointed place, and that they should all take different routes. The plan was executed with success, so far as to rescue the marquis. They then separated. The alarm went forth; but La Fayette, when within twenty miles of the frontier of Germany, was asked for his passport. Having none to show, he was carried before the magistrate of the town, who was upon the point of discharging him, when one of the clerks of the house, who passed by accident through the room, no sooner saw the face of the marquis than he recognized him, and declared the fact immediately. He was reconducted to his prison, where he has been kept ever since with more rigor, but not enough to endanger his health. Huger and his friend were both taken and kept in close confinement eight months, where they suffered very severely, not having the use of books, pen, ink, or paper. Mr. Huger mentions a singular anecdote with regard to the marquis while in his first confinement. In the same prison where he was, there was one of his officers also confined. The officers who visited them being particularly charged to be careful that there was no correspondence between them, they fell upon the following expedient: The rooms of the two friends were adjoining, — that is, they were only separated by an entry; so that the dinner came to the marquis, and was immediately carried to his friend, or sometimes from his friend to him. Their general mess was carrot-soup. The marquis formed a piece of wood into the shape of a carrot, and colored it, making it hollow. Thus he wrote what he pleased; and, slipping the carrot into the large tub, his friend pitched upon that, and, when the jailer had returned, opened his artificial carrot, and feasted upon its contents. Thus they corresponded for some time; until an accident happened, which entirely defeated any future attempt, or rather the success of any. As the attendant was carrying the soup from one room to the other, some one, who felt a great inducement to taste a carrot, unfortunately fixed upon this one, which he found to be hard, and, upon further examination, observed it was of wood. Thus the business was discovered, and an end put to their mode of correspondence. What expedients will not the human mind resort to, to obtain that most precious blessing, liberty? What sacrifices will it not make, and what risks not run? This deprivation to the marquis must be peculiarly aggravating. His anxiety, too, for his wife and children must be great indeed, particularly if he has by any means heard of the dreadful slaughter there has been in France, regardless of sex, age, or degree. His own family has been among those who have lost some of their nearest friends and connections. I have the pleasure to learn that the wife of the marquis has left France, and that she has gone to Hamburg.

"Saw the Drury-Lane performers, and Mrs. Siddons, and her brother, Mr. Kemble, in 'Isabella.' Their performances were almost beyond praise. Had

Mr. Kemble a better voice, he would appear to much greater advantage.

"23d. — This day, left London in a post-chaise for Bristol, where my intention is to take passage for America, either in the 'Richmond' or the 'Severn.' Mr. Pollard takes the chaise with me; and our intention is to go out of the general route, and take Oxford in our way.

"29th. — Arrived at Oxford in the evening of the day on which we left London, which is fifty-five miles."

One result of this visit to Europe is thus mentioned in the autobiographical sketch already referred to: —

"The circumstance of my interference in sending young La Fayette to this country was the cause of one of the most interesting events of my life. It was known to Gen. Washington, through the father or son, or both, that I had been active in effecting the removal of the young man to this country; and, from the great partiality he had for the marquis, he was pleased to regard the actors in a favorable light.

"In the summer of 1796, I visited the city of Washington, which was decided upon as the future seat of government, though Congress still sat at Philadelphia. While I was there, Gen. Washington passed some days at the new seat of government. He lodged at the house of Mr. Peters, who married a Miss Custis, grand-daughter of Mrs. Washington. At a ball given by Mrs. Peters, to which I was invited,

I was introduced to the General by Col. Lear, his private secretary, and was graciously received, and invited to visit Mount Vernon, and pass some time there. This was not to be declined; and, a few days after, I went, as invited, to pay my respects to the man I cherished in my mind beyond any earthly being. There was no company there except Mr. Thomas Porter, formerly of Boston, who then lived at Alexandria, with whom I was intimately acquainted, and who was a great favorite at Mount Vernon. He took me to the residence of Gen. Washington, and returned after dinner to his own residence.

"It is well known that the General was not in the habit of talking on political subjects with any but those connected with him in the government. Indeed, he was what may be called a silent man, except when necessity called upon him to be otherwise. He conversed with me on internal improvements; and observed to me, that I should probably live to see an internal communication, by canals and rivers, from Georgia to Massachusetts. The State of Maine had not then been separated from the old Bay State. He little thought, at that time or ever, of the railroads which now span the country. Gen. Washington, it is understood, was the first projector of the Dismal Swamp Canal, between Chesapeake Bay and Albemarle Sound, in North Carolina, at that time a great undertaking, as well as the lockage of the Little Falls of Potomac. As was before remarked, I was the only guest at Mount Vernon at the time spoken of. Mrs. Washington, and her grand-daughter, Miss Nelly

Custis, with the General, were the only inmates of the parlor.

"The situation of Mount Vernon is known to every one to be of surpassing beauty. It stands on the banks of the Potomac, but much elevated above the river, and affords an extensive view of this beautiful piece of water and of the opposite shore. At the back of the house, overlooking the river, is a wide piazza, which was the general resort in the afternoon. On one occasion, when sitting there with the family, a toad passed near to where I sat conversing with Gen. Washington; which led him to ask me if I had ever observed this reptile swallow a fire-fly. Upon my answering in the negative, he told me that he had; and that, from the thinness of the skin of the toad, he had seen the light of the fire-fly after it had been swallowed. This was a new, and to me a surprising, fact in natural history.

"I need not remark how deeply I was interested in every word which fell from the lips of this great man. I found Mrs. Washington to be an extremely pleasant and unaffected lady, rather silent; but this was made up for by the facetious and pleasant young lady, Miss Custis, who afterwards married Major Lewis, a nephew of the General, and who is yet living. During the day, the General was either in his study, or in the saddle overlooking the cultivation of his farm.

"I shall never forget a circumstance which took place on the first evening I lodged at Mount Vernon. As I have said before, it was in July, when the day trenched far upon the evening, and at seven or eight o'clock we were taking our tea; not long after which, the ladies retired. Knowing the habit of the General, when not prevented by business, to retire early, at about nine o'clock I made a movement in my chair; which led the General to ask me if I wished to retire to my chamber. Upon my answering in the affirmative, observing there was no servant in the room, he took one of the candles from the table, leading the way to the great staircase; then gave me the candle, and pointed out to me the door at the head of the stairs as my sleeping-room. Think of this!

"In the room in which I laid myself down — for I do not think I slept at all, so much was I occupied with the occurrences of the day — was a portrait of La Fayette the elder, and, hanging over the fireplace, the *key of the Bastille;* which, I believe, retain the same places to this day. On the afternoon of the second day after I arrived, I took my leave of Mount Vernon, more gratified than I can express.

"In the autumn of the year of my visit, Mr. Stuart (Gilbert) painted the full-length portrait of the General; which is much the best likeness I have ever seen of him. The bust I have, also by Stuart, is a *fac-simile* of the original. The portrait of Mrs. Washington too, by Stuart, now in the Athenæum, is an excellent likeness of that excellent lady. I remember her amiable expression of countenance, and courteous, unaffected manner, as well at this time as half a century since.

"The President, having inquired of me if I had visited the Great Falls of the Potomac, and being answered in the negative, observed to me, that I ought not to leave that part of the country without visiting them. I made the excursion, though pressed for time, and to my great satisfaction.

"I consider the visit to Mount Vernon as one of the most interesting of my life. It was the only opportunity which I should have ever had of conversing familiarly with this great and good man. Two years after my visit, he died, at his residence, of croup. It is stated that he was not well treated for the disorder, and that with more skill his life might have been preserved; though I doubt if his happiness would have been preserved to him, had his life been spared. Detraction and calumny had assailed him.

"The new city of Washington, when I was there, had but few houses. The Capitol was not built for many years afterwards; and, when Congress first sat there, it occupied, I think, a building erected by means of a tontine speculation, got up by a Mr. Blodget, who went from Massachusetts, and was well known as a great projector of speculations of one sort and another."

About this time he was made commander of a military corps, — the battalion which constitutes the guard and escort for public occasions of the Governor of the Commonwealth of Massachusetts, — with the rank of lieutenant-colonel, having for some time previously held that of major in the same corps.

With some persons, it may excite only a smile of derision to mention this as worth remembering, and particularly to add, as the cause of any allusion to it, that he was so generally known afterwards as *Col.* Perkins, that his numerous acquaintances throughout the country might be in doubt whether he is the individual spoken of in this memoir, if that appellation were omitted. But there are some considerations connected with this that deserve notice. The foreigner smiles or frowns, as he feels disposed, when he hears any reference among us to military rank beyond the field or day parade, unless it be of the regular army; but in this he overlooks the fact, that the customs of a nation are usually connected with its history and political character. Military rank among quiet citizens is not so empty a distinction here as it may seem, but constitutes a pledge which it may become necessary to redeem in earnest. A large portion of the bloodiest and most important battles that have ever occurred among us have been fought chiefly by the militia. The deference paid to it here is not greater now than that with which the same force was regarded in England, when the regiment of Coldstream Guards formed a large part of the standing army, then no greater than ours is at present; when, indeed, the only army which the law had recognized in that country but a short time before was the militia.

"The king was the sole captain-general of this large force. The lords, lieutenants, and their deputies, held the command under him, and appointed meetings for drillings and inspection. . . . There were those who looked on the militia with no friendly eye. . . . The enemies of the liberties and religion of England looked with aversion on a force which could not, without extreme risk, be employed against those liberties and that religion, and missed no opportunity of throwing ridicule on the rustic soldiery. . . . In Parliament, however, it was necessary to express such opinions with some reserve. . . . The array of the counties was commanded almost exclusively by Tory noblemen and gentlemen. They were proud of their military rank, and considered an insult to the service to which they belonged as offered to themselves. They were also perfectly aware, that whatever was said against a militia was said in favor of a standing army; and the name of a standing army was hateful to them." *

As that standing army was gradually enlarged, however, and the profession of arms became an occupation for life, a change naturally followed; the exclusive feeling in favor of professional rank gained strength; and the recognition of any similar claim for the militia was discouraged as a matter of taste, because it affected privilege.

But no such change has taken place here. We have no intention of having a standing army, beyond a mere nucleus, from which we can extend, when necessary, with an academy for the thorough education of officers, — having no need of more.

It is not a mere channel or a narrow sea, but the broad ocean, that separates us from those nations whose power could ever endanger our safety; and if such power should be directed against us, our coast and frontier being equal in extent to those of several of the kingdoms of Europe taken together, no army that we are likely ever to have could guard the line of

* Macaulay.

exposure. We rely, therefore, mainly on the local force of the country for security in war, and for the maintenance of order in peace. Some attempts have been made among us to break down the militia by ridicule; but it seems probable, that, until vast changes take place in other respects, we shall not dispense with this system, which by its efficient action gains deference for itself, in comparison with what is done elsewhere. Many proofs that it does so might be given. One will answer.

In 1849, the year succeeding that of revolutions in Europe, a serious disturbance occurred in the city of New York, in the dramatic performances there, arising from displeasure towards an eminent foreign tragedian. The theatre was surrounded by a vast multitude, many of them in a state of great excitement; acts of violence were committed; property and life were endangered; and that state of things existed which is thought to warrant the use of military force. It came promptly when summoned: numbers of people were killed and wounded; the mob was dispersed, and order was restored. When the account of this reached England, it was remarked in one of the leading journals there, with reference to a similar event which had just then occurred under British rule, that we had, at any rate, given an example to governments of greater energy in form than our own how to deal with rioters. In the same steamer that carried this account, or the one that preceded it, there went the particulars of a riot, just over our frontier, in Canada. There, the nobleman who represented the majesty of England was driven by the mob from the seat of government, and pursued towards his country-seat; the Parliament House was burned, with the archives, a library of great value, and other public property; and, if any punishment has ever been inflicted for this, it must have been so slight that it has scarcely been heard of out of the province.

There is likewise something of exaggeration in reference to the use of military titles in this country. Where a dozen instances can be given of it, often arising accidentally from assiduous attention, personal appearance, or otherwise, probably a score of others might be adduced where there is no further allusion to rank in the militia after the service is performed, even including some officers who have met a foreign enemy successfully in battle.

But Col. Perkins was a man distinguished for energy, for a lively interest in all that concerned the welfare of the community in which he lived, and for a desire to maintain and promote its respectability. He acted with vigor in times of great excitement. A prominent part was frequently assigned him, either to assist in the direction of public meetings, or as leader on important committees; and, his name being necessarily often in print, he was designated, naturally enough, in the way that indicated its connection with public order, and thus added something to its weight. The military rank, therefore, which might otherwise have soon been forgotten, as it generally has been in regard to those who have held it in the same corps, but with less distinction in other respects, became widely associated with his name, and so continued until his decease. This was the more natural, because the tone of his character and his ordinary bearing were obviously in keeping with the sentiment which he once proposed for a toast at some military festival: "That high and honorable feeling which makes gentlemen soldiers, and soldiers gentlemen."

Soon afterwards he was chosen President of the Boston branch of the United States Bank; quite a distinction at that time, when there were few banks in the country, and a remarkable one for a man so young as he was then. The choice was owing to a warm rivalry for the honor between two distinguished merchants, much older than himself; whose friends at length mutually agreed to end the contest by selecting a third candidate, on whom all could unite. He was too much engaged in his own enterprises to retain the place long; and in a year or two he was succeeded by the Hon. George Cabot, eminent not only as a commercial man, but as a Senator of the United States.

In 1805, he was elected to the Senate of the State, as he frequently was afterwards; and, for eighteen or twenty years following, he was, most of the time, member of one branch or the other of the Legislature, but generally of the Senate, unless absent from the country. Being a man of few words, he rarely took part in debate; but his opinions were marked by decision. What he said was to the point; his language was good; and, when he was strongly moved, he spoke with power. One of his colleagues in the

Senate, who afterwards had long experience in Congress, and was favorably distinguished there as well as at the bar, has remarked since, that he had rarely heard public men make a short, off-hand speech with more effect than Col. Perkins occasionally did, when his feelings were deeply engaged in the subject of debate.

He was never in Congress himself, although his election would have been certain if he would have accepted a nomination as candidate; and there were several occasions when it was desirable to his political friends, who predominated by a large majority in his district, to have had a commercial representative there like him. It is understood that he might at one time have been made Secretary of the Navy, if he had been disposed to take charge of that department of the national government. But he does not appear to have been desirous of political distinction; and the engagements in commerce which required his attention were too important to be made subordinate to any other demands on his time.

In the narrative addressed to his children, after relating the foregoing circumstances of his visit to Mount Vernon, he proceeds as follows: —

"But to return to the object of these *dottings-down*, — my own concerns. The north-west trade led to a continued communication with China; and, in 1798, we bought, and sent to Canton direct, the ship 'Thomas Russell;' and Mr. Ephraim Bumstead, then the eldest apprentice in our counting-house, went out as supercargo; and, in 1803, we entered into an engagement with him to go to China, and there establish a house for the transaction of our own and other business when offered. Mr. Bumstead took passage in a ship from Providence, belonging partly to merchants there, and to J. and T. H. Perkins.

"Mr. J. P. Cushing, then in our counting-house, went with Mr. Bumstead as his clerk. He was then sixteen years old, wrote a fine hand, was a very steady lad, and had a great taste for going abroad. Soon after their arrival in China, Mr. Bumstead was obliged, from illness, to leave Canton, with the intention of recruiting, and then returning to China. But he never returned, having died on the passage to the port for which he was bound.

"Mr. Cushing was, therefore, left at this early age to manage the concerns of the house, which were increased by consignments, and which required a good head to direct them. This, fortunately, Mr. Cushing possessed; and the business which fell into his hands was as well conducted as if Mr. Bumstead had been on the spot. We afterwards sent a nephew of my brother's wife, Mr. Paine, to join him. He remained but a short time in China. Mr. Cushing was taken into copartnership with us; and so continued until his return to America, or rather to the dissolution of the house in 1827. He had visited the United States in 1807; but soon returned to China, and did not leave it until twenty years after that time. He was well repaid for his undertaking by the result."

When the tidings of Mr. Bumstead's death reached Boston, Col. Perkins immediately decided to go to China himself, as there seemed to him to be no alternative in such an emergency; and he made preparations for his departure accordingly. But, just before he was ready to sail, a vessel arrived in a short passage from Canton, with letters from Mr. Cushing, who was his nephew, giving so clear a report of the business of the house, and showing so much ability in the management of it, that he felt safe in postponing his voyage at first, and afterwards in relinquishing it altogether, as it became obvious that Mr. Cushing, young as he was, needed no aid in performing the duties thus devolved upon him.

Under his guidance, the house there was at length so favorably known, that consignments increased until they interfered with the business of the house itself, and it became desirable to give them some other direction. A distinct commission-house was, therefore, established at Canton for this purpose, under the auspices and with the favor of Perkins and Co., which continues to this day, although the first partners withdrew from it, rich, many years ago. A long line of successors, following them, have managed the same establishment by turns, and retired from it successively with fortunes, with which they have returned to the United States. If all those were enumerated whose success in life might thus be traced to that first voyage of Col. Perkins to China in 1789, the number would cause surprise.

"Embargoes and non-intercourse," he continues in the narrative, "with political and other causes of embarrassment, crossed our path; but we kept our trade with China, and, during the war of the Peninsula, embarked largely in the shipment of provisions to Spain and Portugal. Our general plan was to freight vessels, load them with flour at the south for Europe, and have the funds remitted to London. To make some necessary arrangements respecting them, I took passage in the brig 'Reaper,' belonging to my friend Henry Lee, for London, in August, 1811. The intention of Mr. Lee was to proceed to India in the brig, taking funds from England, and returning to Boston with Calcutta cloths, which then paid a great advance. I sent funds in her; and she returned in the year 1812, during the war with Great Britain, and with great profit. Long-cloths of India then brought twenty-five cents per yard, though an inferior article to what is now made in this country and sold at six cents, being less than one-fourth of the price the India cloths then sold at. I remained in London during the year, or until the summer, and returned after war had been declared. While in London, I bought, with the elder Mr. Higginson, goods brought into England for France; which resulted in great gain.

"In the spring, I bought a carriage, with Mr. Alexander Everett, and was made bearer of despatches for France. At that time, the only communication was by Morlaix from Plymouth. There I took a vessel of about forty or fifty tons in which to cross the Channel. As we had no use but for the cabin, we gave passage to a dozen or more Frenchmen, who had been exchanged, and had no means of getting to France but by the privileged vessels which left Plymouth from time to time. Among the persons to whom a free passage was given, was one who had resided some years in our good city of Boston, and who doubtless had known me as active in resisting the principles of the Jacobins. This individual was the cause of my detention at Morlaix nearly three weeks, — having reported me to the commissary at Morlaix as opposed to the French, and a great friend of the English. In consequence, I was ordered to remain at Morlaix until orders were received from Paris. After writing to Mr. Barlow, the then minister of the United States, and using other means, we were permitted to proceed to Paris. During my stay at Morlaix, my limit was the town, unless accompanied by one of the *gens d'armes*. I visited the lead mines in that vicinity, and made other excursions within thirty or forty miles; and was, upon the whole, very civilly treated by Moreau, the commissioner, after he was satisfied that my object in visiting France was commercial, and not political. Moreau, the general, although from the same town, was not a relative of the commissioner, who was a great Bonapartist.

"An incident which caused me much anxiety, and which might have been attended by serious consequences, occurred in, or was connected with, this journey. On my leaving London, Mr. Russell, who was then *chargé d'affaires* of the United States at the court of St. James, on my going to his house for despatches, put into my hands a package of some sheets in a volume, directed to Col. Tchernicheff, chancellor to the Russian minister, Prince Kourakine, at Paris. Had I considered a moment, I should have doubted the ——"

Here the narrative is broken off. It was suspended, probably, at his departure from Saratoga, where it is dated, and was never continued. But, in conversation, he gave a graphic account of the solicitude which he felt, while he was detained in Morlaix, at having with him despatches so directed, which might be discovered in his possession; of the momentous state of affairs which he found on his arrival in Paris, shortly before the open breach of Napoleon with Russia, that led to the fatal campaign in the North; of the difficulty that he had in safely delivering the despatches; the acknowledgments that he received from the Russian embassy for doing it successfully; the angry look which he saw the emperor cast, from his seat in the theatre, towards the box of the Russian ambassador, as if he had meant that it should be observed; and the departure of the latter from Paris the following day.

While he was at Morlaix, an incident there called into action some of those qualities of heart and head which were repeatedly exercised afterwards on a greater scale, — the spirit that freely contributes to the alleviation of distress, and the intelligent skill which can make one liberal contribution the means of eliciting the action of a community in a good cause. The story is told in a letter to Mrs. Perkins, too long to be inserted entire, but interesting throughout; and some passages will show his habits of observation as a traveller, with something of the state of France at that time: —

"CHERBOURG, June 2, 1812.

"MY DEAR SARAH, — I can easily conceive, from my own feelings, how much pleasure the receipt of this letter will give you, — being the only one I have written you for two months, excepting a short one from Morlaix, which was not calculated to afford you much satisfaction, as I was then under a degree of restraint, which has not left me from that time to this. I am now here waiting the arrival of the 'Wasp' (sloop-of-war) from England, where she returns again to land me with the despatches from the minister at Paris to the *chargé d'affaires* at London. You may well suppose what my anxiety is to hear from home, having received no letters of later date than February. My anxiety is much increased from the uncertainty as to our situation in regard to the war. If we are engaged in the contest, I shall find it difficult to return. My passport to leave the country was kept back; and, but for exertions which I made through some persons whom I had interested in my behalf, I might have been some months longer detained.

"You will want to know what has been the disposition of my time since I arrived in France. I was detained at Morlaix fifteen days; and, but for the exertions of my friends, might have been there this hour, as a gentleman who arrived there a month before me has been detained there till this time, and can get no permission either to return to America or to go to Paris. Another bearer of despatches was there a month. I was not so much *ennuyé* as those gentlemen who were looking to Paris as the place where they were to realize golden dreams of pleasure. As I am fond of spying out wonders, I got permission to visit a lead mine, which is at no great distance from Morlaix, and which afforded me the highest gratification. There are upwards of twelve hundred persons employed at the works. The descent from the surface to the deepest part is eight hundred feet. I was astonished to find the price of this severe labor so low. Twelve hours' labor is exacted in the twenty-four. The time employed in going down and returning is not included. And for this the men receive about eighteen to twenty cents per day, *and find themselves!* Men only, with a few boys, are employed in the mines. Women, both old and young, and children down to five years old, are employed in selecting the good from the bad ore, breaking it in pieces, and working it. They receive from four to seven sous (equal to as many cents) per day. They find themselves, and work, from the getting up to the going down of the sun, the year through. You will ask how they subsist. I can hardly imagine how they get along: but so it is; and I do not see but they appear as healthy as people, in general, who are employed in hard labor of a different kind. Black bread, moistened with a kind of lard or bad butter, furnishes them their food, and the spring quenches their thirst. Once in a while, they have a few pounds of beef boiled to pieces in a pot containing half a barrel of water and a few vegetables. This soup, as it is called, is a sort of luxurious living, which is too good to be served often. I found, that, were twice the number of women wanted, they might be had; and even of men of a certain age, which does not include the term when they are wanted for the army.

"When I returned to Morlaix, I found my passport had arrived; so that I could not go again to visit this very interesting work. Upon the whole, my fifteen days went away much more pleasantly than I had expected; and I should not have hung myself, had I been obliged to remain there a week longer.

"There is a tobacco manufactory at Morlaix, on a very large scale. Twelve hundred and sixty persons are daily at work at it. All the manufactures of snuff, and tobacco in every shape, in the empire belong to the government, who purchase the raw material, and work it into the form in which it is used. I contrived to get admission, and was astonished at the extent of the establishment.

"It is astonishing to observe the difference in numbers between the men and women you see in the streets in every town through which you pass. At Morlaix, they say there are fourteen females to one male in the town. You would hardly suppose there was any part of France — I mean of France as it was under the old government — in which the inhabitants of whole districts do not speak French. This, however, is the case in Brittany. The people who live a mile from the town speak no more French than they do Greek. Their language is the Welsh, and is the only one spoken by them until they leave their villages and come to the towns to reside, or go to the army, when they are obliged to learn the French. The people who live in the towns are obliged to learn the language of Brittany, or they could not go to the market, or have any communication with the country people. Before taking my leave of Morlaix, I must relate to you a fact that came under my knowledge, by which you can appreciate the tenure by which liberty is held here.

"The family in which I lived was one of the most respectable in Morlaix, in point of property, previous to the revolution. Like many others, it was reduced to very narrow means by the then existing state of things, as their wealth consisted principally in vessels, which either perished at the wharves, or were taken by the powers which then ruled, and were totally lost to Monsieur Beau, who was their proprietor. Having been the agent for the lead mines for a long time, this was a resource to him; and although the stipend arising from this was a moderate one, yet it served to feed his wife and children, who were some six or seven in number. M. Beau died a few years since, and left his widow without any resource for the support of her family. Being a woman of a good deal of character, the company to whom the mines belong concluded to continue the agency in the hands of Mrs. Beau, who, with the aid of her youngest son, has carried on the purchases and sales to this time. The two eldest sons got clerkships in the tobacco manufactory, and a daughter was married; so that but one daughter and one son were upon the shoulders of the old lady. Their means were, to be sure, small; but their wants were few; and, although their whole income was not more than six hundred dollars per annum, the son who aided his mother in the lead-mine agency had made a matrimonial engagement; and, not believing that 'Love would fly out of the window, though Poverty looked in at the door,' a day was designated for the marriage; and I was invited as a guest at the meeting of the family, which was to take place in the evening. The marriage ceremony took place in the morning, at the parish church; and at about ten o'clock I was introduced to the bride, whom I found to be, as I had heard her represented, a beautiful woman of about twenty, with a very prepossessing countenance, which, it was universally acknowledged, was a perfect index of her amiable mind. She seemed perfectly happy; and nothing but joy was visible in every countenance in the family. All was happiness and gayety and laugh and frolic. Mark the sad change. At twelve o'clock, the bridegroom received notice that he had been drawn in the conscription; and that on *Sunday* he must be at Campège, a distance of thirty leagues. This was on Thursday. In such cases, entreaty is vain, and never resorted to, because always ineffectual. To go to the army was to *go*, to return when the exigencies of the State no longer required his services. The whole family was in a state little short of distraction when I left the town, which was early on the next morning. The lowest price at which a substitute could be procured was three thousand francs; and the family could not command half the money in all its branches. The peculiar situation of this family seemed to paralyze the whole town, and led to an exertion which is seldom made, and which proved effectual in preventing this young man from being torn from the embraces of his charming wife and amiable mother. I have the satisfaction of having put the thing in train, and shall always consider the opportunity as one of the most gratifying which ever presented itself to me. After my arrival in Paris, I received a letter, saying that my example had been followed, and that it had produced the effect desired. This is an anecdote, or rather this part of it, for your own private ear; and you will not, of course, show this letter."

Some years afterwards, he was again at Morlaix; and, as a proof of the affection and respect with which the remembrance of him was cherished, he found that the room which he had occupied at the time of this occurrence had been kept in the precise order in which he left it, no article having been removed from its place.

War between the United States and Great Britain was declared, as it appears from the foregoing letter he apprehended that it might be, even before he reached home in 1812. After his return, being himself among the leaders in political affairs, as he was prominent in commerce, he took an active and very decided part in the discussions and movements of the time, which are now matters of history. His sensations on the return of peace are forcibly expressed in the following letter* to Mr. Cushing, his nephew and partner in China: —

"WASHINGTON, 16th February, 1815.

"MR. JOHN P. CUSHING, Canton.

"My dear John, — I am here on public business in behalf of the State of Massachusetts. The joyful event of peace has suspended the mission on which I came. You will hear with delight of this event. No sacrifice is made of territory or commercial rights. It is a treaty formed on the basis of that of 1783. All the claims upon which the war was founded have been relinquished. The right to go to the British possessions was a municipal privilege extended to us, and which a commercial treaty may restore. The Senate has ratified the treaty, and the president's proclamation will issue to-morrow. Then, thanks to the Giver of all good things! we are once more restored to peace; and I trust I shall never see another war.

. . . .

"Heaven bless you! Your sister is well, and all your particular connections are so.

"I shall be here a week longer, and then I shall look homewards. Yours, affectionately, T. H. PERKINS."

About this time, he became actively engaged in measures for establishing the Massachusetts General Hospital with an Asylum for the Insane, the necessity for which had begun to be deeply felt. He was one of

* See Appendix.

those to whom an act of incorporation had been granted for the purpose, with a valuable donation from the Commonwealth, on the condition that the sum of one hundred thousand dollars should be raised by subscription within a limited time. His name was at the head of the first list of trustees; and he undertook the work which his position involved with characteristic energy. His influence and his services were highly appreciated by those with whom he was engaged in that undertaking. The subscriptions were made on the condition that the full sum of one hundred thousand dollars should be obtained; so that the whole depended on entire success. Besides his exertions in rousing other subscribers, he and his elder brother contributed five thousand dollars each towards the fund; and it was completed agreeably to the terms of condition. It is well known that the efforts of those who were engaged in this movement have been productive of all the good which they hoped to effect. The institution bears a favorable comparison with those of the same kind in other places, and has become celebrated throughout the world for the first successful application of the great discovery in the use of ether for surgical operations.

His elder brother and partner, James Perkins, Esq., died in the year 1822. The following passages from a notice of his death, published at the time, show the estimation in which he was held: —

"While his real and most eloquent eulogy is to be sought in the course of an industrious, honorable, and most useful life, it is due to the virtues he practised, to the example he set, to the noble standard of character on which he acted, not to be entirely silent, now that nothing remains of them but their honored memory. He had received in boyhood, under the care of an excellent mother, the preparatory instruction which might have fitted him for an academical education; but the approach of the Revolutionary War, and the discouraging aspect of the times, dictated the commercial career as more prudent.

"In enterprises extending over the habitable globe, employing thousands of agents, constantly involving fortunes in their result, and requiring, on many occasions necessarily incident to business of this extent, no secondary degree of firmness and courage, not a shadow of suspicion of any thing derogatory to the highest and purest sense of honor and conscience ever attached to his conduct. The character of such a man ought to be held up for imitation."

Mr. James Perkins left a large fortune, acquired in this honorable course, and is still remembered for distinguished liberality in all appeals that were made when he lived, for charity or public good, to the affluent and generous in the community; for his liberal donations to several institutions; and especially for a munificent gift of real estate, of the value of about twenty thousand dollars, to the Boston Athenæum, and the bequest of twenty thousand more to the University at Cambridge. The decease of such an associate in the commercial vicissitudes of nearly forty years was deeply felt by his surviving partner and brother.*

In 1826, it was proposed to raise a considerable sum for additions to the Athenæum. Something over thirty thousand dollars was required. Col. Perkins, and his nephew, Mr. James Perkins, son and sole heir of his deceased brother, contributed one-half of it, paying eight thousand dollars each, on the condition that the same amount should be subscribed by the public; which was done. He made other valuable donations to the Athenæum, and was for several years president of that institution.

Soon after this, having witnessed the successful commencement of railroads in England, he resolved to introduce them here; and, having obtained a charter for the Granite Railway Company, he caused one of two miles in length to be made, for the purpose of transporting granite from the quarries in Quincy to the water. This was the first railroad built in this country; though there was a rough contrivance in Pennsylvania, for the removal of coal, which is said to have preceded it. It has been the means of adding

* The experience of Franklin, as our representative in Europe, led him to remark, that diplomatists and statesmen would find great advantage in attending more closely than they do to the information that may be had from commercial men, who have strong inducements to get the earliest possible intelligence of all political movements that affect the intercourse of nations, and are sometimes better informed as to what may be impending than the governments under which they live.

To show what extended and comprehensive views are taken in conducting the correspondence of a great commercial house, and what variety is sometimes combined in the anticipations necessary for planning voyages of great length or complicated design, some of the letters of the house of J. and T. H. Perkins are given in the Appendix. The first was written by Mr. James Perkins, to his brother when in France, in 1794, to give him what information could be gathered here, for his aid in deciding whether any commercial enterprise could be undertaken with advantage in Europe. Some of these letters indicate, in both partners, the discernment and power to direct which go far to qualify men for acting either as diplomatists or statesmen.

large quantities of granite to the building materials of our cities, and its effect is seen extending as far as New Orleans.

In 1833, a movement was made to obtain funds for the establishment of a school for blind children in Boston. Having been deeply interested by an exhibition given to show their capacity for improvement, he made a donation of his mansion-house in Pearl Street as a place for their residence. He gave it on the condition that the sum of fifty thousand dollars should be contributed by the public as a fund to aid in their support. Efforts were made accordingly to effect that object, and proved to be entirely successful. The school was thus placed on a stable foundation, and by means that insured it continued care. The incitement which had thus been offered to the community, to secure so valuable an estate as a gift to the public, roused general attention to the subject that could induce such a donation. Mutual sympathy in endeavoring to effect the purpose was a natural result. This became widely diffused. An institution which thus offered intelligence, enjoyment, and usefulness, in place of ignorance, sorrow, and idleness, was recognized by the government of the State as deserving aid from the Commonwealth; and liberal public provision was made for the education there of blind children whose parents need assistance for unusual expenses.

Under the direction of Dr. Howe, it has been eminently successful, and is known through the country as an important example of what may be done. Indeed, it may be said further, that the country itself is more widely and favorably known in the Old World from the annual reports of what has been effected there, not only by improvements in the art of printing for the blind, but by new discoveries in the possibility of instruction, which he has demonstrated.

The publications from the press of the institution, under his care, probably comprise more matter than all other works in the English language that have ever been published for the use of the blind; and, at the recent "Exhibition of Works of Industry of all Nations" in the Crystal Palace of London, the prize medal was awarded to his specimens for the best system of letters, and the best mode of printing such books. But, beyond this, Dr. Howe has enlarged the science of mind by reaching and developing the intellect of the blind and deaf mute, shut up from human intercourse by obstruction in all avenues of the senses but one, and proved that the single sense of touch can be made the medium for effectual instruction in reading and writing, and for the free interchange even of the most refined and delicate sentiments that are known to the heart of woman. In this he was the first to reduce to certainty what had before been only a problem; and has shown that there is no solid ground for the principle of law on the subject, as laid down by Blackstone, that "a man who is born deaf, dumb, and blind, is looked upon by the law as in the same state with an idiot; he being supposed incapable of any understanding, as wanting all those senses which furnish the human mind with ideas."

The estate given by Col. Perkins, although spacious

in extent, was becoming, from its position, better suited for purposes of trade than of residence. From the same cause, however, it was rising in pecuniary value; and not long afterwards it was exchanged, with his consent, — he releasing all conditional rights of reversion, — for a large edifice in the suburbs, built for another purpose, but admirably adapted, by location and structure, for the residence of young people. It overlooks the harbor, is secure by its elevation from any interruption of light or air, and affords ample room for all who may desire to come.

The institution bears his name. That something important would have eventually been done in Massachusetts for the education of the blind, even if he had rendered no assistance, cannot be doubted. Dr. John D. Fisher, a physician of great worth, to whose memory a monument has been erected at Mount Auburn for his early exertions in the cause, moving almost unaided, had previously obtained an act of incorporation from the Legislature for the purpose; and Edward Brooks, Esq., and Mr. Prescott, the historian, with some other gentlemen, had united with him to promote it. What followed is, in a great measure, to be attributed to their preparatory movements. But Col. Perkins, by the impulse of a powerful hand, suddenly roused the community to aid in the project, and placed it at once in an advanced position, which otherwise it probably would have required the lapse of many years, with arduous exertions, to attain. At that time, the institutions for the blind in England were little more than workshops, affording hardly any instruction except for manual labor, and no printing, though two small books had been printed in Scotland. But, through his aid and advice, the means were obtained and effectually applied for an establishment on a more liberal plan, giving the precedence to intellectual and moral education. There is little doubt, therefore, that a large portion of the good which has been effected thus far within the institution, and by its example elsewhere, is the result of his munificent donation, and the wise condition which he attached to it.

It should be remarked here, however, to guard against any mistake detrimental to the interest of the blind, that, while the pupils are placed, through his means, in a building which might give the impression that its inhabitants are likely to be in want of nothing, the institution is by no means richly endowed. The money that has been liberally given has been liberally spent in the cause of education; and those who are inclined to give or leave any portion of their wealth for the relief of misfortune, should be informed that the blind still need, and humbly hope, to be remembered. There can hardly be any class of persons to whom books, and a large library of books, can afford so great delight as those whose sources of enjoyment do not include that of sight; and after reading, in the report of the juries on the awards at the exhibition of the Crystal Palace in London, ten close pages that are devoted to the subject of printing for the blind, with an historical sketch, in which marked prominence is given to what has been done at "The Perkins Institution in Boston," it can hardly be heard without sorrow that the printing there is suspended for the want of pecuniary means; and that the publication of the "Cyclopædia," in twenty volumes, probably the most valuable work, with the exception of the Bible, that has ever been attempted for the blind, was necessarily stopped with the eighth volume.

A few extracts from that report, on a subject so deserving of interest, will hardly be out of place here:—

"A few years ago, printing for the blind was considered only a curious or doubtful experiment; but it is now established, beyond all question, that books are true sources of profit and pleasure to them. Whilst embossed books have recently very rapidly increased, it is delightful to notice that the blind readers have multiplied far more rapidly.

"The invention of printing for the blind marks a new era in the history of literature. The whole credit of this invention, so simple, yet so marvellous in its results, belongs to France. It was Mr. Valentine Haüy who, in 1784, at Paris, produced the first book printed with letters in relief, and soon after proved to the world that children might easily be taught to read with their fingers. The blind really received but little advantage from an invention that promised so much. The fault, however, seems to have been not so much in the plan as in the execution of it. This noble invention, except perhaps within the walls of the institution, soon sank into oblivion, and very little more was heard of it until 1814. The institute of Paris, since its foundation in 1784, has at times been in a deplorable condition; but about the year 1840 it underwent a thorough re-organization, and is now justly entitled to the front rank of institutions of this class in Europe.

"It was in Great Britain and in the United States that the first improvements were made in embossed typography. Before 1826, when Mr. James Gall, of Edinburgh, first began to turn his attention to the intellectual and moral education of the blind, it is believed that not a single blind person, in any public institution of this country or America, could read by means of embossed characters. To Mr. Gall is due the credit of reviving this art."

In 1827, he published a small volume for teaching the art of reading to the blind; and, in 1834, he published the Gospel of St. John, and afterwards several other books: but they do not appear to have been generally used. It is added in the report, that, with one exception, "it is believed they are adopted by no public institution in Great Britain."

"While the puzzling question of an alphabet best adapted to the fingers of the blind and the eyes of their friends was under warm discussion on this side of the Atlantic, Dr. Howe was developing his system at Boston, in the United States. In 1833, the Perkins Institution for the Blind was established at Boston; and Dr. S. G. Howe, a gentleman distinguished through a long series of years for his philanthropic labors, was placed at its head, and soon made those improvements and modifications which have rendered the Boston press so famous. His first aim was to compress the letter into a comparatively compact and cheap form. This he accomplished by cutting off all the flourishes and points about the letters. He so managed that they occupied but a little more than one space and a half instead of three. So great was this reduction, that the entire New Testament, which, according to Haüy's type, would have filled nine volumes, and cost twenty pounds, could be printed in two volumes for sixteen shillings. Early in the summer of 1834, he published the Acts of the Apostles. Indeed, such rapid progress did he make in his enterprise, that by the end of 1835 he printed in relief the whole of the New Testament, for the first time in any language, in four handsome quarto volumes, comprising 624 pages, for four dollars. These were published together in 1836. The alphabet thus contrived by Dr. Howe in 1833, it appears, has never since been changed.

"As the Boston books can now be obtained in London at a price cheaper than any of the five different systems of books printed in Great Britain, it is to be hoped that they will come into general use here."

It is then shown, by a table of comparison, that Dr. Howe's books are much less in bulk, and cheaper by more than one-half, than those printed in any other of the six systems used in the English language. And it is added, —

"His system has been fully described, and to it the jury give the preference above all others. The jury beg to suggest that a uniform system should be adopted, and that, in future, all books printed for the blind should be printed in the same character. Dr. Howe's appears simple, and fit for general adoption."

In 1835, Col. Perkins went to Europe for his health, and travelled for some months on the continent; extending his tour afterwards in England and Scotland, where he was accompanied by his friend, Joshua Bates, Esq., of London, the munificent donor of a large fund for a public library in Boston.

At that time, he went into Italy, where he had not been before, and, as might be supposed, looked with lively interest on the wonders of history and art to be seen there. An American statesman of the highest distinction, who recently passed a winter in Rome, mentioned to an acquaintance who called on him, that, when he arrived there, he heard accidentally, while inquiring for places of residence, that a house once occupied by Col. Perkins could be had, and that he lost no time in securing that house, being confident that it had been well chosen; which, to his great comfort, he found to be as he had anticipated.

As usual, he kept a journal while travelling. The objects most likely to attract attention in such a tour have been often described by others; but a few extracts, referring to objects or incidents not usually noticed by travellers, may be found interesting: —

"Saturday, July 25th, 1835, Meaux. — I arrived here the last evening." (He was then returning from Italy and Germany towards Paris.) "The day was hot, and the ground dry. I breakfasted at Chalons, which is a large town, and celebrated in the olden times as having been the place where Attila was defeated by the Romans, and, more recently, from its having been the town where the Emperors of Russia and Austria, with Great Britain and the others, assembled and made the proposition to Bonaparte, in his last retreat from the North, to give to France the Rhine as its boundary, and which he had the folly to refuse.

"From Chalons-sur-Marne to this place, this useful, though not very beautiful, river runs through a highly cultivated valley the whole distance, and makes the ride a very interesting one. The hills are cropped to their summits; and, from the difference in size of the portions in which are sown the different kinds of grain and other vegetables, they are as brilliant and as various as the figures shown through a kaleidoscope. Château Thierry, which was the birthplace of La Fontaine, is the only large town we have passed through; though many have been in sight on either side, which show the places where cultivators congregate. The district where the most famous of the Champagne wines are grown is quite small; and many tuns of wine have passed the world over for Champagne, under a misnomer. I have observed the villages on this side the French territory more attentively than those passed in going to Lyons. This was the great highway of armies going to and returning from the Rhine. The street is wide which leads through them; and, from so many of them being new, I think the present towns are the sites on which stood, some years since, the old villages, with their narrow streets and wretched houses. I was pondering on this when the post-boys pulled up before a very stately edifice, which, from its appearance, commanded respect and attention. It is an old Gothic church, built in the fourteenth century, and has been honored with the visits of kings and princes through all time since, and is the very odor of sanctity. There was nothing particularly worthy of note except a dead Christ, in marble, with full-length figures of Joseph of Arimathea and Nicodemus at the head and foot of the body; with the three Marys and Sarah, also large as life, weeping over Him whom they mourned.

"I was about to depart, when an old woman offered me a book, which she said was sold for the benefit of the church, and that it was a history of this Church of Notre Dame de la Pine, and that all that was stated in the book was true, and the evidence of the fact, long since deposited with the papers of the church, might be seen by any one who would take the trouble to apply to the authorities. I found, upon examining the book, that the church had not been so much visited for itself as for the miracles which had been wrought here. A long description is given of the time when the church was built, in 1472; but the interesting point is the cause which induced the erection, and designated the spot where it was to be placed. It seems, by this historical account, that there was near this place a small church, which would not accommodate the population; and the holy Virgin, mother of God, came to their relief. One night, when some shepherds were watching their flocks, they saw, at a small distance from where they sat, a sight; upon approaching which they became sore afraid, and fled, — not, however, before they discovered, in a large bush of thorns, the figure of the blessed mother, with the infant Jesus in her arms, in the centre of the bush, which was on fire. The light shone to a great distance. The sheep took fright, and ran away; but the lambs, changing their natural timidity into courage, approached the bush; which encouraged the shepherds, and many others, to return and see the miracle; and they attest to the correctness of the report of the transaction. The wonderful interposition of Heaven pointed out to the faithful the object of this supernatural appearance, as one that should be commemorated by erecting a splendid church on the spot where the burning bush was seen.

"Charles VII. aided largely in the erection of the church, in accordance with the wishes of the *pious* Louis XI., who, when Charles of Burgundy entrapped him at Peronne, made a vow, that, in case he escaped from his very dangerous situation, he would build churches, and do other things that should gratify the Virgin, to whom he so often kneeled; and at the same time taking care to add, that he would also do something to gratify himself, by making those suffer who had betrayed him into the scrape. The history of the Cardinal Bellère can tell how well he performed his promise. The example of Charles was followed by many other adorers of the Virgin; and the pious determined to erect a church worthy of the blessed mother. The building was costly; and although the subscriptions and contributions were great, yet the want of funds was supplied by other miracles which were wrought, and which brought adorers and contributors from all the Christian cities. The dead were raised; the particulars of which are given in this most veracious account. Those who came to church on crutches went away upon their ten toes. A child, which had been buried three days, was taken from the grave, and changed from decay to bloom; but, either from a want of faith or from some other cause, it finally went back into the state in which it was when taken from the grave. These things are so well attested, that he who does not believe them is 'little better than one of the wicked.' The after-miracles did the job; and the church was finished in a very elaborate manner. The sculpture on the outside is varied, and emblematic of the adoration of the shepherds, and the history of the Virgin. There are some figures, however, which are better suited to a brothel than a church; but I dare say they have a pious story to vindicate them from the charges which unbelievers would bring against them.

"Sunday, July 26th. — I arrived yesterday in Paris, and had the pleasure to receive my letters, and to learn that all was well. I write this from Mrs. Welles's country-place, to which I came to pass the Sunday.

"The celebration of the three days — 27th, 28th, and 29th of July, 1830 — is to be got up with more than usual parade. The first day is appropriated to funeral services in the churches, in commemoration of those who fell on that day. Sixteen girls, who received a wedding-present from the city, are married on that day in the City Hall. How they are selected, or what gives them the preference, I am not aware. On Tuesday there is to be a review of the troops of the line and the National Guard, probably some fifty or sixty thousand, by the king; and, as they march through the square I am lodged in, it will give me a good opportunity of seeing them and the king, with his family, who are to be near the Hôtel de

Bristol. The third day is appropriated to a great display of fireworks and illuminations, for which there are great preparations in the Tuileries, Champs Elysées, and other parts of Paris. As the French give fine exhibitions of this sort, I am glad to be present.

"Monday, 27th. — The day is pleasant; and, in the afternoon, showers, which are favorable to the military duties of to-morrow.

"Tuesday evening, 28th. — This has been an interesting day, and had nearly caused an event which might have thrown France into a state of great perplexity. The custom is for the troops to be drawn up on the Boulevards, making a line of one or two miles, when the king rides with his staff down the line, in front of the troops, whilst thus drawn up. Having got to the extreme left of the line, he leaves the Boulevards, and comes to the Place Vendôme, where all the troops defile before him, and receive the marching salute. Having thus marched before his majesty, they each go to their cantonment, and the king and his suite to the Tuileries. I had secured windows, one of which looked into the Rue Castiglione, and the other upon the Square. All the avenues to the Square are guarded, to prevent any assemblage of people there which would interfere with the troops. At twelve o'clock, the king passed through the Rue Castiglione and Place Vendôme to the Boulevards with his sons, and the officers attached to him, amongst whom were the Maréchal Mortier, Duke of Treviso, with the ministers De Broglie and Thiers. At about twelve, the queen, and her daughters and the ladies in waiting, came in their carriages to the house of the chancellor, and seated themselves in balconies, which were covered with awnings. Later, the king with his suite came to the Place Vendôme, and, alighting from his horse, as did those who were with him, went to the apartments where the ladies were. A few minutes afterwards, the column came in view by the Rue de la Paix, and, having paid the marching salute, defiled by the Rue Castiglione. I observed a great degree of enthusiasm as the National Guards — which are the militia of the country — came near to the king. This was unusual, and was observed by some of the Frenchmen who were in the room where I was, and who could not account for it. In many cases, the common soldiers left their ranks, and ran up to the king, whose stand was near to the right of where the platoons passed, and took him by the hand. They all cheered, and gave tokens of great excitement. In one case, a whole company surrounded the king; when, from the movement of his sons, it seemed that they were alarmed for their father, and rode towards him. We could discover by their action that they wished him to withdraw a little farther from his loving subjects; but, so far from doing this, he rather advanced into the midst of them.

"About this time, my courier came to me to say that the king had narrowly escaped assassination by an infernal machine, whilst reviewing the troops; and that the Maréchal Mortier, with some nine or ten others who were near the king, was killed, and several wounded. This accounted for the enthusiasm of the troops, and the return made by the king. His majesty narrowly escaped one of the balls which were simultaneously fired by twenty-five barrels placed on a level, and a train so laid as to discharge all at the same time, wounding his horse slightly. It was within a few seconds of laying the king low, and probably deluging the country in blood. We had seen one of the officers ride across the Place Vendôme, before the king returned from the review, with a precipitancy which seemed uncalled for, and for which I could not account. He stopped at the place where the ladies of the royal family were. The evening papers state that it was an express sent from the king to her majesty, to inform her of the attempt, and his escape. The paper this evening gives the particulars. All further doings for the three days are given up, I suppose indefinitely. The assassin's name is Gerard,* — thirty-six years old. He was badly wounded himself, and was unable to speak, so that we cannot yet get the particulars; nor is it known whether he has associates or not. It is probable there are others behind the curtain, and that the poor instrument will be left to suffer alone.

"29th. — In place of fireworks and other demonstrations of joy, every thing, it is said, is to wear the trappings of sorrow. A funeral ceremony is said to be in preparation.

"Harrowgate, Sept. 6th. — We are on our way to York, which we pass on our route to Scotland.

* The name was Fieschi.

"On Tuesday, and the two following days, there is to be a musical festival in the Cathedral, which will be numerously attended by the nobility and gentry. One of the great attractions will be the Princess Victoria, who, if she survives William IV., is to be Queen of England. The princess, with her mother the Duchess of Kent, visited the Museum Gardens to-day, where I saw them. The future queen is about seventeen years of age, good-looking, and in manners very courteous, but not remarkable for her beauty.

"The road from Leeds here is pleasant. We passed Lord Harewood's grounds, which are very extensive. The ride through the park was, for the moment, interdicted on account of the expected visit of the princess. I walked to one churchyard to see if there was any stone to mark the place where lie the ashes of my friend, the late Dr. Gardiner; but there was none. I shall inquire further.*

"7th. — Rose early, with the intention of learning more respecting the resting-place of Dr. Gardiner, and concluded that to visit the clergyman was the most certain way of effecting this. I went to his house, about a mile from my lodgings, and, upon inquiry, found the gentleman was ill. I told his wife the object of my visit, and she made the inquiry I wished. She told me she was not married at the time of Dr.

* Dr. John S. J. Gardiner, Rector of Trinity Church in Boston, who died in England, July, 1830, deeply lamented in America as a distinguished clergyman and an accomplished scholar. He was President of the Literary Club, by whom the Boston Athenæum was founded; and the incipient measures which have produced a library of sixty thousand volumes, a building probably more spacious and costly than any other in the United States devoted solely to books and the arts, with the large funds for future increase mentioned in this memoir, were all framed and adopted at his house.

Gardiner's death, but that her husband remembered well the melancholy event. He said the body was interred about two miles from the spring, and that the service was read by an Irish clergyman residing near the ground of interment. He informed me that the stone had been erected which was the particular object of my inquiry. He spoke in high terms of respect of the memory of the doctor, and of the general sorrow felt at the event. The clergyman who read the service lies now at the point of death."

Col. Perkins returned from this visit to Europe with renewed health, and, although past seventy years of age, engaged with characteristic energy in whatever attracted his attention favorably; making soon afterwards an arduous journey into the interior of Pennsylvania, to visit the mining region.

In 1838, his commercial firm was dissolved; and he withdrew from business with a large fortune, after having been actively engaged in commerce for more than fifty years, though within the last ten his personal attention to its affairs had been considerably relaxed. His success had been great, but by no means uninterrupted. Severe disappointments and disasters, from causes beyond his control, made part of his experience; and, while he had great confidence in his own ability to direct, he well knew the importance of leaving as little as possible to accident in any enterprise that he undertook.

An instance of the readiness with which he could sometimes decide on the advantages to be justly expected from commercial operations, when proposed, will serve to show the extent of his information, and the value of such information in enabling those who engage in commerce at all to act with clear discernment, instead of trusting to blind chance in speculation. He had used such information and discernment himself with striking effect, even so far as to pause in his career, and stand somewhat aside for years, when others, moved partly by an ambitious desire to rival him in commerce, had sought to rise from the grade of successful dealers in purchases from his cargoes, and become the owners of ships, importing cargoes of their own. Insolvency and melancholy oblivion or insignificance have, since then, been the lot of most of them. But when enterprises requiring capital, and, still more, judgment, beyond their resources and capacity, had led them into embarrassment, there necessarily came a pause on their side, of which he and those who were associated with him took skilful advantage in a rapid succession of voyages that have rarely had a parallel for success.

The particular instance referred to was this: About thirty years ago, the price of coffee, which for a long time previously had been as high as twenty-five cents, had declined to fifteen cents per pound; and Col. Perkins being in New York for a day or two, on a visit to a daughter who resided there, a wish was expressed that it might be suggested to him, that, the temporary depression having made it a fit subject for speculation, if he should be disposed to engage in it on the extended scale to which he was accustomed, there was an opportunity to secure a large quantity on even more advantageous terms. As coffee was an article out of the line of his usual operations, and not likely to attract his particular attention, the subject was mentioned to him rather for entertainment, in conversing upon the occurrences of the time and the news of the day, than in the belief that he would give it serious thought. Without hesitation, and with the ease and decision of an able lawyer or surgeon in giving an opinion on any case presented to either of them professionally, he answered to this effect: —

"The depression in coffee is not 'temporary.' Whoever makes purchases now at fourteen cents, or even at thirteen cents, will find that he has made a mistake, unless he means to take advantage of any transient demand to dispose of it speedily. There are more coffee-trees now in bearing than are sufficient to supply the whole world, by a proportion that I could state with some precision if necessary. The decline in price is owing to accumulation, which will be found to increase, particularly as there are new plantations yet to come forward. Coffee will eventually fall to ten cents, and probably below that, and will remain depressed for some years. The culture of it will be diminished. Old plantations will be suffered to die out; and others will, in some cases, be grubbed up, that the land may be converted to new uses. At length, the plantations will be found inadequate to the supply of the world. But it requires five or six years for the coffee-tree to reach its full bearing. Time, of course, will be required for the necessary increase; and the stocks on hand will be diminishing in the mean time. A rise must follow. Whoever buys coffee twelve or fifteen years hence at the market price, whatever it may be, will probably find it rising on his hands; and fortunes may be made, unless speculative movements shall have disturbed the regular course of events."

With so clear an outline for the future, it was interesting to observe what followed. Coffee gradually fell to less than ten cents, and remained low. One consequence, usual in such cases, ensued, — the consumption increased. Misled, perhaps, by this, and an impatient desire to be foremost in securing advantages which by that time were generally foreseen, parties began to move in a speculative spirit about five years before the time thus indicated. They made great purchases, and large quantities were held in expectation of profit. It was curious to notice the action, and hear the remarks, of various persons concerned, in what ensued, according to their different degrees of intelligence on a subject that was not, even then, fully understood by all. Coffee rose considerably. Some of them secured a moderate profit while they could; others, arguing on a crude belief, that, as coffee had been at twenty-five cents, there was no reason why it should not attain that price again, determined to wait for far greater profits. The stimulant given to the demand, by withholding large quantities from sale, developed greater stocks than were supposed to exist. The movement was found to be premature, and coffee fell again in price. Immense sums were lost. Bankruptcy followed, with many a heartache that might have been prevented by counsel from one like him, who had the comprehensive views and thorough knowledge that belong to a complete merchant.

This unwise anticipation somewhat retarded and diminished the well-founded rise that had been foretold. But it came at length, and some moderate fortunes were made by it; though the dreams of the speculator, of a return to the high prices that prevailed in the early part of the century, have never been realized.

After his retirement from commerce, Col. Perkins found sufficient occupation in the management of his property; in various matters of a public nature which interested him; and in the cultivation of trees, and particularly of fruits and flowers, on his estate at Brookline. He was remarkable for his love of nature; and, in travelling, sometimes went far out of his way to examine a beautiful tree or to enjoy an interesting view. Occasionally he made a voyage to Europe, renewing his observations on the changes and improvements that were to be seen there. He had crossed the Atlantic many times besides the instances that have been referred to, always keeping a diary, which he filled with the incidents that occurred, with the results of his inquiries, and with remarks worthy of an intelligent traveller, and sending home works of art, some of which were bestowed as gifts.

He took a lively interest in the progress and welfare of American artists; kindly aiding some who desired to improve by studying the great models in Europe, and liberally purchasing the works of those who deserved encouragement. He was generally very agreeable to those whom he incidentally met as fellow-travellers; and, where he became known abroad as an American, he left a very favorable impression of the character of his countrymen.

Active industry had been, and continued to be, the habit of his life. The day with him was well occupied, and equally well ordered. He had long been accustomed to rise early, to consider what required his attention, and to prepare so much of what he had to do personally as he could perform by himself, that he might meet the world ready to decide and direct promptly and clearly. This enabled him to transact business with ease and accuracy, and made him so far master of his time that he found leisure for various objects, both of usefulness and enjoyment, as well as for courteous and kind attention to the affairs and wishes of others, which it might have been supposed would hardly be remembered by one so occupied. Each day with him was the illustration of a thought which young men, and particularly young men entering on commercial life, will find to be a safeguard against precipitation or perplexity, and against the irritation, as well as the miserable shifts, to which they sometimes lead. The action of the mind in preparing with calm foresight what is to be done, before it is absolutely necessary, is widely different from its action when affairs are left until necessity presses, and the powers are confused by various calls on the attention in the midst of hurry and embarrassment. What is only method in the first case actually becomes a faculty, and sometimes passes for uncommon ability, of which it has the effect. On the other hand, some men, who really show great powers when pressed by necessity for despatch, are in truth *unable*, without being aware of such a defect, to foresee and prepare what they have to do before they feel the pressure. When that ceases, the exertion too often ceases with it; and important matters are left to be done at some future time, which perhaps are never done. The older they grow, the more incurable is the evil; and melancholy instances might be given of bankruptcy late in life, after great success, which might be traced chiefly to this cause. It is said that the Hon. Peter C. Brooks, of Boston, who left a large fortune, after a life well worthy of imitation, on being once asked what rule he would recommend to a young man as most likely to insure success, answered, "Let him mind his business." And to a similar inquiry, it has been said that Robert Lenox, Esq., of New York, well remembered as one of the most distinguished and estimable merchants ever known in that great city, and for his wide hospitality, once answered, "Let him be beforehand with his business." One answer seems to include the other; as no man can be beforehand with his business, and enjoy the tranquil self-possession that accompanies forecast, unless he minds it unremittingly.

At one time, when Col. Perkins had decided to leave home for some time on a long journey of several thousand miles to the South and West, application had been made to him to give his guaranty for a considerable sum, to enable one whose welfare he wished to promote to engage in a commercial connection that seemed to offer great advantages. As the magnitude of the affair required caution, it was expected, of course, that, when he had considered the subject, explanations on various points would be necessary before he could decide to give it; and it was intended to take some favorable opportunity, when he might be entirely at leisure, to explain every thing fully. Suddenly, however, he found it best to commence the journey a week or two sooner than had been mentioned; and engagements of various kinds, previously made, so occupied him in the short interval left, that there seemed to be no time for offering such explanation without danger of intruding; and the hope of obtaining his aid at that time, in an affair that required prompt action, was given up. The applicant called at his house half an hour before he was to go, merely to take leave, knowing that the haste of departure in such cases usually precludes attention to any matters requiring deliberation. On entering the room, however, he found there was no appearance of haste. All preparations for the journey had been entirely completed in such good season, that the last half-hour seemed to be one entirely of leisure for any thing that might occur. After a little chat, Col. Perkins introduced the subject himself, and made pertinent inquiries; which being answered satisfactorily, he gave the guaranty, and very kindly added a further facility, by allowing, until his return, the use of a considerable sum of money which he was leaving in the bank. The arrangements were, in consequence, completed the next day. They proved, in the result, to be eminently successful: all pledges were redeemed; his guaranty was cancelled in due course, without the slightest cost or inconvenience to him; and the person whom he wished to oblige received very large profits, which happily influenced the remainder of his life, and which he perhaps might never have enjoyed, if that last half-hour before the journey had been hurried.

When doing an act of kindness like this, he seemed to derive great pleasure from the consciousness that the action of his life had given him the power to produce such results by the single influence of his name; from all proofs, too, which followed, that he had decided correctly in bestowing his confidence where he believed it to be deserved; and from indulging an impulse of his nature that prompted him to diffuse happiness where he had the opportunity.

Numerous instances might be given of his kindness in promoting the success of others, and particularly of young men engaging in voyages or other commercial enterprises; and he always showed a warm interest in the Mercantile Library Association of Young Men in Boston, to whom he made a donation to aid in the erection of a building.

In a general view of his character, he appeared

as exercising the influence of one having a nice sense of propriety with reference to the opinion of others, love of order, a high standard of action, and a desire to promote whatever tended to general advantage and respectability, with such steadiness of purpose as gave power to his example. His manners, formed in an age of ceremony which has passed, retained something of its courteous dignity, divested of what was artificial, and united with the ease of our own time.

As a leader of the Federal party, that party which sustained the administration of Washington and transmitted its principles, he had personally known most of the distinguished men of the country who belonged to the period next succeeding the Revolution, and was intimate with many of them. He had thus enjoyed the advantages of intercourse with eminent statesmen who had aided in giving the present form to the government of the Union, or in directing its early action; among whom the high principles and the resolute decision of his own political character made him a welcome associate.

His personal appearance so far indicated his character, that an observer of any class who saw him for the first time was very likely to be impressed with a desire to know who that personage might be. "A very noble-looking man!" said a young woman who was called to fetch him a glass of water when he stopped one day at the house of a friend some miles from town. "*Ce beau vieillard!*" — that beautiful old man! — exclaimed the wife of a foreign ambassador, in speaking of his reception of her at his country-seat, when some one was showing her the environs of Boston. And, in repeated instances, foreigners of rank have remarked in a similar tone on his person, and the high-bred courtesy of his manner.

Great personal strength and entire self-reliance made him almost heedless of danger, in the full confidence that he had the power and the presence of mind to do just the right thing at the right moment; and he had, at different times, some remarkable escapes. On one occasion, when driving towards town over a road made in one part on the slope of a hill, with a steep bank on one side, and a descent, guarded by a wall, on the other, some object fell from the top of the bank on his right so suddenly that his horse, a powerful animal, sprang to the opposite side, and dashed into a run. Close before him was the stiff branch of a large apple-tree, projecting over that side of the road, at about the level of his waist as he sat. He leaped at once from his seat over the wall, alighting unhurt in the orchard below; and, in an instant, the top was swept from the vehicle in a manner that must have proved fatal to himself if he had remained in it a moment longer.

Though fond of social intercourse, his opinions were often conveyed in monosyllables, or short and terse expressions; and he was more inclined, whether abroad or at his own table, to promote conversation in others than to talk much himself. But he listened with attention, and contributed readily, from the stores of his experience and knowledge, whatever occurred to him as interesting, — occasionally introducing an anecdote with striking effect, but rather as if he were stating a fact than telling a story. He used language with precision; his expressions were concise; and his words carried the full force that belonged to them, all the more because there was no attempt to exaggerate their true and precise meaning. The instances that he gave were usually such as had occurred within his own knowledge in reference to remarkable events or distinguished men; and most of them might well have found place in history or biography. But occasionally he related incidents of an amusing character, such as the following, and in a manner that afforded great entertainment.

In one of his early visits to London, Stuart, the celebrated portrait-painter, whom he knew well, resided there, occupying apartments as a bachelor, with a boy to attend him. One day, Stuart sent the boy with a message to a man of rank, to say that he could comply with a request to give him a sitting, if he would come at a certain hour. The boy went off, accompanied by a large and favorite dog of his master's, but did not return at the time expected; and Stuart waited, receiving no answer, until he found that the forenoon was lost. He then went out to take his usual walk; and as he strolled on, finding himself in that part of the city where the mother of the boy resided, he made her a visit, and inquired whether her son ever came to see her. "Oh, yes!" she said: he had been there that morning, with a great dog, both of them full of mischief; and there had been such a time! First, they discovered a piece of beef-steak intended for her dinner, which, after great struggles, the dog had been suffered to devour. Then, in a scene of frolic and riot, they had upset her wash-tub, and had just gone off. He desired the woman not to mention his own visit to her; and on returning home, and inquiring what was the answer brought, was told by the boy that he had been unable to find the place, having lost his way, and got back as he could; to all which he said nothing, except as a slight caution to be more attentive to the direction in future. Soon afterwards, his dinner was brought, as usual, from a chop-house, and the boy took his accustomed stand opposite to him; while the dog placed himself at his side, expecting an occasional mouthful. In due course, Stuart, taking a piece of juicy meat on his fork, held it towards the dog; but, after looking at him for a moment, suddenly drew back with well-feigned surprise, exclaiming, "How is this? What! dined already?" And he looked earnestly at the boy, who became alarmed. Turning again to the dog, with the meat still withheld over him, he said, "Ah? and beef-steak! Is it possible?" Casting an angry and searching look at intervals towards the boy, he went on: "What! a wash-tub? — and upset it too?" He at length turned back to the table; and, laying the fork on his plate, folded his arms, and looked intently at the culprit. The boy, aghast at these supernatural disclosures, as they seemed, from the dog, confessed the whole, making solemn promises for his future behavior, which became exemplary. The pretended wonder of the artist, the eagerness and disappointment of the dog, and the conscience-stricken amazement of the boy, were all presented in vivid light, while he only seemed to be mentioning casually what had occurred.

The following is an incident of a different character, which occurred in the National Convention during the French revolution, and of which he was an eye-witness. He related it with great effect. Soon after the death of Robespierre, one of his former associates proposed a sanguinary law; which was objected to, by a member who had been a butcher, as unnecessarily cruel. The deputy who proposed it said, with a sneer, that he had not looked for such fine sentiments from one whose trade had been blood. The butcher, a burly, powerful man, starting to his feet as if he would destroy his opponent, exclaimed, "Scelerat! scelerat! Je n'ai jamais trempé mes mains que dans le sang des animaux. Sentez les votres!" *

It has been thought that he showed a lack of discernment in judging of character. Whatever might be the truth as to any defect of that sort, it rarely, if ever, appeared in making unjust imputations, but rather in giving others credit for good qualities which they did not possess. Although he used strong terms in condemning, on some occasions, what he disapproved, he seldom spoke in disparagement of any one; and, if he listened, it was with no indication of pleasure at hearing any thing to the disadvantage of others. There certainly were cases in which he found

* "Wretch! wretch that you are! I have never imbrued my hands but in the blood of beasts. Smell of your own!"

that his confidence had been misplaced; but, as he was not apt to communicate his motives fully, it was not clear whether it arose entirely from error of judgment, or partly from a readiness to take risks of which he was aware. In some instances, he misunderstood the intentions or difficulties and embarrassments of others, and occasionally spoke with warmth where he supposed there was just cause for displeasure, though he was more likely to be quite silent at such times; but no one was more ready than he to make reparation, if it were explained to him that he had been unjust. Probably he was supposed to be unfriendly in other instances, when he would have appeared to be entirely kind if he had talked more freely. His nature was affectionate, appearing particularly so towards children; and many of them were his intimate friends, habitually exchanging with him the liveliest pleasantry with perfect freedom.

It is not uncommon with those whose feelings are characterized by great energy, as his were, that, from an apprehension, perhaps, lest strong emotion might escape control if expressed in any degree whatever, it is guarded with such entire suppression and reserve, that they seem to those around them almost to have no feeling at all, when, in truth, they feel most deeply. A striking instance of this nature may be mentioned of him.

The death of his eldest son, who was named for him, and in person, as well as in some points of character, bore a strong natural resemblance to himself, occurred about four years before his own. They differed in character, as the son of a widow, moved by strong incitements to assist in relieving her of care, and to secure his own advancement in the world, might be very likely to differ from one born to the enjoyment and expectation of wealth, and advancing in youth under the auspices of a parent who stood high in public estimation, and possessed powerful influence. Like his father, he had preferred action to the life of a student, and went early abroad, having sailed for China, during the war of 1812, in a private armed ship, that was prepared to fight her way for a rich cargo, as was successfully done; and he took part in one bloody naval action, besides other encounters. Daring in spirit, of a buoyant and generous temper, and eminently handsome, he was a favorite abroad, particularly among the officers of our public ships as he met them in foreign ports; and he had seen much of the world, with various adventures, in China, in South America, and in Europe.

He eventually joined his father's commercial house in Boston, and, after a few years of remarkable success, withdrew with a good fortune, and lived in affluence and leisure, amusing himself with field sports, of which he was fond, and varying his life by an occasional tour in Europe. After rearing a beautiful family, he fell the victim of a distressing illness, and died in the prime of life.

At his funeral, his father appeared tranquil as usual, advising on some matters of detail; and, having followed the hearse to the place of interment, chose, rather against the suggestions of those near him, to descend to the tomb under the church, that he might see that all was arranged as he had intended. But when nothing more remained to be done; when the single lamp, by the light of which the coffin had been adjusted in its place, was withdrawn, and the door was closed in darkness and silence on all that remained of one who had been the object of so deep interest from infancy upward, — nature prevailed, for one moment only, over all restraint, and an involuntary burst of grief disclosed the depth of sorrow that remained beneath the habitual composure of his manner.

About two years after this, the death of Mrs. Perkins took place; and the dissolution of a tie which had continued for sixty-three years had a visible effect on him. His younger brother, Samuel G. Perkins, Esq., had died blind, past the age of eighty. His own sight was failing. Of all the family left by his father, he and two sisters only remained. His friend through life, the Hon. Harrison Gray Otis, was dead. The companions of his youth and middle age were nearly all gone. Of the association remembered as the "Saturday Club," consisting of some of the most distinguished gentlemen of the town in their day, — who, while they found mutual enjoyment in dining successively at the houses of each other, gave hospitable admission to such strangers as deserved attention, — only two survived besides himself. The impression had long been habitual with him, that the close of his own life was near; and he awaited it with tranquillity. He had lived as he thought it was right to do. There appears to have been no period in which he had been inclined to vice of any sort. His life was marked by self-control. But, besides that, he seems to have had an innate purity and love of order that made excess distasteful to him. In the order of events, he had found the enjoyment, and incurred the responsibility, of great success in the acquisition of property; and he had shared it freely with the community in which he lived, — his gifts and contributions continuing numerous to the last.

He had become feeble, and moved with difficulty. But an indomitable spirit, which remained ready for action still, if any thing was to be done, carried him once more from home as far as Washington. This spirit had long before borne him through some passages of ill health, that might have proved fatal if it had not been that the energy with which his mind opened itself to excitement and pleasure always imparted corresponding vigor to his physical frame in a remarkable degree.

Twenty-five years before, being greatly debilitated after a severe illness, he had resolved to try the effect of a voyage to England, though some of his friends feared that he might never return; and he sailed with his nephew and friend, Mr. Cushing, in a new ship belonging to his house. He was so weak that it was necessary to assist him, almost to lift him, on board the vessel; but, becoming immediately interested in the management of the ship, and in getting to sea, when the pilot left them in the outer harbor he was already better for the excitement. He continued to improve during the voyage, and returned in vigorous health.

A few years afterwards, being again reduced to much the same state, he left Boston for New York, to embark for Europe in company with his eldest son (who thought it unsafe that his father should sail without his personal care), and with his grandson, — three of the name. He went from home so enfeebled that his family doubted whether he could reach New York in a condition to be carried on board the packet (it was before the day of steamships); and they were surprised to learn, after waiting with solicitude, that he was so well after the journey as to accompany his friend Mr. Otis, whom he met there on his arrival, to the theatre in the evening.

After the decease of Mrs. Perkins, some important business in which he was concerned required attention at Washington; and, his courageous spirit still rising above the infirmities of age, he made one more journey there, resolved to see to it himself. While there, he was concerned to find that labor was likely to be suspended on the monument to the memory of Washington. On his return home, he took measures to rouse fresh interest in the work; and a considerable sum was raised for it through his exertions. His action in reference to this has been publicly alluded to, since his decease, by the Hon. Robert C. Winthrop, late Speaker of the House of Representatives in Congress, who, at the close of an eloquent speech addressed to the Massachusetts Charitable Mechanic

Association, at their annual festival in Faneuil Hall in October, 1854, spoke as follows: —

"The memory of your excellent and lamented president (Mr. Chickering) has already received its appropriate and feeling tribute. I can add nothing to that; but I will venture to recall to your remembrance another venerated name. You have alluded, in the sentiment which called me up, to an humble service which I rendered some years ago, as the organ of the Representatives of the Union, at the laying of the corner-stone of the national monument to Washington. I cannot but remember that the latest efforts in this quarter of the country to raise funds for the completion of that monument were made by one whose long and honorable life has been brought to a close within the past twelve months.

"I cannot forget the earnest and affectionate interest with which that noble-hearted old American gentleman devoted the last days — and I had almost said the last hours — of his life to arranging the details and the machinery for an appeal to the people of Massachusetts in behalf of that still unfinished structure. He had seen Washington in his boyhood, and had felt the inspiration of his majestic presence; he had known him in his manhood, and had spent two or three days with him, by particular invitation, at Mount Vernon, — days never to be forgotten in any man's life; his whole heart seemed to be imbued with the warmest admiration and affection for his character and services; and it seemed as if he could not go down to his grave in peace until he had done something to aid in perpetuating the memory of his virtues and his valor. I need not say that I allude to the late Hon. Thomas Handasyd Perkins. He was one of the noblest specimens of humanity to which our city has ever given birth, — leading the way for half a century in every generous enterprise, and setting one of the earliest examples of those munificent charities which have given our city a name and a praise throughout the earth. He was one of your own honorary members, Mr. President; and I have felt that I could do nothing more appropriate to this occasion, — the first public festive occasion in Faneuil Hall which has occurred since his death, — and nothing more agreeable to the feelings of this association or to my own, than to propose to you, as I now do, —

"The memory of THOMAS HANDASYD PERKINS."

For a long time, he had been deprived of the use of one of his eyes, which was blinded by cataract, how long he could not tell with accuracy, — for the discovery that it was useless, and that he saw only with the other, was made by accident, and much to his surprise, — but it must have been more than twenty years. Opening it one morning while the right eye was buried in the pillow, he found himself unable to perceive any objects about him. For many years, however, he saw well enough for common purposes with the other; but, more recently, even that one had caused him so much trouble that he lived in fear of total blindness. Early in 1853, cataract appeared in that eye also, and was making such rapid progress that in a few weeks all useful vision was lost. Under these circumstances, he resolved to submit to an operation on the one that had been so long obscured. It was successfully performed by Dr. H. W. Williams, of Boston, the cataract being broken up in the month of March. Some time was necessary for the complete absorption of the fragments; but, in less than three months, the pupil had become entirely clear, and, by the aid of cataract-glasses, he could not only see large objects as well as ever, but could read the newspapers, and even the fine print in the column of ship-news. His sight was at times rendered feeble afterwards by the general debility of his system, and he never recovered the power of reading and writing with entire ease; but to do both in some degree was an advantage, in comparison with total loss of sight, that could hardly be appreciated, particularly as it enabled him still to manage his own affairs, which he always wished to do, and did to his last day, — even keeping his books with his own hand, except for a few months of his last year, when the entries were made from his dictation.

In this, the last year of his life, he gave one more remarkable proof of his continued interest in what was going on about him, and of his readiness to aid liberally in all that he deemed important to public welfare and intelligence. A large and costly building had been erected for the Boston Athenæum, by contribution from the public, liberally made for that purpose, that there might be such a one as would correspond to the aspirations of the accomplished scholars, who, fifty years before, had founded the institution. A fund was now to be provided for annual expenses, and for regular additions to the library. With this view, an effort was made to raise a fund of one hundred and twenty thousand dollars. As Col. Perkins had already done a great deal for the Athenæum, no application was made to him for further aid. He, however, voluntarily asked for the book containing the largest class of subscriptions, and added his name to those contributing three thousand dollars each. Soon afterwards, he inquired of the President of the Athenæum what progress had been made, and was told that the subscriptions amounted to eighty thousand dollars, — all of them being, however, on the condition that the full sum should be made up within the year; that every thing possible seemed to have been done; but that, as people were leaving town for the summer, nothing further could be obtained until the autumn; and that it was doubtful whether the object could be effected even then, by raising forty thousand dollars more, as the applications appeared to have been thoroughly made by a numerous committee. He then gave his assurance that the attempt should not be suffered to fail, even for so large a deficit as that, and agreed to be responsible for it, in order that the subscriptions already obtained might be made binding; stipulating only that nothing should be said of this until the expiration of the last day fixed, and that the efforts to obtain it from the public should not be at all relaxed in the mean time. Further assistance from him, however, was rendered unnecessary, chiefly by the noble bequest of Samuel Appleton, Esq., a man of liberality and benevolence like his own, who died during the summer, leaving the sum of two hundred thousand dollars to trustees, to be distributed, at their discretion, for scientific, literary, religious, or charitable purposes. The trustees appropriated twenty-five thousand dollars of this to the fund for the Athenæum; and the remaining sum of fifteen thousand dollars was easily obtained by further subscriptions at large.

But the assurance given by Col. Perkins, although any call on him thus became unnecessary, was useful in warranting that confidence of success which helps, in such cases, to secure it.

In January following (1854), he found it necessary to submit to a slight surgical operation, for the removal of some obstruction that troubled him. He had passed most of the day — the 9th — in attending to his domestic payments for the preceding year; arranging the papers himself, with his usual method in business. The operation was successfully performed by Dr. Cabot, his grandson; and he went to bed with the agreeable prospect of finding himself relieved for the remainder of his life of what had, for some time, made him uncomfortable, — but with a caution, too, from his surgeon, not to rise the next morning, but remain in perfect quiet. In such matters, however, he had habitually judged and chosen to act for himself; and in this instance he gave too little heed to the caution, — refusing, too, to have any attendant in his chamber, as had been recommended. He passed a good night; and, feeling only too well after it, chose to rise rather early the next day. After being partly dressed, becoming faint, he was obliged to lie down on the sofa, and never left it. He became more and more feeble through the day; and, falling into a state of unconsciousness towards evening, he continued to breathe for some hours, sleeping without pain or distress, and died tranquilly on the morning of the 11th, soon after midnight, in the ninetieth year of his age.

The impression of his character left on the community was such as had been sketched a short time before — in language that hardly admits of improvement, and needs no addition — by the Hon. Daniel Webster, in a note written with his own hand on the blank leaf of a copy of his works presented to Col. Perkins: —

"WASHINGTON, April 19, 1852.

"MY DEAR SIR, — If I possessed any thing which I might suppose likely to be more acceptable to you, as a proof of my esteem, than these volumes, I should have sent it in their stead.

"But I do not; and therefore ask your acceptance of a copy of this edition of my speeches.

"I have long cherished, my dear sir, a profound, warm, affectionate, and I may say a filial, regard for your person and character. I have looked upon you as one born to do good, and who has fulfilled his mission; as a man without spot or blemish; as a merchant known and honored over the whole world; a most liberal supporter and promoter of science and the arts; always kind to scholars and literary men, and greatly beloved by them all; friendly to all the institutions of religion, morality, and education; and an unwavering and determined supporter of the constitution of the country, and of those great principles of civil liberty which it is so well calculated to uphold and advance.

"These sentiments I inscribe here in accordance with my best judgment, and out of the fulness of my heart; and I wish here to record also my deep sense of the many personal obligations under which you have placed me in the course of our long acquaintance.

"Your ever-faithful friend,

"DANIEL WEBSTER.

"To the Hon. THOMAS H. PERKINS."

A meeting of the merchants of Boston was held at the Merchants' Exchange, for the purpose of testifying their respect for his memory. The following is a report of the proceedings as published: —

The meeting was called to order by T. B. Curtis, Esq., who proposed that Hon. Abbott Lawrence be invited to preside on the occasion. The motion was unanimously adopted.

Mr. Lawrence, on taking the chair, said, "I thank you, gentlemen, for the honor you have conferred on me in placing me in the chair on this occasion. You all know the cause of this meeting; and a melancholy occasion it is. It was thought fit and proper, by the merchants of Boston, that some special notice should be taken of the death of Col. Thomas H. Perkins. In regard to the appropriateness of such a course, there is no difference of opinion.

"I feel, as you feel, that we have lost our guide, our great exemplar, in the mercantile profession. I have looked, from a very early age, to Col. Perkins as the great merchant of Boston; as a man endowed with great talent; ever devoted to the best interests of his country, — his whole country; a man incapable of a mean thought or action; and a man who has done more to elevate the mercantile character than any man now living among us. We therefore feel it due to the memory of a man and a merchant so distinguished as Col. Perkins, that his death should be noticed by the merchants of Boston.

"There are many topics," Mr. Lawrence continued, "in connection with the memory of Mr. Perkins, which press upon my mind; but this is not the time or place for me to speak of his character, or the general attributes he possessed. We all look with reverence and respect upon them; and this meeting has been called to give some testimony to the world of the honor and respect in which we hold his character, as a man, a philanthropist, a friend of science, of art, and of literature. Though a merchant, he was not confined to the mercantile profession alone; but has taken an active interest, for over threescore years and ten, in all the departments of literature, science, and philanthropy. It is remarkable that a man of his age should have been so fresh in his feelings in these particulars, — a characteristic which was as marked twelve hours before his death as it was twenty years ago.

"But I must leave his character to be spoken of by others. I will only say, that, in all the relations of life, he was faithful. Even to the sitting on juries, he was conscientious; and never omitted it, whether it was for a longer or shorter period. Another duty he always performed, which some are too apt to neglect: he always went to the polls and voted, because he deemed it one of the highest duties, as well as one of the most valuable privileges, of an American citizen. But, gentlemen, I will not detain you longer; and will ask you to complete the organization of this meeting by nominating one or more persons for secretaries."

Joseph B. Glover and James Sturgis, Esqrs., were nominated, and unanimously chosen, for secretaries.

John Amory Lowell, Esq., then addressed the Chair as follows: —

"We have met here to-day, Mr. President, almost without notice, in obedience to a spontaneous and irresistible impulse, to exchange our feelings of regret and of respect for the memory of one so much the senior of even the more advanced among us; whose name we have from childhood regarded as the very symbol of mercantile honor and success. We would fain contribute our mite to the universal testimony of society; for to us he peculiarly belonged. He was emphatically a merchant. His very bearing reminded us of that noble class of men, whose pride centres in the profession they contribute so largely to adorn. Few of his associates in business remain to tell us of his professional career; but around us, on every side, are the enduring monuments of the munificence and public spirit which graced and dignified the retirement of that serene old age.

"Mr. President, I may not trust myself to enlarge on this topic, lest I perchance be deemed to glorify the past,— 'Laudator temporis acti.' I will simply offer for the acceptance of this meeting a few resolutions expressive of those feelings, in which, I am sure, we all cordially unite:—

"*Whereas*, We have met here to-day to exchange and reciprocate the feelings elicited by the death of one of the oldest, of the most distinguished, and of the most public-spirited of those merchants who have so largely contributed to raise the standard of mercantile honor in this community, and who have caused the name of Boston to be respected at home and abroad; and

"*Whereas*, All history and all experience show that literature, science, art, all that ennobles and refines humanity, are intimately connected with the prosperity of commerce; and it is our intimate conviction that that prosperity is dependent upon, and inseparable from, those qualities for which Col. Perkins was so eminently distinguished;—

"*Resolved*, That, while we deeply mourn the loss that this community has sustained, it is a loss not unalloyed with pride in the high honor, the great public spirit, the extensive benevolence, and the noble example, of Thomas Handasyd Perkins.

"*Resolved*, That the history of his life encourages us all by the example of a long, honored, and successful career, and affords a valuable illustration of the connection of private with public prosperity.

"*Resolved*, That, whatever of just estimation may have been awarded to Boston for her enterprise, her sagacity, her institutions for education, literature, philanthropy, or art, a prominent share must be attributed to him who was ever foremost where any good deed was to be done.

"*Resolved*, That these resolutions be respectfully communicated, as the spontaneous and unanimous sentiments of this meeting, to the family of the Hon. Thomas H. Perkins."

Hon. J. Thomas Stevenson seconded the resolutions in the following able and appropriate remarks:—

"Mr. Chairman, may I second the motion for the adoption of the resolutions?

"The report of the death of a noted man and a distinguished merchant has summoned us here, that we may take counsel together as to a fit testimonial of the universal respect felt in our mercantile community towards Thomas Handasyd Perkins, whose face we shall see no more on earth for ever. He was the oldest merchant amongst us. None was more honorable. All the qualities which go to make up, and at the same time to adorn, the character of a merchant, shone brightly in him. He was a pattern of mercantile honor. In that, he was a man fit for an example. He was sagacious, bold, enterprising, honest. His word was a bond; his promise was the performance. His age — his great age, his good old age — prevents tears at the change which has conducted him to his reward. Eighty-nine summers have smiled upon him, and eighty-nine winters have prompted his warm charities. We may not utter lamentations over the needed repose of one who had overstepped so far the allotted boundaries of the life of man; but we are here, rather, to bear willing witness to the love we bore him, and to the respect he inspired us with. Literature, science, art, each received his homage and his sacrifices; but his chosen altar was in the beautiful temple of Charity.

"Public and private charities, — he absolutely revelled in them. No story of distress fell upon his ear, without making his manly heart throb to the overflow of tears. It was not weakness, but greatness, in him. Those tears were the mingled outpourings of sorrow and of joy; of sorrow at the suffering, of joy that he could do something to alleviate it. His full heart kept his full hand open. He, who had achieved a fortune, himself dispensed its bounties. He was liberal to a proverb, and as just as he was liberal. No public charity lacked his substantial aid. His heart beat nobly in response to the wants of the less favored of his race; and that which his heart prompted soon became his deed. His munificent endowment of the Asylum for the Blind, even if it had stood alone, instead of merely overtopping a crowd of others like it, would have been enough to have preserved his memory; for, in that, the hand which had been filled by an honest enterprise was opened wide by a cheerful charity, and many an eye that could not see him blessed him. We need not praise him: his deeds do that.

"May the large place which he has filled in our community not be left vacant by his departure; but may his bright example lead others, who, like him, are enabled to rejoice over a prosperous career, to realize, as he did, that the value of wealth is in its proper and beneficent uses! We will not mourn him; but we will remember him as an upright merchant, a kind friend, a good citizen, an honest man, and an honorable gentleman."

Mr. S. T. Dana offered, as an additional resolution, the following: —

"*Resolved,* That the merchants of Boston will attend the funeral services of the late Col. Thomas H. Perkins to-morrow; and that, during those services, they will close their places of business."

This, with the other resolutions, was unanimously adopted.

There being no further business, Mr. Lawrence — with the simple remark, that if ever a man died in this city who deserved to have written on his tombstone, that "the world is the better for his having lived in it," that man was Col. Thomas H. Perkins — declared the meeting dissolved.

The bells in the city will be tolled from twelve to one; and owners and masters of ships in the harbor are requested to display their colors at half-mast during the day.

Although private interment is most common now, it seemed inappropriate for one who had filled so large a space in public regard. The funeral service took place at the church of Rev. Dr. Gannett, where he had long worshipped, and was marked by one incident peculiarly touching in its association. The solemn music usual on such occasions was impressively performed by a large choir of pupils from the

Perkins Institution for the Blind, who had requested permission to sing the requiem for that friend through whom they enjoy the comforts of their spacious dwelling. A further proof of their regard for his memory was seen but lately, in gleams of pleasure lighting their faces on being promised that they should soon listen to this story of his life.

APPENDIX.

APPENDIX.

PAGE 218.

THE FRENCH CONSCRIPT.

SINCE the account was first published in the "Merchants' Magazine," of the release of Jean Beau, the conscript at Morlaix, in the manner related, his godfather, who is still living at an advanced age, has stated that the circumstances were as follows: —

Col. Perkins having observed the sudden gloom prevailing an hour or two after so happy a wedding, and being unwilling, from motives of delicacy, to make inquiries of any of the family, applied to a respectable bookseller, who kept at the next door, to learn what could be the cause of the apparent change from joy, throughout the house, to dismay and grief. "And you do not know, then," said the bookseller, "that Jean has drawn the black ball, and must go at once to the army?" He answered that he had not heard it before, but desired to know what was necessary to be done to obtain a discharge. The bookseller told him that nothing could be done; that a discharge could not possibly be obtained without the payment of a sum of money so large that Madame Beau and all her relatives could not raise half of it in the time required. "But I will see to that," said

Col. Perkins; and it was well known in Morlaix, that, modestly as he states to Mrs. Perkins his share of the transaction in "having put the thing in train," he paid nearly all the money himself.

Page 219.

LETTER TO J. P. CUSHING, ESQ.

MISSION TO WASHINGTON.

The "public business in behalf of the State of Massachusetts," on which Col. Perkins went to Washington in February, 1815, had reference to the defence of the eastern frontier and seaboard of the United States in the war with England. It had become necessary to maintain a large force for that purpose from the militia, if the war was to be continued; the troops of the Union being chiefly engaged in attempts on Canada. Direct taxes for the support of the war, very burdensome in the general derangement of business, had been imposed by Act of Congress, and were likely to be soon very much increased. Under these circumstances, it was recommended by a convention of delegates from some of the Eastern States, held at Hartford, Conn., in December, 1814, that application should be made to the Government of the United States, requesting their consent to some arrangement whereby the States exposed might be empowered to assume the defence of their territory against the enemy, and a reasonable portion of the taxes collected there might be paid into their respective treasuries, and appropriated to that object. A resolution was adopted, in consequence, by the Legislature of Massachusetts, authorizing a mission to Washington for the purpose of making the request.

Other measures were recommended by the convention; but this was the only one leading to any action except such as would necessarily be subject to the jurisdiction of the Supreme Court of the United States, or to the provisions of the Constitution in regard to amendments.

Col. Perkins was not a member of the Hartford Convention; but knowing most of the members personally, and having entire confidence in the purity of their motives and their devotion to the union of the States, with great deference for their wisdom, he willingly gave his support to the principal measure thus recommended by them, and accepted a place in the mission to Washington, believing that it would be productive of good to the whole country.

He was accordingly commissioned, with the Hon. Harrison Gray Otis, and William Sullivan, Esq., to proceed to Washington, "and make respectful and earnest application to the Government of the United States, requesting them to consent" to such an arrangement for defence.

Just after his arrival there, as appears by his letter, news was received that a treaty of peace had been effected; and any further action became unnecessary. It was his opinion, however, from indications at Washington when he reached there, that, if the commissioners who had been sent to Europe, early in the year preceding, had failed in their negotiation for peace, the proposal recommended by the Hartford Convention would have been readily acceded to by the General Government, as the best mode that could be adopted for the further conduct of the war.

Owing to a concurrence of circumstances at the time, a mistaken and very unfavorable impression in regard to the purposes of that convention prevailed for many years. The subject is now better understood, and bears thorough investigation, without hazard to the character of its members for patriotic attachment to the Constitution and the Union.

The respect for that body entertained by such a contemporary as Col. Perkins, is, in itself, historical testimony of some value. He had the best opportunity to form a correct judgment of its character and designs. He seems never to have desired political advancement for himself, and his judgment was probably unbiased by any wish for it. Impatience for the return of peace might at first seem likely to predominate with one engaged so largely in foreign commerce as he was; but it would rather appear, from his correspondence, that his establishment in China and other extensive arrangements gave him such peculiar advantages for success during a state of war, when he had few competitors, as left no motive of that nature for assisting in any improper attempt to impede or influence the action of the General Government.

Page 222.

COMMERCIAL LETTERS.

Boston, Feb. 7, 1795.

Mr. Thomas H. Perkins, Bourdeaux.

Sir, — We have this day received certain information of the conclusion of a treaty of commerce and navigation between the United States and Great Britain, said to be bottomed on terms of reciprocal advantage. We are also informed that Holland has concluded a separate peace with France, and that we have every reason to suppose that Great Britain will stand alone in the war. If these facts are to be relied on (and we presume they cannot be doubted), the advantages we have long experienced will be continued, if not augmented; new sources will be opened to our commerce; and the late obstructions in the north of Europe so far removed as to offer a market for our West-India goods, and revive the demand for our navigation. Under these circumstances, I conceive many opportunities for speculation will present themselves during your stay in France; and my object in writing you at this moment is to urge the importance of your early attention to the advantages which may be derived from the existing state of affairs in Europe. I find several vessels have been advantageously employed in plying between Hamburg, Rotterdam, and France, and that neutral vessels have been permitted a free trade *even from* England. Williams, who is in our friend H.'s brig "William," has pursued this business to great profit; and I am very well assured he has, notwithstanding, neglected many very important advantages, and that, in his choice of the articles he has carried from port to port, he has been mistaken, though they have yielded a profit worthy of attention. The "Betsy" will be with you, ere long, with a cargo of rice. This cargo, I conceive, will afford capital sufficient to be employed in the pursuance of this object; and, the vessel being exactly calculated for the purpose, you will be enabled, in case of a continuation of the war, to keep her employed to more advantage in Europe than in suffering her to return here. H. informs me that some articles purchased by Williams have given a profit of one hundred and fifty per cent, and that any person well qualified to pursue this object might render it infinitely productive. You will be enabled to inform yourself on this head; and, if satisfied of the facts, you will undoubtedly pursue it. For my part, I am so far impressed with its advantages, that I am resolved (if H. will consent) to send the "Dolphin" out to you, that she may be employed while the opportunity exists.

If you can sell your different cargoes for cash, or sure bills on Hamburg or Amsterdam, I would by all means advise it in preference to trusting to paper, which I observe is depreciating, and which will probably experience the same fate as ours at the close of the war. Many people say, France having obtained her ends, her paper must be better. The success of our contest did not produce this effect; and we may justly conclude that the same causes will produce the same effects, whether on this or the other side the Atlantic. My motives for advising your establishing a fund in

Holland are bottomed on a conviction that the best speculations which can be made will be on the goods carried from the northern ports to the republic, and not on the exports from France, which are at this moment at most extravagant prices, and will probably bear but a small or no profit. By having your specie at either of those places, or in London, you will not be detained to make your sales, but can provide your cargoes for France with greater benefit and despatch. The number of voyages made while the war lasts is certainly an important consideration. Williams has already made several trips on this plan, and his principal benefit has arisen from the despatch he has made. If you should have a surplusage of funds, you will establish a credit for our drafts in one of the above places, on which we can undertake new voyages from hence. You will probably hear of the "Delight." She was to take a freight from Hamburg for some part of Europe. I hope you will find employ for her also.

The "West Point's" duties become due in twenty days, and of consequence her cargo must be shipped. H. and myself have been looking at a vessel this morning, which we probably shall take and load for Havre. Carter will go in her.

Yours, &c.

BOSTON, Dec. 8, 1795.

Mr. JAMES BUSH, London.

Dear Sir, — I arrived, after a tedious passage, at the port of New York, and, a few days since, at this place; and I feel sensible it will give you pleasure when I add that my family and friends are well.

The brigantine "Mary Hughes" was taken by the ship "Assistance," of fifty guns, and sent to Newfoundland. The pretence for restraining her was that she was laden with provisions. How long coffee, which was her only lading, has been thus classed, I know not. She was to sail with convoy for England about the 1st of November. The injury this interruption has been to our property is very great. I hope your exertions will insure us reparation. The captain is furnished with every document necessary: the papers he took from hence are full and explicit as to the property, destination, &c. . . . .

To fill up the measure of injustice, I have no doubt the captain of the "Assistance" will endeavor to get an order for taking the "Mary's" cargo at the ten per cent. This you will oppose. . . . .

The prospect of a permanent good understanding between your court and the republic, gives me the fullest hopes of a favorable issue to the "Charlotte's" cause. My brother has forwarded to Mr. Bayard a claim of damages for the injury done us in detaining a vessel and cargo at Jamaica under the order of Nov. 6, 1792. The vessel is the same brig "Delight" (though at that time a schooner) of which you already know something. I hope to get the freight due the brig "Delight" also. . . . .

Yours,

T. H. P.

BOSTON, Feb. 8, 1796.

Mr. JAMES BUSH, London.

Dear Sir, — The above is duplicate of my last to you. We are a long time without any European arrivals, and are anxious to hear from your side the water. You will see, by our papers, how much it is the wish of this Government to live in peace with all the world. A few mad-heads have said much, and their noise has been heard afar; but they are as impotent as they are desperate, and their ill intentions have already been frustrated. This goes by a vessel of ours with flour for a market in Europe, where, I have but little doubt, it will bring a good price.

I am,

T. H. P.

BOSTON, April 15, 1796.

Messrs. T. H. CAZENOVE, NEPHEW, & Co., London.

Gentlemen, ... From the cessation of hostilities on the Rhine, we have been led to expect a general peace; but we observe, by your letter of the 6th February, that another campaign will probably take place: indeed, from the exertions made in the islands, we presume the war cannot terminate the present year. We flatter ourselves our next will advise you that all necessary measures for carrying our pending treaty with Great Britain into effect will be completed, the disorganizers of this country notwithstanding. From the unequalled firmness of our president, we have every thing to hope; and, from the general good sense of the people, we conceive the Constitution will long remain unshaken by its present enemies.

We remark with pleasure your approbation of the president's speech in the opening of Congress. We now enclose you his message to the House in reply to the requisition for the papers relative to the treaty, which, if possible, does him more honor than the former.

We are, &c.

BOSTON, April 30, 1796.

Messrs. WILLIAM & E. CRAFTS & Co.

Gentlemen, ... We have daily accounts from Europe of the low prices of American produce in proportion to home prices. We hope you have not speculated deeply in your staple commodities, but have been contented with being the carriers for those who have been full in the faith of the last year's prices in Europe. In consequence of the disposition shown in the House of Representatives of the Union not to grant the supplies for carrying the British treaty into effect, business has been very slack for these two weeks.

All new appropriations are entirely suspended. The alarm is very general lest the dearest interests of our country — *peace and national honor* — should be sacrificed to party-spirit and Antifederalism. The doings of this place, and those in its vicinity, have allayed fears; and we are full in faith that an appeal to the people will save us from the precipice over which we had like (involuntarily) to have been precipitated. Yours,

J. & T. H. P.

BOSTON, Aug. 4, 1796.

Mr. JAMES BUSH.

Dear Sir, — I have none of your letters for a long time past, though I have been in expectation of some to tell me favorable news respecting the causes I am unfortunately interested in at your courts. We — I mean the owners of the "Charlotte" — hope for a favorable termination of her appeal through the commissioners. I was in hopes the freight of the "Delight" would have been awarded her ere now. I send you the speech of Mr. Ames, member of our Congress, on the subject of the appropriation to carry the treaty with Great Britain into effect. I also send one, which please to present to Dr. Nicholl with my respectful compliments.

With my most cordial wishes for the health and prosperity of all who interest you,

I am, my dear sir, yours,

T. H. P.

BOSTON, Oct. 18, 1796.

Mr. JOSEPH RUSSELL, jun., American citizen now in Europe.

Dear Sir, ... Business in this country is becoming very dull. A great number of vessels are flocking to the American ports which have until this time been employed in Europe and the East Indies. What they will find to do now, we cannot anticipate. American produce is high,—every article of provisions at prices which exceed those quoted in any country we are in correspondence with. Articles of exports for Europe, which are the growth of the West-India islands, are also at nearly the same prices as in the places they are exported from. Thus you see we have but indifferent prospects of employing our navigation. The East-India voyages have turned out to more profit than any other trading voyages for some time past; and, we think, will still do well if managed with skill. . . . .

We anticipate the pleasure of yet seeing you this way in the spring. We lament the circumstances which have retarded your eagerness to revisit your native place, and hope you are persuaded there are yet amongst us those to whom you are very dear. Our young friend* Motier is with our beloved President. He is fostered by this great man, and is considered by him as a son. Frestel is with him. Our T. H. P. was with him at the president's seat in Virginia the past summer. He spoke with much gratitude of your goodness to him and his hapless family.

With respects to our friends who are with you, believe us, dear Russell, &c., Yours,

J. & T. H. P.

Boston, Dec. 27, 1796.

Mr. George Perkins, Smyrna.

Sir,—The deranged state of the European trade, consequent on the existing war between Great Britain and the continental powers, having opened some new channels for the American commerce in the Mediterranean, and the experiments which have been made in those seas exciting a further spirit of enterprise, we avail ourselves of a conveyance

* G. W. La Fayette.

by way of Naples to make a few inquiries respecting the commerce of your city. On this subject we have conversed with our friend and your brother, Mr. Thomas Perkins; but the unfrequent communications between Smyrna and this continent have prevented his receiving the necessary information. The meditated negotiations between these States and the powers of Tunis and Tripoli, we think, will soon remove all impediments between us; and, if permission for the entry of American vessels can be obtained, we have strong hopes a sufficient incentive to an experimental voyage, at least, may offer.

We have heard that many of our cargoes of coffee and sugar have been reshipped from Leghorn, Naples, and other ports in the Mediterranean, and have paid a valuable freight at Smyrna. The uncertainty, however, of this fact, and the great loss which might result from a merely speculative essay, render us anxious to obtain certain information of the state of your markets. We will therefore thank you to write us on this head, and inform us if an American vessel would be permitted an entry at your port, and under what restrictions; what articles of West and East India produce are in demand at your market, and what prices in English sterling they bear; what returns suitable for this country can be made, and at what rates.

An intercourse reciprocally advantageous, we conceive, may be formed between the two countries; and as the information we require, and the measures which may result from it, will be for the joint benefit of your brother, Mr. Thomas Perkins, our mutual friends and connections, Stephen Higginson & Co., and ourselves, we feel a hope that you will favor us with your communications as early as possible. They may be addressed to us under cover of Messrs. Thomas Dickason & Co., merchants, London; or Messrs. Degen & Iwertz, at Naples.

We are, sir, with respect,

Yours, &c.,

J. & T. H. P.

BOSTON, June 21, 1799.

Mr. LAREINTY, Martinique.

Dear Sir, — We subjoin a copy of our last letter to you, dated 22d April. Since then, we have received yours of 21st April. We feel much satisfied with the advice we formerly gave you as to the disposition of your funds in this country. Such has been the uncertainty with respect to the political situation of America for some time past, that great fluctuations have been experienced in our stocks. Since three months, some particular species of stocks have declined eight to ten per cent.

The present unanimity in our councils gives us confidence that we shall not become altogether the dupes of Mr. Talleyrand. We shall at all times take great pleasure in doing all in our power to secure your interest. We agree to the proposition that you shall have liberty to retire your funds, giving us a little previous notice as you propose.

We have all our concerns in the India trade at present, which we find more lucrative than the colonial trade, particularly under the present embarrassment in getting returns. . . . . We are, &c.

P. S. — Our T. H. P.'s best regards to Mr. and Mrs. Lareinty. Mrs. Perkins and our children are well, — the present number, four, — who will be all very happy to see you again in America.

BOSTON, Nov. 1, 1799.

Capt. STEPHEN HALL, of brig "Sally."

Sir, — Your brig being now ready for sea, our instructions to you are to proceed from hence, with all possible expedition, to the Pacific Ocean, and touch at such islands as you may think proper for the purpose of taking seals. Kerguelen's Land we think you will do well to stop at first; and from thence to St. Paul's and Amsterdam, or any other islands you, with Mr. Peron, your chief mate, may think best.

As the success of the voyage depends altogether on your unremitted exertions to procure seals, we do not doubt you will use them on all occasions. We put a great plenty of provisions on board your vessel; but we calculate upon your making use of fish and seal-flesh occasionally for your people, and that your beef, pork, and bread will be used with the utmost economy. In voyages like that you are now embarked upon, every thing depends upon harmony and good understanding. Good treatment and tenderness to your crew will do more than can be effected by different conduct. Mr. Peron is so well acquainted with the sealing business, that we shall not pretend to point out to you the mode of procedure, but leave to you and him to devise and execute your future operations. Should you be able to purchase prime seal-skins at one-quarter to one-half a dollar, payable by drafts on us, we authorize your doing it on account of those concerned in the voyage. When you have collected as many skins as may make it an object for you to go to China with them, you will proceed there, and lay out the amount they may net in such articles as you may think best, being governed in this by the capital you have to invest. You will recollect, that, unless the price of skins is high in Canton, the expenses in the river will take away all your cargo. You can learn the price at Macao, and be governed accordingly. Should skins be very low in China, as we think probable may be the case, the first eighteen or twenty-four months, it would be best to place the skins in the hands of the American consul, Mr. Snow, at Canton, until a favorable opportunity for sale arrives, and proceed to the islands again, or go to the North-west Coast for sea-otters, if a favorable cargo can be had in China. We only intimate these things for your consideration, and leave you to be the judges of carrying them into effect. We depend upon hearing from you as often as opportunities may offer, and on having a circumstantial account of your proceedings. Should we have any vessels bound to China, we shall probably order them to stop at Amsterdam, to visit you, and take your skins to China. As it is probable you may have an opportunity of purchasing skins from persons left on the islands in the Pacific Ocean, it may be necessary to say something on that subject. It is very far from our wishes or intentions that you should on any account purchase skins of any persons left for the purpose of sealing by any vessel which has contracted to take off the persons left. It may be (and we have reason to suppose it is the case) that some persons have been left on their own account to collect seal-skins, and are fully empowered to dispose of them; in which case you will purchase them, provided you can make such a bargain as you may think will answer. You can better afford to pay half a dollar for good skins the present season than a quarter of a dollar the next season, provided you can get a sufficient quantity to induce you to go to market with them. The reason of this difference is, that, the next season, there will probably be a great glut of skins in China; whereas, the present season (or, in other words, in November next, or earlier), the sealers will not have arrived. In all cases, when you purchase skins, you will be well persuaded that the persons have a good right to dispose of them; and they will probably have it in their power to convince you of their property in them. Although we have pointed out to you the objects of the voyage generally, yet we authorize you to make such changes as you and Mr. Peron may think most for the interest of the voyage. We depend much on Mr. Peron's judgment and information in the sealing business, and recommend your consulting him on all occasions. We hope and presume there will be a perfect good understanding between you and Mr. Peron, whom we recommend particularly to you as a man who has our confidence, and deserves yours.

We again repeat to you the necessity of the most rigid economy in the use of your provisions, particularly of the bread kind. While at the islands, you will be able to economize in your beef, as you will there find plenty of fish. We think, if you should purchase skins to go to China with, and find them sell well, — that is, if you should get twenty thousand to thirty thousand, and be able to sell them at one dollar and three-fourths to two dollars each, — you would raise capital sufficient to load the brig with Nankins; and it would be best to proceed home with them, as you may be nearly as soon at the islands again as the people left would be able to make up a second cargo.

Should you leave a large party at St. Paul's and Amsterdam, and go to China, we think Mr. Peron's being at the head of it would be important.

BOSTON, Nov. 9, 1799.

Mr. SAMUEL G. PERKINS, London.

Dear S., ... We wrote you the "Eliza" had succeeded on the North-west, and had proceeded to China; that is, she was about leaving the coast for China. We presume, from the letters which are dated off St. Blas, that she would dispose of her dry-goods for about one hundred per cent advance. The collection of skins exceeded that of Magee in the "Margaret," or Swift in the "Hazard;" although they were two years, and the "Eliza" ninety days. This is a *coup de hasard* rarely to be met with. Should she get safe to China, of which we have but little doubt, she will make a great voyage.

We are still of opinion the "Russell" had best be despatched for Batavia with $40,000, unless she can make a freight here which will net a handsome sum. Indeed, if there is no difficulty in clearing for Batavia from London, there ought to be no question as to sending her forthwith.

It may be that a freight from London may be had out to Batavia, or that the revolution of Holland is so far completed as that the ship may be loaded at Amsterdam without being implicated with the English. We are, however, of opinion, that the more simple the plan, the better; and, for this reason, we prefer the voyage direct to Batavia and home. If two hundred tons could be procured for China, on freight, and the freight paid there, it would be best to send her perhaps to Canton, in preference to anywhere else; and, in this case, the proceeds of freight out, and our own stock, could be invested in Nankins, and brought home. All these things are matters of calculation, and you must decide upon them.

The "Massachusetts" goes to Batavia direct, with $80,000. The other voyage is too speculative and uncertain. We shall occasionally drop you a line, and hope the return of the "Minerva" will see you once more with us.

God bless you!

BOSTON, Nov. 9, 1799.

Mr. JOSEPH MARRYAT, London.

Sir, — We have written to Mr. Samuel Perkins on the subject of the destination of the ship "Thomas Russell," and give you an extract of our letter to him herewith. Should no difficulty present to oppose our plan of sending the ship to Batavia, we wish $40,000 put into her for that place.

We fear there will not be arrangements made with Holland which will authorize the projected voyage from thence to Batavia; and we are induced, upon reflection, to adopt the plan just mentioned, as the most eligible one to be pursued. We rely on your kind interference and aid in getting the ship to sea upon the most economical plan.

We are, &c.

BOSTON, Dec. 30, 1799.

Mr. SAMUEL G. PERKINS, London.

Dear Sir, — We now send you a triplicate of our last. A recent arrival from India brings accounts of the Government of the Isle of France having declared war against us, and that several vessels have sailed from thence to cruise against our commerce. This very much alarms us; and we are concerned for the fate of all our vessels in those seas. We cannot suppose the "Russell" is still with you. Should she have been detained by any cause until this gets to hand, if bound to Batavia, let her go through the Straits of Lombok; or, if going to China, let her go round the south cape of New Holland. Sever and Preble, in the frigates "Congress" and "Essex," sail for the Straits in a few days. They will, however, be too late to protect those vessels which will be on the return from Batavia and China in the spring. We have no news in the political line. The General Government now is, and the State Governments as they get in session are, making arrangements to pay honor to the memory of the man whom the world delighted to honor. . . . . .
Hoping soon to hear from you, We are, &c.

BOSTON, May 24, 1800.

Messrs. HENRY JACKSON and JOSEPH TILDEN.

Sirs, — Herewith you have invoice and bill lading (duly attested) of the cargo on board the ship "Thomas Russell," Henry Jackson, master, for the sole account and risk of the owners of said ship, and which goes to your address jointly. You will proceed from hence direct to Malaga, and, on your arrival there, inform yourselves of the state of the markets in the Mediterranean; and if, on investigation, you should find your cargo will sell at that place for such prices as may be preferred to further hazard, you will there dispose of the whole.

If, on the contrary, you may be convinced, from minute inquiry and calculation, that it will be most expedient to proceed further up, — say to Barcelona (Genoa, if open for American ships), Leghorn, Naples, Smyrna, or any ports between those and Trieste, — you will conduct accordingly; taking care, in all instances, to estimate the expenses of detention, extra premium, wages, &c. From your own knowledge of the trade of the Mediterranean, you will be enabled to judge of those markets where your teas, Nankins, and light articles will answer best; and we would recommend your embracing the first good opportunity to dispose of this part of your cargo. Your coffee, sugar, and cocoa being (more or less) in demand at every port, they will, of course, govern your movements above Leghorn, and will alone be an object for you to proceed beyond that place. Having disposed of your cargo, you will convert the amount into Spanish dollars, with which you will proceed direct to Calcutta, and there invest the whole amount in such articles as you may think best calculated for this market from the memorandum furnished you, and return with this cargo direct to Boston. If it should so happen that you cannot procure dollars in the Mediterranean, and you can obtain well-indorsed bills on London, you may proceed to Lisbon, and there dispose of those bills for specie. In case it should be necessary, for the satisfaction and security of the purchasers of your bills, to receive our guaranty of their payment, we authorize you to use the names of the owners to that effect. We shall furnish you with a power of attorney, and letters to respectable houses in that place, to facilitate your operations. Vessels have obtained freights, on advantageous terms, to go from the ports in the Mediterranean to Lisbon, London, and other ports within the Straits; which would be quite an object for the vessel, in case you are obliged to go out of the Straits to look for dollars. We should recommend your selling at a good profit, whenever you may find it, in preference to going in search of extravagant markets, particularly if specie can be got in payment. You will be able to get advices of the state of the markets generally in the Mediterranean on your arrival at Malaga. Selling at one of the first ports will very much facilitate your voyage, and lessen expenses. Those are calculations which you must make on the spot, the ultimate object of your voyage being the purchase of a cargo in Calcutta; and the speedy conversion of your present lading into dollars must be a governing object in your operations.

Relying on your discretion, and having stated to you the general plan of the voyage, we leave you to exercise your judgment in its management; not doubting that your measures will be taken for the best interest of the concerned. In case of taking a freight, you will take the earliest opportunity of communicating your destination; and we beg you to write us as often as you have an opportunity which promises safety to your letters, although it may be circuitous. We agree to allow you five per cent upon the sales in the Mediterranean over and above the commission you will be obliged to pay to the merchant you may employ to do your business. This commission is to be divided between you as follows: Three per cent, or three-fifths, to Capt. H. Jackson; and two per cent, or two-fifths, to Mr. Tilden. We also allow you five per cent for laying out the money arising from your cargo and invested at Calcutta, and to be divided in the same proportions. Capt. Jackson is allowed five per cent privilege in the ship, estimated upon what she carries under deck. To Mr. Tilden we allow three tons privilege. Should you go as far as Trieste, you will deliver the letters we enclose you for Messrs. John & George D'Isay of that place; and if, upon inquiry, you are satisfied that they can do your business upon as good terms as any other house, and that their reputation for solidity and fidelity is well established, you will give them the preference. For aiding you to transact your business, you will have the names of many houses at the ports where you may probably fall in; of all which you will be the best judges on the spot. Perhaps better information can be had of the reputation of a house at another port than the one of its establishment, where persons, from motives of interest, are sometimes led to blast the reputation of another, to enable them to establish their own on the ruin of those they have traduced. You will return quadruplicate certificates for the landing your present cargo, being particular as to packages. You are furnished with memoranda for a return cargo from Calcutta, which will preclude the necessity of our saying any thing on the subject. We feel so much impressed with the idea that a perfect good understanding will prevail between you, that we think it almost unnecessary to mention that mutual communication in every thing which concerns the voyage is important. Mr. Parsons is to have two tons privilege. You will avoid touching at Gibraltar, that port being blockaded, but proceed direct to Malaga. Offend no law of either of the belligerent powers; and recollect that it is important strictly to observe a conduct perfectly neutral, and break no acts of trade.

It being impossible for us to provide for contingent events, we finally leave you to exercise your discretion if it should be necessary to deviate from the letter of instruction; and, wishing you success in your operations, we are, in behalf of the owners of the ship "Thomas Russell,"

Yours, &c.

BOSTON, Oct. 16, 1800.

WEL EDEL HERR SIBURG, Batavia.

Sir, — Since writing the letter of the 7th, of which we have the honor to annex a copy, we have received letters from Capt. Hutchings, who informs us he has some expectations of going to Japan in the service of the Dutch East-

India Company. This is very gratifying to us, as we are in hopes, from this intercourse, to be preferred in furnishing the annual ship to Japan from Batavia. We repeat that we shall be ready to provide a ship of such force and capacity as may be thought most appropriate to the service for which she is wanted. It would be highly gratifying to us to be useful to you in this country. We have nothing very interesting of a political nature of which to advise you. It was the general opinion, both in this country and in Europe, that a pacification would take place in the course of the coming winter. From some circumstances which have transpired from the cabinets of the belligerent powers, within a short time, all hope of peace has for the present vanished. When this much-wished-for event will take place, it is impossible to calculate with any degree of precision.

We are, &c.

Boston, Oct. 16, 1800.

Mr. R. B. Forbes, New York.

Dear Sir, — We understand the United States frigate "New York," Capt. Morris, is destined for Batavia; and we enclose letters which we wish to have forwarded by that ship to Capt. Hutchings, &c. It is possible the frigate may arrive before the "Massachusetts" leaves Batavia for home. Hutchings, we understand, took a freight for Japan. This is the report of a captain who has arrived here from Batavia. A letter from Hutchings mentions his expectations of doing this; but, when he wrote, it was not completed. He was to have $100,000 for the run. We expect he will not leave Batavia until late in January, or early in February. We also send you a letter to Mr. Peter Peron, who was landed, by our brigantine "Sally," at the Island of St Paul's, which lies in the route to Batavia, and which island is generally run for by vessels bound to the Straits of Sunda. There are eight men with Peron, and eight men on the Island of Amsterdam, which lies about fifteen leagues to the southward of St. Paul's; so that the object would be answered if the letter could be put on either, as we presume they have the means of communicating with each other. Capt. Hall's letters were unfortunately lost; so that we are uncertain if his return home was originally intended when he left the islands, or whether it grew out of circumstances which transpired at Batavia. At any rate, it would be highly gratifying to us to let them know our intention of sending a vessel to take them off. We hear they are well supplied with provisions for two years. If it should not be inconvenient to Capt. Morris to let his boat put this letter on shore, as he passes the island, he would very much oblige us, and serve his countrymen who are in those desert islands in a high degree. It would not detain his ship more than a couple of hours. Please to call on him, with our respects, and request this favor of him. We hope soon to hear of your safe arrival *chez vous*. Our regards at home.

We are, &c.

BOSTON, Dec. 4, 1813.

Messrs. PERKINS & Co., Canton.

Gentlemen, — You will hear from us particularly and generally; but, that nothing may escape us, we take notice of any thing that strikes us at the moment, and make a record of it, that it may not be omitted in our general letters. . . . .

We shall not be surprised to find the war continue a year or two longer. Much will depend on European events. If the allies are successful, our rulers may be more disposed to meet Great Britain upon terms that are attainable. A fast ship, belonging to ourselves and others, will be with you. You must not keep her long in port; though it would not be best to buy her teas in anticipation of her arrival. We hope you speculated in sea-otter skins: none can go down from the North-west Coast to lower the market. No vessels can be fitted from hence. It is said the British have sent frigates to the coast of Peru. If so, they will go to the islands, and our vessels in that quarter will be in danger.

BOSTON, Jan. 1, 1814.

Messrs. PERKINS & Co., Canton.

. . . . We shall send a couple of fast schooners to Manilla, in all probability. We presume there is no difficulty in landing a cargo of teas there, to be exported, and without duty. This you must ascertain through some of the Spanish residents at Canton or Macao. What would a cargo of Congo tea cost, — say three thousand chests, which would load the "Levant," worth now, short price, $250,000, and cost say $36,000? Coming round Cape Horn, and arriving on the coast in winter, she would stand a good chance of getting in. We should be willing to try it, and hazard one-half, if Honqua would take the other. . . . .

You say a cargo laid in at Canton would bring three for one in South America, and your copper would give two prices back. Thus, $30,000 laid out in China would give you $90,000 in South America; one-half of which, laid out in copper, would give one hundred per cent, or $90,000; making $135,000 for $30,000.

60,000 pounds indigo, even at 80 cents	$48,000
120 tons sugar, at $60	7,200
Fill up with cotton, or some other light freight, say skin tea . .	20,000
	$75,000

would be worth here $400,000, and not employ the profits of the voyage to South America. Manilla sugar is worth $400 to $500 per ton clear of duty. The ship should be flying light, her bottom in good order, the greatest vigilance used on the passage, and make any port north of New York. Perhaps those on the eastern shore are easiest of access. There would be no very great chance but in the winter. We should not be surprised if the British send some frigates to the South-American coast, as one of our ships has been there; but yet the danger cannot be very great of going to a single port. . . . .

In times like these, the resources of the head must make up for the limited state of trade. We have been fortunate in getting home our property from abroad, except what is in Canton; and that we think in good hands, under your care. We shall perhaps add to this. If the Chinese act with spirit, the supercargoes will prevent capture above Macao. This must be all-important. If not stopped at Macao, we think we shall see some other vessels along.

BOSTON, Jan. 6, 1814.

TO THE SAME.

Gentlemen, — We have good grounds of hope that the present year will restore this country to a state of peace. Teas have risen to enormous prices, but are now declining. We hope that you may have bought a few thousand chests, for the European market, when they were low. . . . .

Teas will rise with you immediately after a knowledge of peace takes place. Many voyages will be undertaken after the war, and the country will be again flooded with teas. . . . .

Although we believe in peace, that event is not certain. A light load of Congo and Hyson teas would bear a war-risk, and would do well in peace. If Honqua would load half the ship with a cargo purposely for the European market, — say black teas of two or three years old, and bought low, — and you can see your way clear out of the river, and in a good sailing vessel, — say the "Levant," — letting her go by way of Cape Horn, and calculate to reach the coast in December or January, making the first port on our eastern coast, our belief is that the ship will find us at peace ; and, if not, prices will be so high as to warrant the operation. . . . .

The North of Europe will be bare of teas; and the first vessel which may arrive there after peace, and with only peace charges on her, will make a brilliant voyage. In all cases, they should call here for orders. Mr. Williams will write you what to expect. . . . .

BOSTON, Jan. 12, 1814.

TO THE SAME.

We have already written you by this conveyance; since which, circumstances have arisen which authorize an expectation that peace between this country and Great Britain will certainly take place in the course of the present year. Your calculations, therefore, may be made, with a great degree of certainty of their being realized upon a basis of an uninterrupted trade.

BOSTON, July 15, 1814.

TO THE SAME.

. . . . The power of France in Europe has been nearly overthrown. Her armies have been driven before the allied powers, and forced to recross the Rhine. All Germany is already, or soon will be, in league against her. The Hanse towns and Holland will no doubt be relieved from their shackles; and it is confidently hoped and believed that the balance of power in Europe will again be restored. A messenger has recently arrived in this country, offering, in the name of the Prince Regent, propositions for concluding a peace between this country and Great Britain. Under all circumstances, we regard it as a thing beyond a doubt that an adjustment of differences must follow. The President has accepted the overture; and ministers will immediately be named to treat at Gottenburg.

A final settlement, such as will enable us to navigate in safety, may be protracted, by the diplomatic habits of our Government, to the ensuing autumn. It may be concluded sooner. All will depend on the complete prostration of Bonaparte. God grant that this obstacle may not long intervene! How far we shall, in time of peace, be permitted to pursue our former commerce, is a question difficult to decide. Great Britain has neither affection nor respect for us. Her interest will guide in relation to her future stipulations. When she can, consistently with her own rights, restrict us, she will naturally do so. . . . .

The duties on all merchandise were doubled on the breaking out of the war, and are to be continued so until twelve months after a peace with Great Britain. Of course, Hyson tea pays 64 cents per pound; Young Hyson Skin, 40 cents; Souchong, Campoi, and Congo, 24 cents. The ship "Sally" arrived safely in our bay without knowing of the war. Two British frigates were off this harbor. She received advice from a fishing-boat, and ran into Plymouth. The cargo was all brought by land to Boston. . . . .

BOSTON, May 6, 1814.

TO THE SAME.

. . . . Since the sailing of these vessels (19th January), the events which we had anticipated have been gradually developing. Ministers were appointed to treat with Great Britain at Gottenburg. They sailed from New York towards the end of February, furnished, as we are taught to believe, with full power to conclude a peace with that power. No advice of their arrival has yet reached us. If there existed strong inducements, when we last wrote you, to put an end to this ruinous war, there are now more urgent reasons for its termination, foreign as well as domestic. The allied powers have been extending and uniting their forces. Holland is in possession of the Dutch. Denmark has thrown off the manacles of France, and formed a treaty with Great Britain, and has joined in the war against her former tyrant. All Germany, and the other Northern powers, are now pouring their armies into the heart of France. Two hundred and fifty thousand men, under the most able generals, were opposing the remains of the French forces, at the last dates (say 1st March), within forty miles of Paris. . . . .

[The same letter.] May 14.

. . . . We learn, since we began this letter, that the allies are in possession of Paris. Bourdeaux is in the hands of Lord Wellington; and the white flag is now flying in that part of France. The Duke of Angoulême is with Lord Wellington, and is well received by the French, who acknowledge their joy on the occasion. Mr. Ammidon will give you the particulars. A peace must soon follow these events, both in Europe and in this country. . . . .

BOSTON, NOV. 17, 1814.

TO THE SAME.

. . . . We hear that the "Jacob Jones" went safely into Canton, and presume she may be despatched before the river is blockaded. In such case, she ought to be here at the time appointed, unless captured. Our coast is closely invested, and the hazard of getting in very imminent. Some insurance has been done on her, owing to her being a war-built vessel, and having the reputation of a *swift sailer*, at fifty per cent; but very little can be had. We have only $8,000 written at present, and fear we shall not be able to effect more, by safe men, even at that. Vessels built before the war cannot be insured at seventy-five per cent, which premium has been given on prizes taken near this coast and ordered in. Owing to the decline of public credit consequent on a continuance of the war, and the many failures which have taken place, it is extremely difficult to effect sales of any sort, except for immediate consumption; and those are made only for cash, no one being inclined to sell on credit at this critical juncture. Under these circumstances, we can ill afford to pay a high premium and double duties.

We are yet unable to say when you may look for a termination of the war. Our negotiations at Ghent have been suspended; but reports say they are again renewed. It is possible that peace may take place in the spring, but not probable, unless the embarrassments and ruined credit of our Government shall oblige them to aceept the terms Great Britain may offer. Mr. Williams will be able to give you better data than we can, on this side the Atlantic, to judge the result that may follow. Europe is still in a state of agitation; and a war between France and Great Britain may be renewed. Public funds here (six per cent) are down to sixty-five, and growing worse. Nothing but peace can prevent an utter downfall of governmental credit and means. . . . .

We have no expectation that the duties will be reduced for several years, if at all. Keep the "Levant" safe in port till you hear of peace. Then she may do well with black teas for European markets.

Feb. 14, 1815.

To THE SAME.

Yesterday, an express arrived, saying that peace was concluded between the commissioners at Ghent and the British Government on the 26th December last, and that the treaty had arrived at New York by a special messenger, and was sent immediately to Washington, accompanied by a British diplomatic character. All this is true. It is now probably before the Government, and will no doubt be ratified in a few days. The terms we know nothing of, — probably the restoration of all territorial acquisitions on both sides ; the same state in which our relations stood before the war ; with some new stipulations respecting the security of the frontiers. . . . .

Before this vessel sails (the schooner from Philadelphia), we presume peace will be proclaimed. Our T. H. P. is now at Washington, as one of the commissioners sent by this State to treat with the General Government respecting its affairs. He will no doubt write you. . . . .

March 19, 1815.

To THE SAME.

. . . . It has been remarked that the return of peace generally brings with it more mercantile embarrassments than the first year of a war ; and the reason is obvious. Having been long restrained from their accustomed trade, all classes of men are led into speculations without calculating the result, hoping that chance may enable them to retrieve lost time. This will be the case now ; and you must expect to see evidence of it in the adventures you will see in China.

BOSTON, June 7, 1815.

TO THE SAME.

Gentlemen, — Letters are received in town from Holland, stating that teas are interdicted in that country, unless under the authority of a newly established company, which has extended to it the special privilege of exclusive trade to China.

We have no letters so late as those in question, which are dated 10th April. This arrangement must have been made under the expectation that Europe was to remain in peace, and incipient measures taken before the bold steps of Napoleon were known. Upon the issue of the struggle, which has ere this begun, to put down the power of this extraordinary man, will depend the mercantile arrangements of France, Holland, Sweden, &c. So long as they are at issue with France, the Northern powers will be very wary, and not put their property on the ocean, lest some of them should again be compelled to wear the tri-colored cockade, and be forced into a war with Great Britain. It is our opinion that such will not be the issue of the contest. If Russia, Austria, and Prussia act with good faith to each other, and Great Britain enters heartily into the plan of putting down the dynasty of Bonaparte, though much blood would be spilt, yet the allies will eventually succeed. Were there any reliance to be placed on the promises of Bonaparte, it is probable the Bourbons would be left to mourn the loss of the throne, and the power of Napoleon would be left undisturbed: but, from past experience, no reliance can be placed on him; and he would only remain at peace to enable himself more effectually to carry on a war of conquest and ambition. It may take some time to effect the destruction of the French power under the new order of things; and, so long as the struggle continues, so long will commercial regulations be unstable on the continent. . . . .

BOSTON, July 10, 1815.

TO THE SAME.

. . . . You will be surprised to find that we have no advice of hostilities in France. Reports up to the 1st June say the "dreadful note of preparation" is not yet complete, but that an early, if not an immediate, conflict must take place, — a conflict which must exterminate the power of Bonaparte, or degrade all Europe. We conceive his fate almost certain. If he moves, he will draw on him the united forces of Great Britain and the Continental powers. At any rate, they will not suffer him to reign. For their own future safety, they must annihilate his power. We have been long without letters from England. Many vessels are hourly expected, which will probably give us important information. . . . .

BOSTON, Aug. 19, 1815.

TO THE SAME.

. . . . The last accounts from Europe give us the strongest grounds of hope that there will be long peace on the other side the water, and on this side of course. Napoleon having been annihilated, *root and branch,* we think there will be no more war between France and the other hostile powers; though it seems highly probable that they may have some *domestic throat-cutting.* If we are correct in our conjecture, and the Continental powers should feel such security in their situation as to induce their people to enter extensively into manufactures, they may reduce the benefit on China silks. Yet there is such an advantage on the part of China, from the low price of raw silk, and even from the price of labor, that we do not think that either the Italians or French can come in competition with the Chinese in those manufactures. . . . .

Oct. 4, 1815.

To the same.

. . . . It seems that the price of raw silk, and the diminution of working hands, both in France and Italy, have made a very considerable rise in the article of silk manufactures, which must continue for some time, until the raising of silkworms can be increased, and workmen be taught the business. Even at the high price of silks in France and Italy, they would bring two for one in this market. Three years of war, and twice that number of restriction upon commerce, had made our people very rigidly economical; and they bought only what was necessary, not what was luxurious. In place of a silk gown or pelisse, they purchased cotton for the first, and dispensed with the last altogether. So with tea. Although they did not wholly forego it, they were careful in the use of it; and now, to make up for lost time, they feel as if they may indulge in the fashions of the city, and gratify their palates with the beverage of the East. This being the case, it will take a long time to overstock the market with silks; though, from the quantity of teas on hand when the war began, the importations since, and the economy spoken of in the use of it during the war, we think the spring ships will cause a great fall of it in the market. . . . .

THE END.

Made in the USA
Monee, IL
20 October 2026

66035293R00171